Worldlessness

Incitements

Visit the series web page at: edinburghuniversitypress.com/series/incite

Worldlessness After Heidegger

Phenomenology, Psychoanalysis, Deconstruction

Roland Végső

EDINBURGH
University Press

Edinburgh University Press is one of the leading university presses in the UK.
We publish academic books and journals in our selected subject areas across
the humanities and social sciences, combining cutting-edge scholarship with
high editorial and production values to produce academic works of lasting
importance. For more information visit our website:
edinburghuniversitypress.com

Edinburgh University Press Ltd
The Tun – Holyrood Road, 12(2f) Jackson's Entry, Edinburgh EH8 8PJ

Typeset in Bembo
by R. J. Footring Ltd, Derby, UK, and
printed and bound by CPI Group (UK) Ltd, Croydon, CR0 4YY

A CIP record for this book is available from the British Library

ISBN 978 1 4744 5761 3 (hardback)
ISBN 978 1 4744 5763 7 (webready PDF)
ISBN 978 1 4744 5762 0 (paperback)
ISBN 978 1 4744 5764 4 (epub)

Contents

Acknowledgements

The ideas presented in this book were first articulated in the context of a series of seminars organised by John Brenkman and Sorin Radu Cucu over a four-year period at the annual conventions of the American Comparative Literature Association. I owe them and the other more or less regular members of these seminars a great deal for providing the material occasions for the birth of the ideas pursued here. Above all, I thank them for their patience. I would also like to thank my research assistants at the University of Nebraska–Lincoln, Kirby Little, Dillon Rockrohr, Luke Folk and Joseph Turner for their indispensable contributions to this project. The same goes for the graduate students who participated in a long sequence of seminars over the years without necessarily suspecting what conclusions I might draw from our discussions. Over the last ten years, the general support of the Department of English at the University of Nebraska–Lincoln created a fully hospitable environment for thinking about even such seemingly irredeemable ideas as worldlessness. I owe many personal thanks to Marco Abel, Joan Copjec and Jeff Nealon for their unfailing support of my work. In a similar spirit, I am also grateful to the anonymous readers of my manuscript whose contributions helped me present my arguments in more convincing ways. Furthermore, I would like to thank Carol Macdonald, Peg Brimingham and Dimitris Vardoulakis for their warm welcome of my manuscript in the Incitements series. Finally, my infinite gratitude goes to Emily Hammerl for our common adventures in worldlessness.

For Oskar, Felix and Ilona

Orbis non sufficit (An Introduction)

According to a widely accepted historical narrative, the three central characters of world history today – the world, the globe and capital – can be brought together in the following melancholy story: under the sway of capital, we gain the globe but we lose the world. As the story goes, according to its very logic, capital wants to conquer all available spaces. But when the conquest is complete, we find that the empirically given unity of the globe (which is given as a brute fact and is simply there without any human effort) does not guarantee the unity of the world (which is always a construction and the product of communal activities). At the end of the story, the irreducible difference between the globe and the world becomes visible. In one sense, the illusory promise of capital has always been that the globe can be identical with a world in the form of a world-market. The insistence that the world is not a globe or that the globe in itself will never establish a world under the conditions of capitalism constitutes the alleged critical force of this narrative.[1]

As we can see, in this historical context the concept of the 'world' is reinvested with a new ethical value in opposition to that of the 'globe'. In the age of globalisation, not only are the two phenomena (the globe and the world) at odds with each

1

other: it is precisely the complete conquest of the globe that might be the most efficient way of destroying the world. The suspicion grows every day that the unification of the world market deprives us of a phenomenological experience of what is common to human existence. Soon, the only thing we will have in common is that we have nothing in common at all. In a moment of historical panic, when the only certainty we still cling to so desperately is that the current situation is reprehensible, we react by elevating the concept of the world to the level of a fetish object. For the world appears to us now as something like the last resort of the well-trained nihilist who must still demonstrate the moral superiority of his position: 'I am wholly untouched by your banal tragedies, but at least I would still mourn for the world.' We congratulate ourselves for the sad fact that there is at least one virtue left that we might be suspected of: we still love the world.

Under these conditions, it is no surprise at all that the greatest possible danger we can imagine today is the loss of this world itself. Thus, the concept of 'worldlessness' has entered the history of modern Western philosophy as a tool to justify our unconditional love of the world. It designates the epochal catastrophe threatening humanity with the loss of its very essence. At the same time – and this point might be harder to accept – the category also functions as a means of a philosophical disavowal. Without a doubt, the idea of worldlessness possesses a certain pragmatic value for us. The philosophical rediscovery of the problem of worldlessness in the twentieth century made it possible for many of us to encounter a fundamental historical problem and to give a recognisable shape to our experiences of modernity. In this sense, the concept has been quite useful for us. But the concept also immediately declared an absolute limit to thought that we dare not move beyond even today. In the background of all the renunciations of the worldless nature of our times, we might perceive a snug retreat from an abyss that appears to be darker and deeper than our most pessimistic visions of capitalism: an existence that is not in any relation to a world. But what if our task today is precisely to imagine worldlessness without an apocalypse?[2]

★ ★ ★

The primary objective of this book is to recast the commonly accepted narratives of postwar continental philosophy around the idea of worldlessness. Upon first glance, this concept will undoubtedly appear as an unlikely candidate for carrying such a heavy argumentative burden, since more often than not it has been relegated to the margins of philosophical discussions. But it will take merely a modest act of our imagination to perceive that worldlessness forms something like the continuous under-current of postwar and contemporary thought and poses a special challenge for thinking today.

If we were to trace the adventures of worldlessness in postwar continental philosophy, we would discover a story full of meta-morphoses and surprising reversals. This would indeed be a fable of many different plotlines and often incommensurable conclu-sions. But the persistence of the common theme should still give us pause. It appears that the problem of worldlessness was im-possible to avoid in this historical context. The list of potential authors and ideas that we would have to investigate to get to the bottom of things would grow longer and longer with every discovery we make along the way. To illustrate the pervasiveness of this problem, in addition to the authors that will be discussed in the following chapters (Heidegger, Arendt, Freud, Lacan, Derrida and Badiou), we could highlight the following episodes of this history: Georges Bataille's concepts of 'inner experience' and the 'impossible' (Bataille 1998); Maurice Blanchot's reflections on literary language, death, disaster and the 'unavowable community' (Blanchot 1988); Emmanuel Lévinas's definition of the 'il y a' as the dark indeterminacy of a truly impersonal Being (Lévinas 1978); Michel Foucault's return to the Epicureans, Stoics and Cynics of ancient Greece in his final years (Foucault 2012); Jean-Luc Nancy's experimentations with 'being singular plural' (Nancy 2000); Gilles Deleuze and Félix Guattari's reinvention of schizophrenia and the 'body without organs' (Deleuze and Guattari 2009); Giorgio Agamben's rediscovery of monastic life as the basic paradigm of the coincidence of life and its forms (Agamben 2013); Michael Hardt and Antonio Negri's politics of 'exodus' in the face of Empire's relentless global onslaught (Hardt and Negri 2011); as well as Slavoj Žižek's new materialist ontology of the 'absolute recoil' of Being (Žižek 2015).

The list is diverse and in no way exhaustive. But in all these cases, a careful reading of these authors would show that the concept of worldlessness is located at the limit of their thought: it is simultaneously an object of fear and desire. In spite of the fact that worldlessness designates the epochal catastrophe of our times, faced with the threat of the loss of the world, our philosophers have proceeded to produce ever more mesmerising figures for this worldlessness. The proliferation of these positive figures testifies to a certain fascination with the obscure possibilities worldlessness promises to harbour. We are imbued with the secret desire to inhabit worldlessness as if it were the coziest of all possible and impossible worlds. This desire is not misplaced. But because worldlessness is the disavowed centre of contemporary thought, the desire of contemporary philosophy constantly mis-recognises itself in its very own projects. Philosophy incessantly promises to save us from the very thing it is assiduously preparing for us. It is in this sense that we could consider worldlessness to be something like a limit-concept of our historical moment.[3]

★ ★ ★

But what remains constant in this encounter with worldlessness in spite of the unruly diversity of possible themes and positions? To answer this question, we will have to revisit Martin Heideg-ger's use of the concept. The Heideggerian encounter with the problem of worldlessness has bequeathed to the second half of the century a double paradox: 1. On the one hand, as Heidegger argues, the world is originary and constitutive. Yet, the Heideg-gerian oeuvre is inundated with a moral panic concerning the loss of this world. As Heidegger repeatedly argues, in the age of modernity, we are threatened by the spectre of worldlessness. 2. On the other hand, since modernity threatens us with world-lessness, our historical goal is to overcome modernity. But what the Heideggerian text dissimulates is that beyond modernity we find precisely the worldlessness that this philosophy was supposed to protect us from. The task of overcoming modern worldlessness once again exposes us to worldlessness (albeit to an altogether different kind of worldlessness).[4] The postwar history of the philosophical reflection on worldlessness unfolded in the field defined by these two paradoxes.

Since the ideas that can be lumped together under the category of worldlessness are quite varied, we often risk talking

5

about entirely different problems when we evoke the term. In order to avoid the dangers of equivocation inherent in this situation, we could start by clarifying a few basic approaches to worldlessness. To account for the strange duplicity of worldlessness as an object of fear and desire, we should first separate three levels of meaning that have dominated our discussions so far. One way of paraphrasing the Heideggerian paradoxes would be to say that for postwar philosophy worldlessness became a positive ontological premise, a necessary phenomenological condition and a negative political phenomenon.

1. *The ontological argument*: Ontology has come to accept the fact that being is constitutively worldless. The radical indeterminacy of being implies that being cannot be reduced to yet another object. The totality of existing beings is not just another being in the world but something else (either nothing or a regulative idea). The very discourse of this kind of ontology is based on the lack of a solid foundation: the world does not exist and everything else follows from this fact. In this sense, in spite of its privative formulation, the ontological thesis of worldlessness is a positive thesis.

2. *The phenomenological argument*: The phenomenological argument in favour of worldlessness is based on the assumption that the conditions of experience cannot be part of experience. To put it differently, the agency that makes the world appear itself cannot be on the same level as what it makes appear. If the conditions of appearance themselves do not appear, the world of appearances must be conditioned by something that is essentially worldless (for example, the transcendental subject). Once again, this is essentially a positive form of worldlessness, because we are dealing with

the enabling condition for the very appearance of the world as we know it.

3. *The political argument*: Political critiques of worldlessness assume that human relations are impoverished by recent historical developments to such a degree that essential features of the human condition are being crippled by technological, social and political developments. Under these historical conditions (totalitarianism, capitalism, the reign of social media, etc.), the human individual is isolated to the degree that it loses its capacity to construct a common world of meaning with others. The political task, therefore, is to restore the human being to its proper place in the world.

We should note the peculiar status of phenomenology in this constellation. It takes upon itself the role of a mediating agent between ontology and any possible morality. Since ontology is increasingly unwilling or incapable of establishing a hierarchical order of being, it is less and less likely to be able to produce solid foundations for a system of values. To put it differently, today philosophy is reluctant to argue that it is possible to logically derive from ontological assumptions a solid system of universally valid values. The link between ontology and morality is broken. But, precisely at the right historical moment, phenomenology comes to the rescue and assumes the role of this 'missing link'. It is possible that ontology cannot give us a hierarchical order, but phenomenology postulates the necessity of appearance. This necessity is absolute. Therefore, even a radically 'relativist' ontology can be ultimately tied to a system of values that follows from this minimal absolute necessity. Being is contingent, but appearance is necessary. Consequently, we do have a foothold in being that provides us with a more or less smooth transition between ontology and morality: the idea of the world. For if appearance is necessary, the phenomenological experience of contingent being constitutes something absolute. The world becomes the non-ontological guarantee of values. This minimal morality (based on the immemorial judgement 'the world is good') is, in turn, the foundation of a politics that is now oriented by the idea of the world. Under the conditions of modernity, our politics have increasingly become world-politics in the sense that the ultimate value that defines its horizon is the wish to save the world.

It appears then that the field of phenomenology remains a privileged site of intervention today. Without rejecting the obvious (namely, that things appear), we have to be able to question what phenomenology holds to be obvious: the worldliness of appearances. The goal is not just the formation of a phenomenology of worldlessness (that would account for the different ways worldlessness appears in the world), but the invention of a genuine phenomenology without a world. To the degree that we still think about worldlessness in terms of a tension between the ontological impossibility and the phenomenological necessity of the world, to the degree that we believe that the ultimate philosophical and political task is to save the world, we are still Heideggerians today.

Thus, it might be worth recalling here the banal fact that the phenomenological critique of worldlessness was the product of a specific set of historical conditions: early to mid-twentieth-century Fordist capitalism against the backdrop of new types of global warfare. In the historical context of what appeared to be the apocalyptic onslaught of instrumental rationality and in-dustrialised mass murder, the phenomenological reinvention of the world promised us nothing less than the 're-enchantment of the world'. Even later commentators in this tradition inhabited essentially the same fallen world in which European thought reluctantly but heroically assumed the role of trying to save the world from the ravages of consumer capitalism, totalitarianism and perpetual war. But today the programme of the re-enchantment of the world might have already exhausted its historical possibilities. It is no longer self-evident that the phenomenological critique of worldlessness still applies in a post-Fordist age, when neoliberal finance capital appears to run on the very values of phenomenological world-formation: it presents constantly renewed risk and uncertainty as the projections of authentic possibilities of subjective self-creation and world-constitution in opposition to the centralised, planned economies and unitary subject positions of the Fordist era of modernism.[5]

It is, then, possible that a new future is now emerging on the horizon, a future beyond the Heideggerian paradoxes of worldlessness. It appears to be a sign of our times that the unqualified affirmation of worldlessness has once again become possible and desirable. Therefore, it is a remarkable fact that the contemporary affirmation of worldlessness proceeds in the name of 'realism'. A new generation of thinkers are now convinced that the affirmation of worldlessness is something like a precondition for philosophical thinking today.[6] This book aims to provide additional theoretical tools for the partisans of worldlessness whose numbers, if ever so slowly, appear to be growing with every passing day.

★ ★ ★

The individual chapters of the book trace the way a decision concerning worldlessness ends up structuring the general outline of a philosopher's thinking. The word that needs to be emphasised here is 'decision': in each case, we can detect a specific moment in an author's argument when the problem of worldlessness forces a theoretical decision that, in one way or another, exceeds the scope of the author's general argument. To put it differently, the decision concerning worldlessness has consequences that go beyond what at first appears to be its intended restricted field. What the chapters show is that the discovery of worldlessness is always coupled with a decision to frame worldlessness in a particular way that is, nevertheless, not always consistent with the possibilities of the original discovery.

Chapter 1 is devoted to Heidegger as the originator of the whole problematic that we want to examine here. The expression 'metaphysics of worldlessness' in the title of the chapter refers to the central complication of the Heideggerian critique of metaphysics. To put it simply, the Heideggerian critique of the essential worldlessness of metaphysics in the end leads to something that Heidegger himself cannot acknowledge: the possibility of a metaphysics of worldlessness as the means of the destruction of metaphysics. Heidegger's critique of the worldlessness of metaphysics leads from the worldlessness of the stone (the material object) to the discovery of the worldlessness of Being itself. Yet this connection between Being and worldlessness remains an essentially unexplored insight in Heidegger's work. Heidegger decides not to follow this line of argumentation. But this decision cannot be logically derived from Heidegger's philosophical arguments themselves (if by 'logically' we mean the logic of Heidegger's discourse itself). Thus, the decision is essentially political in nature, in the sense that the philosophical argument does not make it absolutely necessary. At the same time, Heidegger's philosophical argument also opens up the possibility of very different treatments of the worldlessness of Being, even if Heidegger decides to close down these avenues of inquiry by way of a historical argument.

After the opening discussions of Heidegger, the primary objective of the subsequent chapters is to trace the afterlife of the unfinished philosophical programme of reinventing worldlessness in the works of a select number of thinkers who directly engaged the Heideggerian heritage. Thus, following a path suggested by Heidegger himself, first I will examine the worldlessness of life in Arendt and Freud. After this, taking the expansion of the scope of worldlessness to its ultimate limit, I will argue that the works of Lacan, Derrida and Badiou should be interpreted precisely as experiments in the worldlessness of Being beyond the limitations of Heideggerian philosophy.

In order to explore in more detail the implications of Heidegger's political decision concerning worldlessness, Chapter 2 focuses on Hannah Arendt's works. Here the 'politics of worldlessness' means that Arendt discovers the worldlessness of freedom, but still defines politics as a necessary elimination of worldlessness. When she comes to acknowledge the 'structural' necessity of worldlessness, she simply makes a more or less explicit decision not to explore these possibilities any further. She starts with the worldlessness of life as the domain of biological necessity (pure necessity is worldless) and assumes that it takes an act of human freedom to be able to construct a world out of this necessity. But then she herself shows that in order for this world to remain irreducible to mere necessity and, therefore, remain a true world, it must be open to something non-worldly in order to remain free: the possibility of the undoing of this world belongs to the experience of freedom. The unworldly event that guarantees freedom within any world is the miracle of a new birth – in other words, a biological instance of necessity itself. In the end, worldless necessity is the foundation and the guarantor of freedom.

Just like in the case of Heidegger, once again the philosophical and metaphysical arguments about worldlessness are short-circuited by a historical narrative and a political decision. The political decisions made by Heidegger and Arendt are, of course, quite different, but they are identical in the sense that they both try to mobilise an argument against worldlessness as the metaphysical justification of their politics. Among other things, this state of affairs shows that the attack on worldlessness can be compatible with wildly different politics.

As the first two chapters show, in Heidegger and Arendt we encounter two fundamental paradigms of phenomenological worldlessness that are at odds with each other. In an interesting turn of fate, the actual meaning of worldlessness has now taken on two opposing contents: radical objectivity and radical subjectivity. In Heidegger's famous formulation, it is the stone (the mere material object) that is worldless. There is no such thing in Heidegger's world as a worldless subject, since being-in-the-world is constitutive of Dasein. Radical objectivity is the extreme point against which an ontology of living beings can be constructed. On the other hand, in her critique of Heidegger, Arendt gives a completely new content to the term worldlessness: a central thread of her arguments holds that it is radical subjectivity (the loss of all relation to the public world we share in common) that will have to be the operative meaning of the term. Privacy taken to its extreme limit renders us worldless. This is the point where the specificity of psychoanalysis emerges. In a quasi-dialectical overcoming of these two positions, in psychoanalysis the unconscious functions in a way that renders the poles of this opposition inoperative: the unconscious is the object within the subject. It is the most subjective part of the subject that nevertheless remains alien to it like an object. Worldlessness is now the radical objectivity at the heart of radical subjectivity.

Chapter 3, therefore, raises the following question: in what sense is psychoanalysis the paradigmatic case of a 'science of worldlessness'? In stark contrast to the phenomenological tradition (as it is exemplified at this point in our argument by Heidegger and Arendt), psychoanalysis reasserts the historical primacy of worldlessness. On the one hand, Freud's entire meta-psychological project is based on the theoretical 'myth' according to which the worldless organism functions as the historical origin that determines the genesis of the entire psychic apparatus. The organism's constitutive turning away from the world remains one of its fundamental operative drives. On the other hand, we often encounter in psychoanalytic literature a decision concerning contemporary forms of worldlessness. Although it does not necessarily follow from its Freudian premises, psychoanalysis also established the historical conditions of the pathologisation of worldlessness. There is a fundamental tension in the psycho-analytic treatment of worldlessness between worldlessness as a positive enabling condition (or agency) and the pathological manifestations of this persistent historical origin.

Psychoanalysis, therefore, offers us the possibility of a radical reorientation of the problem of worldlessness. The historical dimensions of Heidegger's and Arendt's arguments no longer apply. In comparison with Freud, these historical narratives now take on a strangely teleological form. Psychoanalysis, however, does not connect the metaphysical and the historical/political dimensions of worldlessness (or, in this case, the metapsycho-logical and political aspects) with the same ease. History is not

13

the history of worldlessness in the sense of a simple decline: we used to have the world but, having been poor guardians of the Greatest Good, we lost it all. The Freudian framework offers us a different model that we could reduce to the following two statements: 1. History is repetition: thus, it is the trauma of worldlessness that organises history from the very beginning. 2. What we suffer from currently is not worldlessness but an excess of worldliness. As the thesis of the historical intensification of the superego also suggests, the world intrudes too much into our psyches. The imperative of the superego is precisely to heed the world at all costs.

The fact that psychoanalysis also introduced to us the language of the pathologisation of worldlessness is not so much Freud's fault as that of some of his readers. Yet, Freud himself stops short of a full affirmation of worldlessness as a possibility of fighting the excesses of the worldly superego. Especially in Lacan, it becomes clear that psychoanalysis is the science of worldlessness because it is an ethical practice that forces us to live with our worldlessness. But the enjoyment that we might gain from suffering our symptoms (the compromises of our constitutive worldliness and worldlessness) is still not an active exploration of the positive possibilities of worldlessness. The pathologisation of worldlessness remains a great danger today precisely because it comes to us so naturally that the only way we can conceive of what is wrong with the world today is by claiming that we are in the process of losing it.

But the quintessential decision concerning worldlessness that constitutes psychoanalysis as such is the wager that psychoanalysis is a science. To many, Freud's decision to frame psychoanalysis in these terms immediately appeared to be a decision against worldlessness. To the degree that psychoanalysis is a science, it must partake of the worldview of science and, therefore, cannot even acknowledge the existence of worldlessness. Yet, this could not be farther from what Freud actually says. This decision concerning the scientific status of psychoanalysis, then, is treated as the metaphysical as well as pragmatic foundation of the pathologisation of worldlessness. If psychoanalysis is a science, it must be a science of the world. If it is a science of the world, worldlessness is only possible to acknowledge as a pathological formation. But Freud's metapsychology does not say that worldlessness is pathological: it says that pathology (the decision concerning the dividing line between the normal and the pathological) is constituted against the backdrop of the ontological primacy of worldlessness. The point is not that worldlessness is pathological but that pathology is a way of dealing with the fact of worldlessness. Lacan is the one, then, who takes the Freudian decision concerning science and explicitly formulates the thesis that psychoanalysis is in fact a science but the science of worldlessness.

In light of this encounter with psychoanalysis, Chapter 4 continues the interrogation of the phenomenological tradition by examining Derrida's analyses of worldlessness. In this chapter, the designation of deconstruction as the 'phenomenology of worldlessness' means that deconstruction moves beyond the classic confines of phenomenology by redefining phenomenology in relation to the experience of worldlessness. Thus, deconstruction constituted a quintessential step in the direction of reconsidering the function of the 'world' in the discourse of phenomenology. To the degree that phenomenology defines itself as the phenomenology of worldliness, it is defined by a methodology (the transcendental epoché) and a privileged object (the world as the ultimate horizon of all possible experiences). Derrida shows that the phenomenological critique of the worldless subject is, in

15

fact, based on the hypothesis of an even more fundamental form of worldlessness (radical auto-affection). This move constitutes the ruin of phenomenology in the sense that both its method and its object are now deconstructed. Classic phenomenology cannot make the world appear without excluding worldlessness from its proper field. Its object is constructed by the exclusion of a field of possibilities and this exclusion constitutes the essence of its method. To put it differently, even if it remains a form of idealism that starts by bracketing the 'natural' world to make accessible the world of meaning, phenomenology shows that what exists in experience must be construed in reference to a world (and not worldlessness); and this demonstration is the essence of its method. Therefore, the phenomenological method postulates that we must exclude from the field of appearance that which cannot appear because it is the very negation of the principle of appearance. Worldlessness is therefore excluded from the proper field of phenomenology because it represents an inadmissible agency. The scandal of deconstruction, then, is that it aims to make the excluded appear in the field of appearance. It wants the conditions of appearance to emerge in the field of appearance. As such, it is the phenomenology of worldlessness. But, in the end, Derrida makes a decision not to fully explore the worldlessness of différance. This is a pure decision on his part in the sense that (as he himself admits) he cannot fully justify it. At best, this decision marks an inherent limit of deconstruction as an ethical investment in the world at the expense of worldlessness; at worst, it is a sentimental choice that unnecessarily restricts the potential scope of deconstruction.

As a final step in this engagement of the post-Heideggerian tradition of phenomenology, Chapter 5 turns to Alain Badiou's radical ontology of worldlessness. The quintessential decision

16

that we need to trace here is the one that takes place in the interval between *Being and Event* (1988) and its sequel *The Logics of Worlds* (2006). The essence of this decision is that we must account for the necessity of appearance and the necessity of the world. Ontology alone, however, is unable to accomplish this task. This is why mathematics as ontology must be complemented by a new phenomenology, which Badiou defines as a 'Greater Logic' (a logic that exceeds in its scope all previous forms of formal logic). The term 'logics of worldlessness', therefore, aims to articulate an internal impossibility of Badiou's philosophy. For Badiou, 'logic' and 'appearing' become identical. As a result, the 'logics of worlds' means that there is a logic only of appearing and only of the world. But this decision to identify logic with the world excludes possibilities of worldlessness: what if worldlessness itself has its own transcendental organising principle?

This question is significant in this context because Badiou's decision to supplement the mathematics of worldlessness with a logics of worlds also functions as the philosophical foundation of his major political decisions. Badiou remains today one of the most consistent proponents of the thesis according to which the problem with contemporary capitalism is that it makes the constitution of a common world impossible. Thus, we encounter in his thought a structure that (in spite of all the crucial differences) resembles the basic Heideggerian paradigm: the ontology of worldlessness is tied to a phenomenology of worldliness which, in turn, becomes the foundation of a politics that aims to ward off the contemporary onslaught of worldlessness in the name of saving the world. The assertion of a possible logics of worldlessness is, therefore, necessary in order to be able to establish the thesis that 'worldlessness' is not some disorganised chaos but the site and result of specific operations that structure it in specific ways. This inherent organisation of worldlessness is what renders it relevant for politics.

In addition to providing detailed readings of the works of a select group of thinkers, the five chapters of the book also define five possible approaches to worldlessness: metaphysics, phenomenology, logic, science (or knowledge in more general terms) and politics. As we have already seen, in this series, metaphysics stands out for the simple reason that the project of producing a genuine ontology of worldlessness has already proven to be a viable enterprise. Our philosophers have by now produced several workable models based on the premise that the world does not exist. What remains still difficult for us today is to systematically connect this metaphysics to the other four registers in such a way that we retain our fundamentally positive, affirmative stance towards worldlessness as we move among these domains. Our inherited instinct is that even if we have a positive ontology of worldlessness, we immediately revert to dismissive if not panicky critiques of worldlessness once we begin to talk about phenomenology, logic, knowledge and politics. But the real issue here is not that we begin to hesitate when we try to locate worldlessness in these four registers, but that the very identity of these domains is first established by the exclusion of worldlessness from their fields. Phenomenology, logic, science and politics exist for us only if worldlessness is completely removed from their respective fields. The readings provided here are, among other things, preliminary attempts at rectifying this situation.

★ ★ ★

The arguments of this book were motivated by two theoretical intentions: one critical, the other speculative. The goal of the critical approach is to re-examine the history of the reduction of worldlessness to an unquestionably negative category. The habitual attribution of worldlessness to a wide variety of phenomena with the intention of simply dismissing them from our theoretical agendas has become a critical reflex for us. This unthinking attitude turned worldlessness into something like a theoretical garbage can. Any concept or historical tendency that did not meet our expectations could be simply dismissed as a factor contributing to our worldlessness. By once again paying close attention to how individual authors construed this category and what phenomena they, then, declared to be prime examples of worldlessness, we might be able to recover possibilities of being together that were in the end dismissed all too hastily by our philosophers.

And this is where the speculative adventure begins. For the ultimate goal of this recovery should not be the predictable demonstration that these summarily rejected ideas were in fact not worldless at all. The objective is not to clear the name of the falsely accused and to restore worldlessness to its worldly glory. The speculative approach to worldlessness is based on the strategic necessity of formulating affirmative theories of world-lessness today. Our starting point, therefore, will be the position best captured by the notorious literary formula: *orbis non sufficit*. The world is not enough because there is much more in being than the world itself. By construing the world as an ultimate limit of thought, we willingly discard possibilities of being and of being-together that might in fact contribute in a positive way to shaping our historical destinies on earth. And what is beyond this insufficient world is the mostly unexplored yet surprisingly diverse domain of worldlessness. When the powers that be promise us today nothing less than an infinity of possible worlds, the historical task ahead of us appears to be the invention of new forms of worldlessness.

Notes

1   For a number of quite different formulations of the thesis according to which the critique of scientific, technological, philosophical, economic or political (post-)modernity and globalization must proceed through a recovery of a common world, see the following recent works: Nancy (2007); Irigaray (2008); Malabou (2008); Stiegler (2008); Stengers (2010); Sloterdijk (2013); Crary (2014); Oliver (2015).

2   As merely one possible example of the predominance today of this kind of argument about worldlessness, I would like to refer here to Jonathan Crary's book *24/7: Late Capitalism and the Ends of Sleep*. I find Crary's book to be especially relevant here because it clearly demonstrates the complications that will form the starting points for our analysis. Crary argues that neoliberalism is in the process of producing 'a generalized state of worldlessness' (Crary 2014: 18) by eroding traditional socially constructed barriers necessary for the human management of time. As a result, it institutes a permanent regime of exploitation without a possible outside. To be more precise, sleep remains one of the last domains that it still could not colonize. As a result, sleep is invested in Crary's discourse with the revolutionary promise of resistance to the 24/7 regime. What remains, of course, interesting is that sleep itself could easily be defined as a form of worldlessness (since during sleep the individual radically withdraws from an active engagement of the world). In fact, Crary derives the very necessity of a new politics of care from the fact that during sleep the human being is radically exposed to all possible dangers. In other words, we could argue that two forms of worldlessness organize this argument: on the one hand, we have the negative worldlessness of neoliberal capitalism; on the other hand, we have the positive worldlessness of sleep that functions as the very condition of human sociality (and, therefore, of the absolute exposure to the world).

3   As a recent example of this philosophical predicament, I will refer here to Sean Gaston's *The Concept of World from Kant to Derrida*. In his conclusion, Gaston defines the central challenge of contemporary philosophy as the necessary resistance to 'the lure of the *sans monde*' (Gaston 2013: 161). Gaston uses the examples of Lévinas and Nancy to argue that the

20

categorical assertion of the non-existence of the world is a doomed philosophical project because the idea of the world always returns in their arguments as the unavoidable correlate of worldlessness: 'For Lévinas and Nancy, the *sans monde* is always *with* the world' (Gaston 2013: 163).

4   This point is probably most clearly legible in 'The Age of the World Picture' (Heidegger 1977: 3–35).

5   I would like to thank Jeffrey Nealon for helping me formulate this point with such clarity. Furthermore, I would like to add here that I will not directly engage the question of the aesthetic in this book (which, nevertheless, was a crucial historical supplement of the phenomenological critique of worldlessness), since I plan to explore this question in more detail elsewhere. For preliminary expositions of the way the arguments presented here might be relevant for a theory of contemporary cinema and for a theory of the novel, see Végső (2018a) and Végső (2018b). In addition, for an analysis of the way the idea of the world was deployed in aesthetic and political discourses in the mid-twentieth-century United States, see Végső (2012). In this book, I try to show how a historical world was constructed against the background of ontological worldlessness in reference to three foundational figures: the enemy, the secret and the catastrophe.

6   See, for example, Gabriel (2015), Bryant (2011) and Morton (2013), who explicitly embrace the language of worldlessness. Although they do not necessarily rely on the same vocabulary, we could also mention here Quentin Meillassoux's concept of 'hyper-chaos' (Meillassoux 2010), Ray Brassier's take on 'nihilism' and extinction, as well as Adrian Johnston's work on 'weak nature' (Johnston 2013) as potentially related philosophical hypotheses.

1

The Metaphysics of Worldlessness

The stone is worldless. This is probably the best-known proposition put forward by Martin Heidegger about the problem of worldlessness. Although it appears in a number of different places in Heidegger's writings, the most often quoted point of reference remains Heidegger's 1929–30 lecture course *The Fundamental Concepts of Metaphysics*. As the title of the course also makes clear, the thesis concerning the worldlessness of the lifeless object is an integral part of Heidegger's reflections on metaphysics and forms part of a hierarchical classification of beings: the human being is world-creating (*weltbildend*), the animal is world-poor (*weltarm*), and the stone is worldless (*weltlos*).[1] The world is one of the fundamental concepts of metaphysics and, as such, a basic principle according to which different classes of beings can be distinguished from one another.[2] Worldlessness, as the absence of the world, therefore, functions here as an internal limit of this system – an internal limit of metaphysics itself – in the sense that it designates within metaphysical thought the non-relation of certain beings to one of the fundamental concepts of metaphysics itself. To the degree that metaphysics is concerned with 'beings as such and as a whole', we could justly say that it is the very field of metaphysics that is being divided up in this classification (Heidegger 2000: 17). We can already see that the very definition of metaphysics is at stake in the articulation of this series. And this definition relies on a limit-concept: metaphysics needs the concept of worldlessness only to exclude it from its proper field.

If worldlessness occupies the role of something like a necessary other in relation to metaphysics, the question emerges if it is even possible to speak about a theoretical construction like the 'metaphysics of worldlessness'? At first sight, the expression might appear to be a contradiction in terms. After all, if the world is in fact one of the fundamental concepts of metaphysics, this is so because metaphysics is always concerned in an essential manner with the world itself. While Heidegger acknowledges that worldlessness is a real possibility with regard to certain types of beings (the stone), it is a negative possibility that must be understood in relation to the metaphysics of the world, which always enjoys a theoretical priority. But if the history of metaphysics is the history of worldlessness, the philosophical programme of the destruction of metaphysics is necessary precisely because, in the final analysis, for Heidegger metaphysics itself is worldless in the sense that it prevents us from having an authentic relationship to Being and ushers in an epoch of worldlessness. The problem of worldlessness is, therefore, doubly inscribed in this hierarchy: while a proper metaphysics excludes worldlessness from its hierarchical system, it nevertheless haunts the entire edifice as the elusive historical essence of metaphysics itself.

We must, however, keep in mind that Heidegger himself was not quite satisfied with this threefold division of the field of beings and offered several adjustments to these theses. I would like to invoke here two of his modifications of the original theses as our guides into the problem of worldlessness. Even if these corrections remain fragmentary observations that are often difficult to decipher, they might provide us with a chance to raise the question of worldlessness in a way that will allow the concept to resonate with new relevance for us today. The first revision can be found in *Contributions to Philosophy*, the collection of Heidegger's personal notes and ponderings from 1936–8, which is often cited as a crucial text for our understanding of Heidegger's move beyond the existential analytic of Dasein in his later works. The following notes force us to rethink the meaning of the worldlessness of the stone:

> The darkening and *worldlessness*. (Earlier as *world-poor*! Liable to be misunderstood. The stone not even worldless, because even without darkening.)
> Rigidifying and reversion of life out of the initial opening. Accordingly, also no seclusion, unless the living being is included – 'earth' (stone, plant, animal). Stone and river not without plant, animal. How does the decision regarding 'life' stand and fall? Meditation on the 'biological'. (Heidegger 1999: 218)

The passage introduces three ideas that we need to consider in some detail. First, by distinguishing darkening and worldlessness, it raises the possibility that the stone is 'not even' worldless. Second, Heidegger directly ties the problem of worldlessness to the concept of 'earth', which is identified here with a principle of concealment. Finally, Heidegger argues that life itself needs to be included in the problem of seclusion (*Verschliessung*), so the earth now encompasses both living and non-living beings ('stone, plant, animal'). Thus, not only the lifeless object but life itself ('the biological') is in some kind of a relation to worldlessness.

It appears that Heidegger is now asking us to consider the possibility that there are different degrees of worldlessness: the radical or absolute worldlessness of the stone that is 'not even worldless' must be separated from a field in which the operation of darkening unfolds and which, therefore, also contains the possibility of a more 'proper' form of worldlessness (that was earlier designated by the category of being 'world-poor'). If the earth now includes stone, plant and animal, the possibility of seclusion must be extended to all of these beings. Seclusion, therefore, universally applies to all elements of the series and, as such, assumes the role of a structural possibility: it designates the withdrawal of entities as the very essence of the earth. Darkening, on the other hand, clearly applies only within the sphere of life (and, presumably, only specific segments of this field). It might be possible, then, to distinguish three forms of worldlessness: there is a split between the historical and structural forms of worldlessness; but there is also a third form of worldlessness external to the field defined by this split. To put it differently: there is a worldlessness that is a historical possibility (the darkening of the world); another kind that is a structural possibility (seclusion as a principle of concealment, which also acts as the condition that makes both the world and the darkening of the world possible); and there is the third kind, which is simply outside this tension itself (the radical worldlessness of the stone).

Even if we do not consider these speculations to be definitive, we must therefore entertain the possibility that, rather than being one simple thing, worldlessness might refer to a whole field of possibilities. There are ways (emphatically in the plural) of being worldless. This field of possibilities, therefore, emerges here as a chance to distinguish beings in their relations to worldlessness. This point needs to be emphasised since, in spite of what these notes suggest, in his writings Heidegger never explicitly affirms this possibility in precisely these terms. Although he all but admits that worldlessness can in fact be understood as a way of taking care of things, this insight does not lead to a detailed analysis of what such a relation could mean for Dasein. Just as Dasein can have different relations to the world, there might in fact be different ways of experiencing and articulating worldlessness.

★ ★ ★

Another correction in a similar spirit, this time from the notorious *Black Notebooks* dated 1938–9:

> The designation of stone, animal, and man by means of their relation to the world (see the lecture course of 1929–1930) is to be maintained in the orientation of its question – and yet it is inadequate. The difficulty lies in the definition of the animal as 'poor in world', in spite of the reservation and qualifications made there concerning the concept of 'poverty'. It should not be a matter of being worldless, poor in world, or world-shaping. Rather, *without field and world, / benumbed by the field and without world, /* and *shaping the world-disclosing earth /* are the more suitable versions of the question's scope. Therewith the designation of the 'stone' as without field and world, at the same time and even ahead of time, needs its own 'positive' definition. But how is this to be articulated? Surely, in terms of the 'earth' – but then indeed entirely out of 'world' [*dann aber vollends gar aus 'Welt'*]. (Heidegger 2014: 282)[3]

The world is not enough. In itself, the reference to the 'world' cannot properly articulate the logic of the series, so it needs a supplemental modifier in the concept of the 'field'. What was once simply worldless (*weltlos*) now becomes fieldless and worldless (*feld- and weltlos*); poor in world (*weltarm*) becomes worldless in such a way that it is captivated by its field (*feldbenommen-weltlos*); and world-shaping (*weltbildend*) becomes world forming and earth disclosing (*weltbildend-erderschliessend*). Two further classificatory terms are introduced in addition to the world: field and earth. While the exact meaning of the term 'field' remains obscure in this context, it is clear what function it fulfils in this classification.[4] It designates a non-worldly possibility of being that is in some kind of clearly recognisable relation to other beings: in this sense, it names a worldless relationality. Its role is to displace the 'world' as the sole category for articulating the logic of the series. It divides and multiplies. As a result, the world is no longer 'one' in the sense that it is no longer imagined to have a 'simple' unmediated identity. The world is now always in relation to something other than itself (field or earth). It is not a surprise then that, beginning with the 1930s, Heidegger projects an inherent antagonism into the very heart of this world (that, depending on the context, he designates with terms like *Riss*, *Kampf*, *Streit* and *Auseinandersetzung*). The world as a problematic or torn entity will now always have to be understood in relation to something that (if not quite worldless) is by definition something non-worldly.

We should note that in this new version the imprecise concept of 'being poor in world' completely disappears and is replaced by worldlessness. Both the stone and the animal are now worldless, albeit in different ways. In fact, we might be able to go even further and suggest that earth itself is a figure of worldlessness in this series. This would mean that all three categories (human, animal, object) are defined here as specific relations between world and worldlessness. Through the addition of the problem of the field and earth, it is the very field of worldlessness that can now be divided. As a result, both the world and worldlessness can be articulated in different ways. The plurality of worlds must be matched by the plurality of different forms of worldlessness. At the same time, the specificity of the human being now appears in a different light: what makes this being special is not simply that it is alone in its unique relation to the world as a world-forming entity. On the contrary, it is also the only being enumerated here that is capable of disclosing worldlessness itself. If the task set forth by Heidegger is to provide a 'positive' (and not a negative or privative) definition of the worldlessness of the stone based on its relation to earth, then it is crucial to note that the human being is the only entity defined here as 'earth disclosing' (*erderschliessend*).[5] The worldlessness of the stone is a direct correlate of its relation to earth, but only the human being can disclose this worldlessness as it forms a world.

★ ★ ★

Although these passages remain fragmentary, the significance of these two revisions of the original formula of worldlessness offered by Heidegger is quite clear: they unmistakably mark within the Heideggerian corpus itself the possibility and even the necessity of a philosophical project that strictly speaking remained impossible to carry out within the framework of the Heideggerian system. We can begin to formalise this unrealised programme in reference to four basic movements: 1. The radicalisation of worldlessness that aims to assign to it increasingly more ontological weight; 2. The positive definition of worldlessness that does not conceive of it in negative or privative terms; 3. The expansion of the scope of worldlessness beyond the lifeless object to include life; 4. The subsequent pluralisation of worldlessness that suggests that there are different ways of being worldless. In the end, this fourfold programme remained unrealised and unrealisable because of Heidegger's investment in a recurrent structure of thought that constantly relegates worldlessness to the status of an ontological threat. Worldlessness and its permutations repeatedly function as necessary structural components whose ultimate function is to reveal to us the inherent glory of the world. In this sense, the theoretical references to worldlessness are reduced to mere foils or necessary detours on the way towards a more authentic experience of the world itself. But if we were to follow these movements to their logical conclusions, we would find ourselves face to face with the possibility that worldlessness is (in some of its modalities) a potentially universal component of Being that contains heretofore untapped possibilities for the human being.

Thus, the ultimate direction of the unfinished programme is clear: Heidegger would have had to argue in the end not that the stone is worldless but that Being is worldless. While the basic outlines of his argument are clearly legible in Heidegger's texts, at every crucial moment he retreats from a direct affirmation of the necessary consequences of this thesis. In this sense, Heidegger's treatment of worldlessness remained limited by a tension (if not an outright contradiction) between his structural and historical accounts of worldlessness. On the one hand, Heidegger on a number of occasions provided 'neutral' structural descriptions that designated worldlessness as a necessary component of his system. On the other hand, the historical critique that animated his entire oeuvre was based on a categorical rejection of worldlessness as an authentic way of relating to Being. He found absolutely no redeeming qualities in historical worldlessness that could have guided the human being on its journey towards Being. And, yet, in his late writings there is clearly an approximation between various figures of worldlessness and the idea of Being. In these texts, Being is precisely that which remains irreducible to anything other than itself. But if Being is forever irreducible to any world (as it is the condition of the opening of worlds), it manifests itself in the form of a nothingness. One of the ultimate limits of Heidegger's reflections on worldlessness manifests itself in the coincidence of Being and nothingness. If the goal of the destruction of metaphysics is to lead us back to Being, it will have to lead us back to worldlessness itself.

In what follows in this chapter, therefore, I will proceed in two steps: following the general trajectory of Heidegger's thought, first, I will examine the position of worldlessness in the existential analytic of Dasein, and then I will investigate its position in the history of Being. Accordingly, I will start with the argument that the encounter with worldlessness already organised the basic arguments of *Being and Time*. I will try to show that the entire project of defining the facticity of Dasein in terms of a being-in-the-world was structured by strategic references to worldlessness that constantly reproduced a tension between Heidegger's descriptive and normative accounts of worldlessness. Worldlessness functions here as the central point of reference for Heidegger's definitions of Dasein's facticity, its historicity, as well as its relation to death. As a result, the ethical programme set forth in *Being and Time* must be described as an ethics of worldlessness: the condition of any ethical disposition is an encounter with the real possibility of worldlessness. In the second half of the chapter, I will examine a select number of later texts in order to highlight a tension between Heidegger's structural and historical accounts of worldlessness. In Heidegger's works after *Being and Time*, we witness a certain intensification of the problem of worldlessness that never reaches a resolution. I will articulate this tension in terms of the conflict between Heidegger's account of the abandonment of Being in beings (*Seinsverlassenheit*) as the historical threat to humanity and the problem of nothingness. The complication that emerges here is similar to what we have seen in connection with *Being and Time*. This time around, however, we might interpret this tension in terms of a politics of worldlessness: in order to fight the world-lessness of modernity, we must embrace the worldlessness of Being itself.

★ ★ ★

Of course, these two fragments that we examined above belong to a specific moment in the development of Heidegger's thinking, as both are products of the late 1930s. Nevertheless, they call attention to the important fact that *The Fundamental Concepts of Metaphysics* did not represent Heidegger's last words on the problem of worldlessness. In fact, it did not even represent Heidegger's first attempts to tackle this question. The idea of worldlessness was already one of the organising concepts of the argument of *Being and Time* (1927). The significance of *Being and Time* for this brief genealogy of worldlessness lies in the fact that it clearly displays a pattern that, in spite of all the changes in Heidegger's thinking, will dominate his treatment of the subject till the very end. As I have already indicated, at the heart of this discussion of worldlessness we find a clearly definable tension. On the one hand, worldlessness is given a specific location in the

Heideggerian edifice and becomes something like a structural necessity. The world and worldlessness enter a perpetual struggle with each other. On the other hand, this descriptive account is clearly linked to a normative hierarchy. It is hard to deny that, in the end, the world does represent a positive value for Heidegger in opposition to the bleak prospects of worldlessness. There is then a palpable tension between the structural and the historical as well as the descriptive and normative accounts of worldlessness in Heidegger's works that will be important for his critique of modernity.

While the term worldlessness (*Weltlosigkeit*) is not part of the vocabulary deployed in *Being and Time*, the adjective 'worldless' (*weltlos*) does play a crucial role in the argument. It refers to a central issue in Heidegger's critique of the Cartesian subject. To put it simply, one of the often-repeated theses of the book is that there is no such thing as a worldless subject. It is a mistake to conceive of the subject as a primarily worldless entity that then, in a secondary modification of its actual existence, receives the world as a possible supplement. Heidegger's critique of the theory of the subject is based on the insight that modern philosophy presupposed the structural primacy of worldlessness over the world. But, as Heidegger keeps insisting, Dasein is constitutively worldly: 'Not too much, but *too little* is "presupposed" for the ontology of Dasein, if one "starts out with" a worldless I in order then to provide that I with an object and an ontologically groundless relation to that object' (Heidegger 2010: 302).

The subject is worldless. This, then, is the philosophical fantasy that Heidegger wants to destroy: the subject as something objectively present. It is in this sense that the whole of the modern theory of the subject from Descartes to Kant is criticised in *Being and Time*. The problem is that this modern subject is understood on the basis of the (modern) object. It is first and foremost a worldless object among other objects that then receives the gift of the world in a specific relationship to objects other than itself. The primary task of phenomenology is, therefore, the destruction of this metaphysical illusion. Accordingly, the programme of the 'phenomenological destruction of the *"cogito sum"'* (Heidegger 2010: 88) proceeds precisely by undoing the primacy of the subject–object relationship based on the definition of being as objective presence:

> If the 'cogito sum' is to serve as the point of departure for the existential analytic, we not only need to turn it around, but we need a new ontological and phenomenological confirmation of its content. Then the first statement is 'sum', in the sense of I-am-in-a-world. As such a being, 'I am' ['bin ich'] in the possibility of being together with innerworldly beings. In contrast, Descartes says that *cogitationes* are indeed objectively present and an ego is also objectively present as a worldless *res cogitans*. (Heidegger 2010: 203)

Heidegger's critique of Descartes' interpretation of the world shows that in Descartes' ontology the world is identified with one specific type of being, *res extensa*. Descartes defines the being of beings as 'substance'. These substances are then declared to have specific attributes among which one eminent property stands out that remains constant: extension. Thus, the problem of the world is reduced to that of extension. This is why the ontological definition of the world provided by Descartes is erroneous. Although he distinguishes three substances – God, res cogitans (ego), res extensa (world) – Descartes avoids the ontological question of substantiality as such and is happy to conclude that substance in itself is inaccessible. As a result, Descartes 'passes over' the phenomenon of world the same way that he passes over the being of innerworldly beings initially at hand.

Heidegger describes this philosophical move by claiming that Descartes switches from 'traditional ontology to modern mathematical physics and its transcendental foundations' (Heidegger 2010: 94) when he reduces Being to the constant presence of what enduringly remains. This is the kind of being that mathematics is concerned with. But Descartes does not raise the question of access to innerworldly beings (he takes 'intuition' for granted). The result is a series of false identifications: first, he identifies Being with constant presence; then, he identifies this Being as constant presence with the being of innerworldly beings; and, finally, he identifies innerworldly beings with the world as such. The meaning of these identifications is clear: Descartes identified the being of a definite innerworldly being with the world itself. To put it differently, he 'forced the ontology of the "world" into the ontology of particular innerworldly being' (Heidegger 2010: 96). The most important consequence of this identification is that Descartes does not have an ontology of the world, only an ontology of nature.[6] This is, of course, not Heidegger's language, but we could also conclude here that the problem with Descartes' ontology of the world is that it produces a specific kind of worldlessness. On the one hand, it is predicated upon the false presupposition of a worldless subject. On the other hand, in its confusion of nature with the world, it reduces the world itself to something essentially worldless (the objective presence of innerworldly beings). A worldless subject produces a world that it then reduces to the mere objective presence of worldless beings.

This rejection of the implicit ontology of worldlessness inherent in Descartes' philosophy also clearly anticipates

Heidegger's critique of science. In fact, in the context of this critique, we could justly speak of something like the 'worldlessness of science'. For Heidegger is very clear about this point: science produces something like the 'de-worlding' [*Entweltlichung*] of the world (Heidegger 2010: 65). Thus, science is worldless, and the worldless form of knowledge that it embodies defines the fate of Western modernity. The possibility of this worldless science, however, is inherent in the very existential constitution of Dasein. It belongs to the possibility of Dasein's being that it relates to the world in a knowing manner. This knowledge can become mere cognition, and the purely epistemological orientation towards beings reduces the world to nature. Thus, nature is not only not identical with the world, but it is precisely a figure of worldlessness: 'Ontologically and categorically understood, nature is a limit case of the being of possible innerworldly beings. Dasein can discover beings as nature in this sense only in a definite mode of its being-in-the-world. This kind of knowledge has the character of a certain "de-worlding" of the world' (Heidegger 2010: 65). Heidegger's paradoxical conclusion is that (as long as we assert the primacy of an epistemological subject–object relation to the totality of beings) 'knowing the world' actually amounts to a certain ignorance of the world. When we know the world in this way, we do not really *know* the world and we do not really know *the world*. We simply misinterpret an essential constitutive factor of Dasein (being-in-the-world) and reduce it to one of Dasein's factical possibilities. In this situation, knowing the world becomes its own opposite. This shows that the metaphysical idea of the world can, in fact, become the means of the production of historical worldlessness. The worldlessness of science, therefore, is based on a misunderstanding of its own status: it does not know that it is worldless. To the contrary, it is convinced that it produces the only reliable knowledge of the world and that it grants us the most authentic access to the world.

* * *

Heidegger's answer to these supposedly erroneous theories of the worldless subject is the thesis of Dasein's constitutive being-in-the-world. But the critique of the philosophical myth of the priority of the worldless subject does not mean that the whole problematic of worldlessness is simply abandoned by Heidegger. To the contrary, worldlessness takes on a central role, albeit in a different capacity. Even if Heidegger no longer presupposes the worldless subject as the necessary theoretical starting point for his philosophy, he still needs to account for worldlessness in order to bring into view Dasein's facticity (the fact that Dasein always already exists in a particular relation to its being-in-the-world). Thus, in *Being and Time*, the analysis of the worldless subject is replaced by the analysis of the facticity of Dasein. But the facticity of Dasein is, nevertheless, articulated in relation to worldlessness: it becomes visible only if it is contrasted with the worldlessness of merely objectively present beings. As a result, the idea of facticity entertains a twofold relation to worldlessness. On the one hand, the entire theory of Dasein's facticity is predicated upon the categorical rejection of the worldless subject. On the other hand, this facticity must include the possibility of an 'inauthentic' relation to Dasein's being-in-the-world in the form of a worldless existence.

This inclusive exclusion of worldlessness from the theory of facticity accounts for one of the most pressing tensions that organise Heidegger's thought on worldlessness: while worldliness is constitutive, the historical threat facing Dasein is nevertheless the prospect of a worldless existence. The force of this theoretical exclusion is most palpable in Heidegger's reflections on what it means for Dasein to be 'in' the world, where Heidegger introduces the classic phenomenological *topos* of 'touching' in relation to the worldlessness of merely objectively present beings:

> A being [Seiendes] can only touch a being present within the world if that first being fundamentally has the kind of being of being-in – only if with its Dasein something like world is already discovered in terms of which beings can reveal themselves through touch and thus become accessible in their being present. Two beings, which are present within the world and are, moreover, *worldless* in themselves, can never 'touch' each other, neither can they *'be' 'together with'* one another. (Heidegger 2010: 55)

The rejection of worldlessness from the constitution of Dasein is articulated here through a basic phenomenological argument. Stones do not touch each other. Touching and the experience of being with other beings belongs exclusively to 'worldly' beings. But this phenomenological argument immediately spills over into another type that we might have to call political in nature for at least two reasons. First, as Heidegger will argue, the historical form of worldlessness that looms over Western humanity threatens (among other things) precisely Dasein's authentic 'being with' other beings. Although Dasein is the only being capable of touching, it can nevertheless lose this special capability that defines its very being as Dasein. Second, however, in this denial of authentic forms of 'being with' to specific types of being (regardless of whether they are lifeless objects, plants, animals or human beings), the possibility opens up that Dasein might find a justification for abandoning its responsibility to care for those beings that are (based on a phenomenological principle) declared to be incapable of touching. To put it differently, what comes into view through the exclusion of worldlessness from the field of Dasein's facticity is the inherent politics of the theory of facticity because it inscribes the necessity of a decision concerning worldlessness into what should appear to be a factual given.

After the initial exclusion of worldlessness from the field of facticity, however, it returns to haunt Dasein's relation to its world. This point assumes a special significance when we continue to read the quoted passage:

> The supplement 'which are moreover worldless' must not be left out, because those beings which are not worldless, for example, Dasein itself, are present 'in' the world, too. More precisely, they *can* be *understood* within certain limits and with a certain justification as something merely present. To do this, one must completely disregard or just not see the existential constitution of being-in. But with this possible understanding of 'Dasein' as something objectively present, and only objectively present, we may not attribute to Dasein its *own* kind of 'objective presence'. This objective presence does not become accessible by disregarding the specific structures of Dasein, but only in a previous understanding of them. Dasein understands its ownmost being in the sense of a certain 'factual objective presence'. And yet the 'factuality' of the fact of one's own Dasein is ontologically fundamentally different from the factual occurrence of a kind of stone [*Gesteinsart*]. The factuality of the fact of Dasein, as the way in which every Dasein actually is, we call its *facticity*. (Heidegger 2010: 55–6)

The problem that Heidegger needs to address here is that, from the perspective of their objective presence, the worldless stone and Dasein might look dangerously similar. The solution to this problem is once again the idea of Dasein's facticity: although

Dasein is constitutively worldly, it always exists in a particular way. What might appear to be mere objective presence is, in the case of facticity, simply a particular realisation of Dasein's being-in-the-world. Thus, Dasein's 'own kind' of objective presence is only accessible to us through an understanding of Dasein's existential structure.

But the passage also raises the possibility of another complication. The entire argument hangs on this distinction: is it possible to establish the difference between Dasein's facticity and mere objective presence in a sufficiently convincing manner? The reduction of Dasein to a worldless objective presence is possible only because Dasein has a world and has the possibility of understanding this relation to the world *as if* it were worldless. In this sense, the worldlessness of Dasein is never an existential fact, only a possible understanding of this fact. Yet it belongs to Dasein's facticity that it can understand its being as if it were worldless. It appears that this facticity (the way in which Dasein actually is) includes the extreme possibility of denying an essential part of its existential constitution. The condition of this state of being is that one must 'completely disregard or just not see' the structure of being-in. Heidegger's language here suggests that this comportment can be either a mistake or a wilful turn against the very constitution of Dasein. One could will to live like a stone without being a stone. In other words, worldlessness is a way of *taking care of* things, even if a negative one (Heidegger 2010: 57).

★ ★ ★

This definition of the facticity of Dasein as the ontological proof against worldlessness, however, also implies that the historicity of

Dasein itself must be understood in terms of a tension between a constitutive part of Dasein's existential structure and one of its possible concretisations. Dasein is historical precisely because its factical being-in-the-world must be perpetually distinguished from a worldless objective presence. As a first step, the definition of history must be based on the renunciation of worldlessness. Only Dasein as being-in-the-world has historicity. There is history only to the degree that there is world:

> The thesis of the historicity of Dasein does not say that the worldless subject is historical, but that what is historical is the being that exists as being-in-the-world. *The occurrence of history [Geschehen der Geschichte] is the occurrence of being-in-the-world.* The historicity of Dasein is essentially the historicity of the world which, on the basis of its ecstatic and horizonal temporality, belongs to the temporalizing of that temporality. (Heidegger 2010: 369, emphasis in original)

In spite of this direct equation of Dasein's historicity with the historicity of the world, however, the possibility of losing this world is still real. In fact, in his explanations of the phenomenological experience of the historicity of the world, Heidegger has to account for the possibility of worldlessness first. Discussing the ontological status of the past to which objects displayed in a museum allegedly belong, Heidegger asks the following question:

> What is 'past'? Nothing other than the *world* within which [antiquities displayed in a museum] were encountered as things at hand belonging to a context of useful things and used by heedful Dasein existing-in-the-world. That *world* is no longer. But what was previously *innerworldly* in that world is still objectively present. As useful things belonging to that world, what is

now still objectively present can nevertheless belong to the '*past*'. But what does it mean that the world no-longer-is? World *is* only in the mode of *existing* Dasein, which, as being-in-the-world, is *factical*. (Heidegger 2010: 362; emphases in original)

Thus, the past is made possible by the structural possibility of losing the world. There is history because innerworldly beings can lose their world. As a result, they lose their status as useful things at hand (the beings that we initially encounter in the world) and become objectively present things without their own contextual totalities of reference. The world that was lost, however, belongs to Dasein. This fact implies that the Dasein whose world is gone is itself 'past'. But this is impossible, since Dasein is never 'past' for the simple reason that Dasein is never objectively present. The claim that 'Dasein is what is primarily historical' (Heidegger 2010: 363) means that innerworldly beings (like antiquities) that are still objectively present in spite of the fact that they belong to the past have a historical character because they belong to the world of a Dasein that 'has-been-there'. This *having-been-there* (*da-gewesen*), however, must be interpreted in terms of Dasein's ecstatic temporality: Dasein stands outside of itself in its essential relations to all three dimensions of time (past, present and future). And, within *Being and Time*, the possibility of authentic temporality (as anticipatory resoluteness) is established in relation to death. Dasein as being-in-the-world is essentially being-towards-death. To be free for death means that Dasein contemplates the loss of its existence as being-in-the-world. Dasein's authentic historicity is, ultimately, oriented by the possibility of worldlessness.

But the logic of phenomenology demands that we start with something other than authentic historicity. Our starting point is an inauthentic relation to this primary historicity from which Dasein can gather itself in order to assume a more authentic existence. The ambiguous name Heidegger gives to this inauthentic relation to historicity is 'world history': 'On the one hand, it signifies the occurrence of world in its essential existent [existenten] unity with Dasein. But at the same time it means the innerworldly "occurrence" of what is at hand and objectively present, since innerworldly beings are always discovered with the factically existent world. The historical world is factically only as the world of innerworldly beings' (Heidegger 2010: 370). The intentional ambiguity of the term 'world history' calls attention to something important. The term contains simultaneously the possibility of referring to the ontological primacy of Dasein's authentic historicity as well as to the phenomenological primacy of its fallenness in the inauthentic historicity of innerworldly beings. The two problems cannot be separated from each other. First, Dasein encounters world history as the history of innerworldly beings. Thus, once again, the articulation of facticity brings in the problem of worldlessness. Dasein 'initially understands its history as world history': 'the being of what is world-historical is experienced and interpreted in the sense of what is objectively present'. Only in the form of a modification of this everyday comportment towards things can Dasein become 'world historical' in the other sense of the expression that refers to the occurrence of the world in the existential constitution of Dasein. To put it differently, Dasein first experiences history in terms of worldlessness (as mere objective presence); and the only way to accede to an authentic 'worldly' relation to history is by reference to another form of worldlessness (the real possibility that Dasein exits from the world through death).[7]

42

★ ★ ★

This necessity of accounting for the historicity of the world through the detour of worldlessness is clearly formalised by Heidegger as a phenomenological principle: the world always manifests itself through such a detour. In fact, *Being and Time* sets us on a path that we could call the phenomenology of worldlessness. If science in essence is the paradoxical and unknowing production of worldlessness in spite of the fact that it cannot acknowledge the existence of anything but the world, the task of phenomenology is to account for the limits of this science. Phenomenology needs the possibility of worldlessness in order to be able to account for the phenomenon of the world.

Phenomenologically speaking, our starting point is the fact that there is world: 'World itself is not an innerworldly being, and yet it determines innerworldly beings to such an extent that they can only be encountered and discovered and show themselves in their being insofar as "there is" world' (Heidegger 2010: 72). Dasein's preontological understanding of the world in everyday taking care of things allows 'the worldly character of innerworldly beings' to appear (Heidegger 2010: 72). If Dasein is always already in relation to world, this world first manifests itself as the referential totality of things at hand (*Zuhandenheit*). What we initially encounter in the world are innerworldly beings that have the characteristics of being useful things. It belongs to the being of these beings that they refer to other things. Here, 'reference' is not the same things as signification – even though they are related problems and are in fact discussed together by Heidegger. Rather, the ontological dimension of 'reference' is the very condition of possibility of signification. Reference here simply means that useful objects that surround us in our everyday circumspect taking care of things point to other objects and, through these relations, also refer to a contextual totality. In its very being, the hammer refers to the nail, to the wood and, eventually, to the totality of the workshop. This totality is what we call world in the phenomenological sense.

But sooner or later, something inevitably goes wrong in the world of useful beings.[8] All of a sudden, an experience emerges that we interpret as the breakdown of reference. For example, a useful being all of a sudden appears to be useless and its mere objective being surfaces (e.g., a broken tool lies before us as a mere thing). In the midst of handiness, unhandiness surfaces, but only for a passing moment, and '[m]ere objective presence makes itself known in the useful thing only to withdraw again into the handiness of what is taken care of' (Heidegger 2010: 73). Heidegger discusses three basic types of this defective experience: a useful thing becomes unusable (and, therefore, conspicuous); a handy thing is not at hand, since it is missing (and, therefore, becomes obtrusive); and, finally, a useful thing gets in the way by appearing in a place where it does not belong (and shows its obstinacy). Although these modes bring objective presence to the fore, they are still bound to the handiness of useful things, and handiness never completely disappears in these experiences (Heidegger 2010: 73).

The question is, how does the phenomenon of world become visible in this experience? What the examples above already anticipate is that the phenomenon of the world emerges precisely when something goes wrong in the world. Thus, the path we have to take is to show how merely objective worldless presence emerges in what is closest to us, the world of useful things (which is not experienced in everyday life as a world). The phenomenology of worldliness, therefore, passes through the phenomenology of worldlessness. We could formalise Heidegger's argument by highlighting the following three moments of this logic: 1. First, we are taking care of things in their usefulness. We are among innerworldly things, but the phenomenon of the world itself eludes us. In its everyday state, the phenomenon of the world withdraws into the background, thereby suggesting that the phenomenological starting point is always the innerworldly phenomenal absence of the world. 2. Then, handiness disappears (or, to use Heidegger's term, 'bids farewell') in unusableness (Heidegger 2010: 73). Something of the worldlessness of mere objective presence shows itself in an innerworldly useful being. 3. Finally, 'Handiness shows itself once again, and precisely in doing so the worldly character of what is at hand also shows itself, too' (Heidegger 2010: 73–4). It is precisely in the experience of the emergence of worldlessness in the innerworldly thing that we are referred to the contextual totality in which innerworldly beings relate to each other. In 'the disruption of reference [. . .] reference becomes explicit' (Heidegger 2010: 74). It is in this disruption that Dasein becomes explicitly aware of the world: 'The context of useful things is lit up, not as a totality never seen before, but as a totality that has continually been seen beforehand in our circumspection. But with this totality, world makes itself known' (Heidegger 2010: 74).

This logic shows that, for Heidegger, the phenomenology of worldlessness is the necessary methodological detour in the phenomenology of worldliness: 'That the world does not "consist" of what is at hand can be seen from the fact (among others) that when the world appears in the modes of taking care which we have just interpreted, what is at hand becomes deprived of its worldliness so that it appears as something merely present' (Heidegger 2010: 74). The condition for the emergence of the world is that the inherent phenomenological worldlessness of the world (the fact that the world withholds itself in everyday taking care of things) must be interrupted by the worldlessness of innerworldly beings that have lost their usefulness. In a sense, the phenomenon of the world is nothing but the surprising emergence of the phenomenological difference between two different forms of worldlessness: the worldlessness of the merely objectively present being, and the everyday worldlessness of the world itself. This state of affairs forces on us a paradoxical conclusion. Once the world emerges, useful things cease to appear as worldly beings and become mere objectively present (worldless) objects. Once the world disappears, useful things become worldly again. It is as if the two phenomena (the world as such and innerworldly beings as useful things) could not ever be present at the same time.

* * *

But are we justified in treating death as if it were another figure for worldlessness in Heidegger's thought? When we say that being-in-the-world is ultimately always being-towards-death, are we saying that being-in-the-world is also being-in-worldlessness? It is clear from Heidegger's discussion that the existential structures of this 'being-in' and this 'being-towards' are two aspects of the same thing. The 'world' always implies 'death': it is only a worldly being that can die. As Heidegger famously insists, only Dasein as being-in-the-world is capable of death (what is merely alive only 'perishes') (Heidegger 2010: 238). Only a being-in-the-world has the capacity or potentiality to become genuinely worldless. In the end, does this mean that after the theoretical renunciation of the worldless subject, Heidegger (if ever so indirectly) ends up arguing that the ethical constitution of Dasein (Dasein's freedom) would be impossible without worldlessness? To the degree that Heidegger's programme is to encourage us to live authentic lives, is he asking us to take the possibility of worldlessness seriously?

Of course, death cannot be simply equated with worldlessness. Rather the two concepts seem to overlap. We could perhaps argue that death remains merely a specific interpretation of worldlessness, since the latter can be equally identified with life as well. Death is, no doubt, worldless, but worldlessness is not necessarily only a form of death. Dasein can assume different relations to the world, among which a few stand out as inauthentic in relation to Dasein's constitutive worldliness. In these situations, however, Dasein himself is not dead and lives an inauthentic life of worldlessness. The way to get out of this life of worldlessness is to orient our existence towards death (as the possibility of absolute worldlessness). Imitating the language of *Being and Time*, we could speak of inauthentic and authentic forms of worldlessness. The negative (or inauthentic) form of worldlessness is a specific kind of life: we live *as if* the world existed, but in reality we completely miss Dasein's authentic worldliness and historicity and live worldlessly. We believe that we know the world, but this knowledge is in fact a mere covering over of Dasein's authentic being-in-the-world. The positive form of worldlessness, in contrast, presupposes that we exist in the certainty of the possibility of absolute worldlessness in order to establish a more authentic relation to the world.

What does *Being and Time* say about death in this regard? The link between death and worldlessness is established at the very beginning of Heidegger's discussion of death in relation to the wholeness of Dasein. It is Dasein's constitutive incompleteness that first gestures towards the problem of worldlessness (Heidegger 2010: 227). Dasein attains its wholeness only in death, in becoming no-longer-Dasein (*Nichtmehrdasein*): 'this attainment becomes the absolute loss of being-in-the-world' (Heidegger 2010: 228). As long as Dasein is incomplete, it has a world. Once it attains to its wholeness, it is worldless. In the section where Heidegger's goal is to dismiss the possibility that the death of the other can provide access to the experience of the death of Dasein, we read the following description:

> Even the Dasein of others, when it has reached its wholeness in death, is a no-longer-Dasein in the sense of no-longer-being-in-the-world. Does not dying mean going-out-of-the-world and losing one's being-in-the-world? Yet, the no-longer-being-in-the-world for the deceased (understood in an extreme sense) is still a being [ein Sein] in the sense of the mere objective presence [Nur-noch-vorhandensein] of a corporeal thing encountered. In the dying of others that remarkable phenomenon of being can be experienced that can be defined as the sudden transition [Umschlag] of a being [Seienden] from the kind of being of Dasein (or of life) to no-longer-Dasein. The *end* of the being qua Dasein is the *beginning* of this being [Seienden] qua something merely [blossen] present. (Heidegger 2010: 229)

The interpretation of the dead body of the other as a mere objectively present thing is erroneous, since the dead body remains 'oriented toward the idea of life': 'This something which is only-just-present is "more" than a *lifeless*, material thing. In it we encounter something *unliving* which has lost its life' (Heidegger 2010: 229). In fact, through the rituals of mourning devoted to the deceased, a form of 'being-with' is preserved that unavoidably leads us back to the world: 'The deceased has abandoned our *"world"* and left it behind. Nonetheless, it is *in terms of this world* that those remaining can still *be with him'* (Heidegger 2010: 230; emphasis in original). This kind of being-together-with the deceased, therefore, does not grant us genuine access to death. We merely stand 'near by' [*dabei*] the death of the other.

A more important connection is established between death and worldlessness when Heidegger outlines the ontological structure of death. The point that we need to emphasise here is the non-relational nature of Dasein's ownmost potentiality of being. Dasein can establish an authentic relation to its being only when it severs every relation to the world. Facing the extreme possibility of absolute worldlessness in death, Dasein has the possibility of moving beyond the worldlessness of everyday absorption in the world:

> Death is a possibility of being that Dasein always has to take upon itself. With death, Dasein stands before itself in its *ownmost* potentiality-of-being. In this possibility, Dasein is concerned about its being-in-the-world absolutely [schlechthin]. Its death is the possibility of no-longer-being-able-to-be-there. When Dasein is imminent to itself as this possibility, it is *completely* thrown back upon its ownmost potentiality-of-being. Thus imminent to itself, all relations to other Dasein are dissolved in it. This nonrelational ownmost possibility is at the same time the most extreme one. (Heidegger 2010: 241)

The dissolution of all relation to others in this most extreme possibility of being evokes the language of Heideggerian critique of worldlessness in very explicit terms. As the 'possibility of the absolute impossibility of Dasein', death is one's *'ownmost, nonrelational, and insuperable possibility'* (Heidegger 2010: 241; emphasis in original). To be more precise, Heidegger defines the full ontological structure of death in the following terms: death is Dasein's 'ownmost, nonrelational, insuperable, certain and, as such, indefinite possibility' (Heidegger 2010: 252). Its ownmost possibility introduces a certain self-reflexivity into Dasein: here Dasein is concerned 'about the being of Dasein absolutely' (Heidegger 2010: 252). At the same time, this ownmost possibility is nonrelational. The anticipation of death individualises Dasein. In this individualisation, 'any being-with others fails' (Heidegger 2010: 252). In fact, 'Dasein can *authentically* be *itself* only when it makes this possible of its own accord' (Heidegger 2010: 252). This does not mean that being concerned with others disappears from the constitution of Dasein – it is simply redirected towards Dasein's ownmost potentiality-of-being. This nonrelational possibility is at the same time insuperable. Dasein must understand that its extreme possibility lies in 'giving itself up', which 'shatters all one's clinging to whatever existence one has reached' (Heidegger 2010: 253). In this sense, anticipation of the possibility of impossibility frees Dasein for death. The certainty of death, however, is not a mere knowledge of the inevitability of death but a mode of *being* certain (Heidegger 2010: 253). This certainty, therefore, is not the kind that allows us to ascertain the being of beings encountered in the world. Its essence consists of being certain of being-in-the-world (Heidegger 2010: 254). (It is this latter that points towards the insuperable totality of Dasein: in being certain this way, Dasein must mobilise the 'complete authenticity of its existence'.) But this certainty remains indefinite in the sense that the exact moment when the absolute impossibility of existence becomes possible remains constantly uncertain. This way death becomes a 'constant threat' most clearly disclosed in the fundamental attunement of anxiety: 'Being-toward-death is essentially anxiety' (Heidegger 2010: 254).

This ontological structure, however, remains covered over in our everyday understanding of death, which is characterised by a certain fleeing from death. What is the meaning of this fleeing from death? The goal of Heidegger's critique of the everyday interpretation of death is to show that its understanding of death in fact 'covers over' (Heidegger 2010: 243) Dasein's ownmost being-towards-death. Death is acknowledged as a possibility in everyday existence, but it is displaced to the 'they': 'one dies' (Heidegger 2010: 243). In its everyday understanding of death, Dasein flees from an authentic relation to death. In this 'evasion of death', everyday Dasein tries 'to veil completely his ownmost nonrelational possibility' (Heidegger 2010: 243). Thus, it tries to evade the extreme possibility of having a singular relation to the structural possibility of a nonrelational existence. As a result, Dasein is 'estranged' [*entfremdet*] from its 'ownmost non-relational potentiality-of-being' (Heidegger 2010: 244). The being-towards-the-end that characterises everyday existence is a way of '*evading that end*'.

It remains an important problem for any discussion of the politics of worldlessness that here the freedom of Dasein is defined in terms of its nonrelational possibility of existence. Freedom is not simply a specific kind of being-together with the world and others. It is the form of being-with that becomes possible only when the possibility of losing all relations becomes real. This possibility, however, is something like a 'pure potentiality'. The actualisation of the extreme possibility of the impossibility of Dasein does not create freedom. The realisation of this possibility simply brings death. In this sense, there is no freedom in world-lessness as such. Heidegger's point is that this extreme possibility must be experienced as such: as a possibility. The existence that is governed by this extreme possibility as real possibility is the existence that has the chance to be free. This, then, is the central proposition of the Heideggerian ethics of worldlessness: there is no freedom in actualised worldlessness, but there is no freedom without the pure potentiality of worldlessness.

* * *

As a result of the basic shift in orientation in Heidegger's works after *Being and Time* (from the existential analytic of Dasein to the analysis of the history of Being itself), we can also detect a parallel transformation in Heidegger's understanding of the world: the world is no longer part of Dasein's existential structure but a necessary moment of the unfolding of Being that assumes the form of a non-substantial, dynamic relation among certain types of being. Consequently, we can also expect a similar transformation in the idea of worldlessness itself: worldlessness is no longer the necessary theoretical detour for Dasein on its way to an authentic relation to the world, but a problem that is internal to the history of Being itself. In this new context, then, we find that the unfolding of this history is still tied in an essential manner to the world (and, to be more precise, to the 'worlding of world'), but Being is clearly always in excess of any world. The history of Being, therefore, takes place in this interval between the fundamental non-worldliness of Being (its ultimate irreducibility to being a world) and the dynamic unfolding of the world (the worlding of world) that is no longer possible to conceive without an internal struggle with a contrary principle (e.g., earth). The excess of Being itself guarantees that the phenomenal world is haunted by a principle alien to worldliness, since every entity that appears in the light of

Being is also determined by its own essence as withdrawal. This excess provides us with the foundation for a positive concept of worldlessness. What we are dealing with here is not the loss of the world but the very condition for the emergence of the world that manifests itself in relation to the world and within the world as an apparently 'negative' principle. Being is the condition of the world but, as such, it also marks this world with the nothingness of an internal limit.

The most immediate consequence of these changes is that the idea of the world is inscribed in an increasingly more complex set of relations. The first major step in this transformation during 1930s was the introduction of the idea of earth as a necessary supplement to world.[9] One of the first systematic formulations of the concept in relation to the idea of the world takes place in 'The Origin of the Work of Art' (1936), where the strife of earth and world makes possible the happening of truth in the work of art. This formula was further complicated by the introduction of the infamous fourfold (*Geviert*), in which the world is no longer directly opposed to earth. In late texts like 'The Thing' (1950) and 'Building Dwelling Thinking' (1951), the world is defined as the simple unity of two dynamic mutually determining oppositional relationships (earth vs. sky, mortals vs. gods). Two major changes should be quickly noted here. First, we should point out that the human being's position is now quite different in this fourfold, since mortals represent merely one of the constitutive elements of the worlding of the world. The world is no longer an internal part of the existential structure of Dasein. Rather, the human being is now one of the poles of the happening of the world. At the same time, we could also say that what was earlier the strife between earth and world is now an 'internalised' set of conflicts within the world itself. The world is not one of the poles of the strife, but the very happening of this complex set of relations.

Yet, the starting point for these transformations could be described as an attempt to account for the world in terms other than the world itself. Since the happening of the world is always dependent on things other than the world, one of the far-reaching yet quite basic assumptions behind these reflections is that, for Heidegger, the world is not everything: Being will always remain in excess of the world. The point that there is more in Being than the world is clearly illustrated by the way the idea of earth functions in 'The Origin of the Work of Art'. We could even argue that the primary function of earth in this essay is to counterbalance the potentially dangerous excesses of worldliness. In other words, the world is not only not everything, but it should not be everything and must be guarded from becoming a totalising force in relation to Being. As a result, in this text, earth functions as a principle of restraint on world both in an ontological and an ethical sense.[10] It appears, then, that it is now important for Heidegger to clearly delimit the proper domain of the worlding of the world in order to safeguard Being itself both from the loss and the excesses of worldly disclosure. While the loss of the world remains a looming historical threat in the background of these arguments, the potential new problem introduced here projects the possibility of a pure worldliness: a world without limits that is let loose in Being without any restraints and tries to bring everything into the light of appearance. Thus, the fundamental formula that seems to organise Heidegger's reflections on worldlessness can be stated in the following terms: while appearing is an absolute necessity, Being must remain forever irreducible to what appears.

In order to establish the necessary limits on the worlding of the world, Heidegger works in this essay with three basic figures of worldlessness: the stone, earth and Being (as nothingness). The worldlessness of the stone remains here a negative example of worldlessness against which it becomes possible to define both the worlding of the world and the necessary positive forms of worldlessness that act as limits on this worlding. In this context, then, the earth represents the principle of worldlessness as it appears within the sphere of revealed Being; while Being (forever irreducible to what is revealed in *phusis*) is a more radical form of worldlessness that is accessible to us only in the form of nothingness. In this sense, as far as the question of worldlessness is concerned, the figure of the earth assumes a mediating role between the worldlessness of the stone and the worldlessness of Being. While the stone is revealed in the field of appearance, it does not provide a space for the worlding of the world. Being, on the contrary, is never present as such in the field of appearance even if it is something like a necessary condition for the worlding of the world. Like the stone, earth does emerge in the light of appearing; but, like Being, it does so as that which does not fully yield its essence to appearance.

We get the first definition of the earth in Heidegger's famous analysis of the Greek temple: '*phusis* lights up that on which man bases his dwelling. We call this the *earth*' (Heidegger 2002: 21). *Phusis* lights up the earth. If *phusis* names the coming forth and rising up of beings in general, this claim suggests that the totality of beings makes visible something other than their appearance. The visible world also makes visible something invisible, but only as something invisible. On the one hand, without this earth, the emergence of the totality of beings would be impossible to conceive, since what emerges needs something to stand on. The earth is what makes the emergence of beings possible. This means that every single being is in relation to the earth. Earth presences (*west*) in beings. On the other hand, earth is what is 'essentially undisclosable' (Heidegger 2002: 25). But it is not what is simply absent from the field of disclosed beings. In fact, one of the essential tasks of the work of art is to set forth the earth, which means precisely to bring it into the open *as the self-secluding*. In other words, the point is to account for the way there is something in beings that withdraws from disclosure. The earth is disclosed as that which withdraws from disclosure. It is not absolute worldlessness but that which appears in beings as something worldless.

This last point, then, takes us to the problem of what Heidegger calls the 'essential strife' of world and earth, a strife in which 'the opponents raise each other into the self-assertion of their essences' (Heidegger 2002: 26): 'To the open belongs a world and the earth' (Heidegger 2002: 31). We can now identify the ontological location for this strife: both the world and the earth belong to the place where Being emerges in the field of beings. While it appears that the world has to do something with the disclosure of beings and earth with their concealment, Heidegger is cautious to avoid simply equating these categories with each other: 'But world is not simply the open which corresponds to the clearing, earth is not simply the closed that corresponds to concealment' (Heidegger 2002: 31). The crucial point Heidegger is trying to make here constitutes an attempt to include concealment itself within the field of disclosure: 'Earth is not simply the closed but that which rises up as self-closing' (Heidegger 2002: 31). This self-closing of beings is, then, presented by Heidegger as a principle of individuation. Heidegger insists that the earth is not some kind of undifferentiated, continuous substance in which beings become undistinguishable. On the contrary, the earth is governed by a principle of 'boundary-setting': 'So in every self-secluding thing there is the same not-knowing-one-another' (Heidegger 2002: 25). It is now earth that becomes responsible for the separation of beings. This 'boundary-setting' and 'not-knowing-one-another' of beings become the worldlessness of the self-secluding thing. Thus, the earth is not an objectively present being but the mark of finitude within the world.

In opposition to the earth, the worldlessness of the stone is defined by Heidegger in relation to the absence of the essential strife of the world and the earth. In the stone, everything is reduced to a mere objective presence:

> *World worlds*, and is more fully in being than all those tangible and perceptible things in the midst of which we take ourselves to be at home. World is never an object that stands before us and can be looked at. World is that always-nonobjectual to which we are subject as long as the paths of birth and death, blessing and curse, keep us transported into being. Wherever the essential decisions of our history are made, wherever we take them over or abandon them, wherever they go unrecognized or are brought once more into question, there the world worlds. The stone is world-less. (Heidegger 2002: 23)

The 'worlding' of world means precisely that we should not try to reduce the world to an objectively present being. Neither world nor earth are mere objects. So, we should keep in mind that the world is not like any of the beings that the human being encounters because the world is in an essential strife with the earth. In other words, the suggestion that the world is 'more fully in being' than beings also implies that (through the mediation of the earth) the world is closer to the worldlessness of Being than mere beings. Yet the worldlessness of the stone falls outside of history precisely because the stone provides no access to the worldlessness of Being.

The question of Being, therefore, introduces a third term to these discussions that takes us beyond the strife of earth and world: the nothing. While the world and the earth are already closer to Being than mere beings, it is the idea of the nothing that will take us one step further in this journey towards Being:

> And yet: beyond beings – though before rather than apart from them – there is still something other that happens. In the midst of beings as a whole an open place comes to presence. There is a clearing. Thought from out of beings, it is more in being than is the being. This open center is, therefore, not surrounded by beings. Rather, this illuminating center itself encircles all beings – like the nothing that we scarcely know. (Heidegger 2002: 30)

The clearing is the location where Being happens. Since Being cannot be reduced to beings, its happening is beyond beings. This 'beyond', however, is not another transcendent location. The open as the location of the happening of Being is immanent to the field of beings. Thus, 'beyond' here simply means that, although the open takes place in the midst of being, it is more in Being than these beings themselves. This clearing is what gives us access to beings (to beings other than ourselves just as much as to ourselves). As such, the open is the very condition of the disclosure of beings, and even concealment of a being is possible only 'within the scope of the illuminated' (Heidegger 2002: 30). In the open, it becomes evident that something happens beyond beings: the nothing.

58

★ ★ ★

This theoretical approximation of the ideas of Being and nothingness functions as something like the ultimate horizon of Heidegger's reflections on worldlessness. In order to begin to unravel this complex topic, we have to briefly consider Heidegger's critique of negation. In 'What is Metaphysics?', this critique is tied to the very definition of metaphysics itself. As is well known, Heidegger argues that negation is always secondary in relation to the nothing that is 'the negation of the totality of beings; it is nonbeing pure and simple' (Heidegger 1998: 85). As a negation of the totality of beings, the nothing is more originary than the negation of particular beings: 'We assert that the nothing is more originary than the "not" and negation' (Heidegger 1998: 86). In fact, in this regard, the nothing functions as the condition of negation itself. But as 'the complete negation of the totality of beings' (Heidegger 1998: 86), therefore, the nothing never 'is'. The predicate of being cannot be attributed to the nothing, for the simple reason that it is precisely that which falls outside every category of being. This, however, does not mean that we cannot talk about the nothing. Just as the only proper way to define the being of the world is to say that 'world worlds', we have to articulate the non-being of nothing as its very essence: 'It is neither an annihilation of beings nor does it spring from a negation. Nihilation will not submit to calculation in terms of annihilation and negation. The nothing itself nihilates [*Das Nichts selbst nichtet*]' (Heidegger 1998a: 90).

The definition of metaphysics that emerges in these pages ties the problem of the nothing to Being in an essential way. If metaphysics is the 'inquiry beyond or over beings' (Heidegger 1998: 93), it is clear that the nothing is a central problem for metaphysics since the question concerning the nothing by definition takes us beyond beings. As Heidegger argues, the question of nothing embraces the whole of metaphysics and implicates Dasein as well. The most important point for us is that Heidegger establishes an essential link between the nothing and Being since they are both beyond beings: 'The nothing does not remain the indeterminate opposite of beings but unveils itself as belonging to the being of beings' (Heidegger 1998: 94). In fact, Heidegger briefly evokes Hegel here and claims that 'Pure being and Pure Nothing are therefore the same' (Heidegger 1998: 95). *Ex nihilo nihil fit* becomes *ex nihilo omne ens qua ens fit* (from the nothing all beings as beings come to be).

Furthermore, Heidegger explains the transcendence of Dasein in similar terms: 'Da-sein means: being held out into the nothing' (Heidegger 1998: 91). It belongs to the essence of Dasein that it goes beyond beings as a whole: 'Such being beyond beings we call *transcendence*. If in the ground of its essence Dasein were not transcending, which now means, if it were not in advance holding itself out into the nothing, then it could never adopt a stance toward beings nor even toward itself' (Heidegger 1998: 91). It is the nothing that separates Dasein's facticity from mere objective presence. Dasein's transcendence in relation to beings as a whole is the condition of Dasein's possibilities of being. Without the distance of the nothing that separates Dasein from beings, Dasein's facticity would be simply objective presence without an ethical dimension. At the same time, however, the nothing also acts as the condition of the unconcealment of beings:

> For human Dasein, the nothing makes possible the manifestness
> of beings as such. The nothing does not merely serve as the

counterconcept of beings; rather, it originally belongs to their essential unfolding as such. In the being of beings the nihilation of the nothing occurs. (Heidegger 1998: 91)

This passage reinterprets the relationship of beings and nothing: the nothing is not the opposite (the external negation) of beings but an enabling condition internal to their being. This double condition (Dasein's transcendence and the internal nothingness of the being of beings) provides the metaphysical formula of worldlessness: in order for there to be a world, the manifestness of beings as such must already include in it that which is forever irreducible to a world, and Dasein must find the ground of its essence in something other than the world in order to be able to exist historically in the midst of beings.

Thus, the metaphysics of worldlessness appears to have two different meanings here. On the one hand, we have the metaphysically determined worldlessness of modern science. Science needs to dismiss the nothing even though 'scientific existence is possible only if in advance it holds itself out into the nothing' (Heidegger 1998: 95). Heidegger seems to argue that, under the conditions of Western modernity, there is no such thing as a science of worldlessness – only a metaphysics of worldlessness, since it is only the latter that can account for the nothing. To be more precise, Heidegger suggests that it is only the erroneous self-definition of science that tries to deny the nothing. The essence of science does not make this denial necessary. There could be another science rooted in metaphysics that could 'disclose in ever-renewed fashion the entire expanse of truth in nature and history' (Heidegger 1998: 95). This would be a science of the nothing rooted in an altogether different metaphysics of the nothing.

On the other hand, if we take the equation of pure nothing with pure Being seriously, we might have to consider the possibility that the nothing is the structural worldlessness of Being itself. This is the most radical claim that we can uncover in Heidegger with regard to the problem of worldlessness. The point is no longer that Dasein is (or has the possibility of being) worldless. It is now Being that is at stake. When Being and the nothing coincide, therefore, we are not imagining a negative state but an enabling condition, the worldless condition of the world itself. It is in this sense, then, that we can distinguish two forms of worldlessness. While there is the kind of worldlessness that can be conceived as the negation of the world, the more originary form is the pure worldlessness of Being itself that is antecedent both to the creation and the negation of any world.

Thus, to think the essence of metaphysics, one must sacrifice the world and thereby establish some kind of a relation to worldlessness. In the 'Postscript to "What is Metaphysics?"', the programme of the overcoming of metaphysics is discussed in precisely these terms. Metaphysics thinks Being as the beingness of beings, but it is unable to ponder the truth of Being. As a result, the truth of being is its 'unknown and ungrounded ground' (Heidegger 1998b: 232). To ask the question of the ground of metaphysics means not only to think metaphysically but also to think in a way that is no longer metaphysical. This non-metaphysical thinking requires what Heidegger calls 'the courage of sacrifice' (Heidegger 1998b: 236–7). It is the freedom to sacrifice the world (beings in their totality) to gain access to and to 'preserve' Being. The 'guardian' of Being must sacrifice the world in an act of 'essential thinking'. In opposition to the mere calculation of beings, this thought must assume 'the courage of sacrifice which has taken upon itself the neighborhood of the indestructible' (Heidegger 1998b: 237). The metaphysics of worldlessness is constituted by this sacrifice: it thinks the essence of metaphysics, but in doing so it paves the way for a non-metaphysical way of thinking.

★ ★ ★

This focus on nothingness also explains how worldlessness is tied to the problem of anxiety in Heidegger. In *Being and Time*, anxiety is a fundamental attunement of Dasein, a fundamental mode of being-in-the-world. The primary object of anxiety is being-in-the-world itself. Heidegger's argument is that anxiety discloses the world to Dasein as a world and, at the same time, individualises Dasein. But this isolation is not worldlessness:

> This existential 'solipsism', however, is so far from transposing an isolated subject-thing into the harmless vacuum of a worldless occurrence that it brings Dasein in an extreme sense precisely before its world as world, and thus itself before itself as being-in-the-world. (Heidegger 2010: 182)

It is precisely the anxious isolation of Dasein (what appears to be its worldlessness) that discloses the world as world and Dasein as being-in-the-world. For Heidegger, anxiety is not the anxiety about worldlessness (the radical isolation of the subject) but precisely the disclosure of the world itself as world. It is the world and not its absence that makes us anxious.

In 'What is Metaphysics?', however, anxiety is described in the following terms:

> All things and we ourselves sink into indifference. This, however, not in the sense of mere disappearance. Rather, in

their very receding, things turn toward us. The receding of beings as a whole, closing in on us in anxiety, oppresses us. We can get no hold on things. In the slipping away of beings only this 'no hold on things' comes over us and remains. Anxiety makes manifest the nothing. (Heidegger 1998: 88)

Experiencing the nothing, Dasein enters into a state of 'hovering': 'In the altogether unsettling experience of this hovering where there is nothing to hold on to, pure Da-sein is all that is still there' (Heidegger 1998: 89). As the example from *Being and Time* also shows, this 'pure Dasein' is something like the worldless subject. However, it is crucial for Heidegger to distinguish the two from each other. Hovering suspended in the middle of nothing as all beings, including the self, are slipping away from it, pure Dasein has a special experience: 'in anxiety the nothing is encountered at one with beings as a whole' (Heidegger 1998: 90). In other words, the specificity of this experience is precisely that the totality of beings as such is identified with the nothing. This identification, however, does not mean the actual annihilation of beings as a whole. It simply means that, 'in anxiety beings as a whole become superfluous'. Pure Dasein is a constitutive being-in-the-world that needs no world. Yet, it needs the experience of worldlessness to prove that it is a constitutively worldly being.

The history of the human being is, therefore, caught between the nothingness of Being and the worldlessness of the stone. If the history of Western metaphysics is truly nothing other than the forgetting of Being (*Seinsvergessenheit*), it is not a surprise that the ultimate historical threat that Heidegger can imagine is precisely that Being abandons beings to the fate of worldlessness (*Seinsverlassenheit*). Ironically, the historical state of perdition imagined by Heidegger in terms of the absence of Being defines worldlessness as the absence of the nothing. Worldlessness is not the state when nothingness takes over the world and the dark night of an empty existence sets in over humanity. To the contrary, worldlessness here is the state when everything exists as it is in its being without the redemptive proximity of nothingness. What is defined here as being worldless is precisely a world without a relation to the nothing.

Thus, the historical threat that Heidegger identifies here is not that the world simply disappears in the night of nothingness but that the world 'turns away'. As we have already seen, according to Heidegger the reduction of *phusis* to the physical world is an exercise in worldlessness. As Heidegger argues in *Introduction to Metaphysics*, *phusis* 'struggles itself forth as a world. Through world, beings first come into being' (Heidegger 2000: 64). This struggle is what Heraclitus calls *polemos*, which is not 'war' but a kind of ontological antagonism that functions as an enabling condition: 'In con-frontation [*Aus-einandersetzung*], world comes to be' (Heidegger 2000: 65). And the creation of this world through strife is the very meaning of the historicity of world: 'This becoming-a-world [*Weltwerden*] is authentic history' (Heidegger 2000: 65). *Polemos*, as struggle [*Kampf*], is not only the enabling condition of the world, since it also remains its operating principle:

> Where struggle ceases, beings indeed do not disappear, but world turns away. Beings are no longer asserted [that is, preserved as such]. Beings now become just something one comes across; they are findings [*Befund*]. What is completed is no longer that which is pressed into limits [that is, set into its form] but is now merely what is finished and as such is at the disposal of just anybody; the present-at-hand within which no world is worlding any more – instead, human beings now steer and hold sway with whatever is at their disposal. Beings become

objects, whether for observing (view, picture) or for making, as the fabricated, the object of calculations. (Heidegger 2000: 65–6)

What kind of a worldlessness is being imagined here? Where struggle ceases, the world turns away. What is this turning away of the world? Obviously, it is not the end of the world in the sense of the complete loss of the world. Beings do not disappear; our relation to them merely changes. They become mere findings since the physical world is worldless.

The turning-away of the world, however, is linked to the possibility that Being abandons beings. This is then Heidegger's definition of historical worldlessness (a state in which Being deserts beings): 'To be sure, beings are still given. The motley mass of beings is more noisily and more widely given than ever before; but Being has deserted them. Because of this, beings are maintained in a seeming constancy (*Ständigket*) only when they are made into the "object" ("*Gegenstand*") of endless and ever-changing busy-ness [*Betriebsamkeit*]' (Heidegger 2000: 66–7). When the historical epoch of worldlessness sets in, everything stays the same – except for a minor detail. The logic of this adjustment evokes Walter Benjamin's reading of Kafka: 'a great rabbi' once said of the Messiah 'that he did not wish to change the world by force, but would only make a slight adjustment in it' (Benjamin 1999: 811). This slight adjustment is the mirror-image of the Heideggerian abandonment of beings by Being. This inverted salvation is a perdition in which hell shows itself as everything that simply 'is'. In a philosophical language, we could say that what happens in this moment of damnation is that the enabling condition (world or Being) deserts the conditioned. Beings become mere objects and the world ceases to world in them – which also means that the nothingness of Being stops happening in beings and everything becomes reducible to what it is as a mere being. According to Heidegger's thesis, this silent catastrophe of the abandonment by Being is the permanent state of affairs that we live in today. What induces anxiety, therefore, is precisely the insight that Being coincides with the nothing – if Being is worldless, the only way to combat our historical world-lessness is to appeal to the worldlessness of Being itself.

★ ★ ★

In Heidegger's writings on the fourfold (*Geviert*), however, we can clearly detect a significant final displacement of the arguments of 'The Origin of the Work of Art'.[11] One possible site for articulating these differences could be Heidegger's definition of the 'thing'. As we have seen, in 'The Origin of the Work of Art', it was the 'work' that provided the key to our understanding of the thing and the equipment. The work was defined there as that special kind of being in which the happening of truth can be put to work through the original strife of earth and world. As such, one of the most important achievements of the work was the very opening up of the world. It was only in relation to this opening of a world that the thingly nature of things and the equipmental character of equipments became accessible. As Heidegger wrote, the thing belonged to the earth (Heidegger 2002: 43).

In the essay 'The Thing', however, the central position is occupied by the thing rather than the work. In fact, in this specific context, there is no reference to the work anymore, and the very possibility of having a world is essentially tied to the thing (and not the happening of truth in the work). The thing takes on the role of a mediating agent between the worldlessness of Being, the human being and the worlding of the world. There is a new proximity between the world and the thing, to such a degree that Heidegger now defines worldlessness itself as a form of thinglessness.

Heidegger describes the worldlessness of the modern age as a kind of distancelessness. Technological inventions like the airplane, radio, cinema and television brought about the 'frantic abolition of all distances' (Heidegger 2001: 165). They might appear to bring the world closer to us, but in reality they deny us any meaningful access to the world. Heidegger's point is that this disappearance of distance also means the disappearance of nearness. In other words, the disappearance of distance does not mean that things reveal themselves to us in a new proximity. To the contrary, the modern world is characterised by a 'uniform distancelessness' that Heidegger calls 'unearthly' (Heidegger 2001: 166). It is a world in which the 'distanceless prevails' (Heidegger 2001: 177). Once again, at the root of the production of this generalised distancelessness, we find the metaphysics of modern science. As Heidegger argues here, the anxiety about the atomic bomb that pervades the era is a completely misplaced fear since 'the terrible has already happened' (Heidegger 2001: 166): 'science annihilated things as things long before the atom bomb exploded' (Heidegger 2001: 170). It is in this sense that the worldlessness of the modern world is a form of thinglessness.

So, what is the thing according to Heidegger? The most important aspect of the thing that needs to be emphasised here is that it is not an object (*Gegenstand*). An object is always an object of representation (*Vorstellung*). But something happens in the midst of beings that establishes a specific set of relations among them. The thing is this happening. The thing, therefore,

is a relational happening rather than a mere object of representation. In this sense, the thing is a more 'dynamic' entity
than a mere object. This dynamism is clearly captured in the
formula: 'the thing things' (Heidegger 2001: 174). What this
means is that the thing is the 'gathering-appropriating staying
of the fourfold' (Heidegger 2001: 174). The thing is a gathering
[*Versammlung*]: it collects and establishes relations among beings
by way of providing a site for the happening of the fourfold.
It is an appropriating event [*Ereignis*]: the four components of
the fourfold establish their identities in relation to each other
through a mutual appropriation. In other words, the ontological
status of this gathering is that of an event. Finally, the thing is
also a staying [*Verweilen*]: there is a temporal and temporalising
dimension to this relation. A way of paraphrasing this definition
would be to say that the thing is a being in which the spatial and
temporal conditions of an event are established.

What is the world in this context? Or, to be more precise,
keeping in mind that the 'thing things', our question should
be: What does it mean that the 'world worlds'? The four components of the fourfold are in a 'mirroring' relation to each other.
They do not exist in isolation before the simple unity of the
fourfold is born. Their identities as parts of the fourfold come
about in the 'fouring' of the fourfold. To put it differently, they
become what they are only when they lose their particularity in
a play of mutual appropriations: 'This appropriating mirror-play
of the simple onefold of earth and sky, divinities and mortals, we
call the world' (Heidegger 2001: 179). Heidegger compares the
dynamism of this mirroring play to a round dance (*Reigen*). The
four are now like couples betrothed to each other in a maddening
circular dance at a wedding. The mirror-play of the world is
this round dance of appropriation. The round dance is the ring

(*Ring*) that joins the four. The way the ring 'is' can be described as the 'ringing' of the ring (*Gering*): 'The gathered presence of the mirror-play of the world, joining in this way, is the ringing [*Das gesammelte Wesen des also ringenden Spiegel-Spiels der Welt is das Gering*]' (Heidegger 2001: 180). The thing then is the being that provides an occasion for the worlding of the world: 'The thing stays – gathers and unites – the fourfold. The thing things world. Each thing stays the fourfold into a happening of the simple onehood of world [*Das Ding verweilt das Geviert. Das Ding dingt Welt. Jedes Ding verweilt das Geviert in ein je Weiliges aus Einfalt der Welt*]' (Heidegger 2001: 181). And this is what the metaphysics of modern science destroys in its generalised distancelessness. What happens in the thinging of the thing is that the nearness of the world nears. Nearness is not something that the thing is 'in'. Rather, the same way that the 'world worlds' and the 'thing things', the near is nearing. The historical worldlessness of modernity consists of the loss of this nearing.

Thus, the world happens through the thing. Historical worldlessness, therefore, is a condition in which the thinging of the thing is rendered impossible. But the current situation is beset by two delusions (Heidegger 2001: 170). On the one hand, as we have seen, Heidegger claims that science annihilates the thing in the represented object. Hence, it is a delusion to think that science can grant us access to the real in its reality. On the other hand, and this is a crucial point, it would be an illusion to believe that 'things could still be things' (Heidegger 2001: 170). The problem is not that we lost the essence of the thing under the reign of modern science, but that we have never had access to the thing: 'not only are things no longer admitted as things, but they have never yet at all been able to appear to thinking as things' (Heidegger 2001: 171). We have always been worldless in the sense that the thing as thing was never accessible to us under the sway of metaphysics.

So the question (which is just as much philosophical as political in nature) is: how do we gain access to the thing today? There appears to be no possible passageway that would take us from the objects around us to an authentic experience of the thing:

> A mere shift of attitude is powerless to bring about the advent of the thing as thing, just as nothing that stands today as an object in the distanceless can ever be simply switched over into a thing. Nor do things as things ever come about if we merely avoid objects and recollect former objects which perhaps were once on the way to becoming things and even to actually presencing as things. (Heidegger 2001: 182)

These lines suggest that the emergence of the thing has to be radically separated from the field of objects. Neither actually existing objects nor the negation of objectivity can grant us access to the thing. The thing is heterogeneous in relation to the object: the thing is something other than an object.

Playing on the different possible meanings of the German word *gering*, Heidegger warns us that we must take the modesty of the thing seriously. On the one hand, the thing is not something 'gigantic'. To the contrary, it is 'unpretentious', 'modestly compliant' and 'inconspicuously compliant' (Heidegger 2001: 182). On the other hand, this modesty also implies the rarity of the thing. In comparison with the commonality of objects and human beings, the thing is a rare occurrence. The enigmatic last lines of the essay leave us with the following definition: 'Men alone, as mortals, by dwelling attain to the world as world. Only what conjoins itself out of world becomes a thing [*Nur was aus Welt gering, wird einmal Ding*]' (Heidegger 2001: 182). The translation, according to which the thing 'conjoins itself out of world', is no doubt onto something. But what I want to emphasise once again is the ambiguity of the expression 'aus Welt'.[12] Commenting on the final sentence of Heidegger's essay, Hans-Georg Gadamer observes: 'This sentence cannot even be translated into German!' After a thorough survey of the semantic possibilities of the neologism *geringen* (understood as a verb), however, Gadamer offers the following interpretation: 'Thus, the final sentence of the essay on "the thing" summarises the way that has been travelled and means: only where world has curled itself around the round ring of a center, regardless of how small it might be, will a thing come to be in the end' (Gadamer 1994: 135–6). Jacques Derrida, in turn, offers the following translation: 'Only what humbly, modestly, is born to the world and through it can one day become a thing' (Derrida 2011: 125). Yet none of these interpretations want to take Heidegger's language literally when he says that 'Nur was aus Welt gering': only what rings 'out of the world' has the chance of becoming a thing. The thinging of the thing might be the centre of the world (as Gadamer suggests), but the thing remains irreducible to the world: the world and the thing are not simply identical to each other. Even if thing and world mutually condition each other, the thing's movement out of the world could be interpreted as a striving towards the privileged location of the worldlessness of Being. The thing is not an object precisely because it is on its way towards Being; and this movement becomes possible only through the worlding of the world, as a move beyond and out of the world.

The connections among man, world and thing can be imagined in the following way: Only the human being has access to the world as world. But the human–world relationship in itself is incomplete. There is a necessary third element, a supplement of sorts, the thing. The thing is the excessive element in relation to the world that makes the human–world connection possible in the first place. The world becomes accessible to the human being as the world only if the thing is present to mediate this relation. Relying on one of Heidegger's puns, we could call the thing a 'condition': if we accept the fact the thing things (*Das Ding dingt*), we also have to add that in this thinging the thing also conditions (*Das Ding bedingt*). As Heidegger puts it, 'we have left behind us the presumption of all unconditionedness' (Heidegger 2001: 181). The world is neither the creation of the human being (as idealism would believe it), nor is it the independent self-presence of material objects. There are subjects and objects, but there are also things. In this sense, the thing is neither inner-worldly nor other-worldly. It is a worldless space of the happening of the world. It is the way the worldless condition of the worlding of the world emerges for the human being in the midst of beings.

★ ★ ★

However, the question remains, what is the politics of worldlessness imagined by Heidegger? If metaphysics is by definition worldless, the goal of politics will be to bring the era of metaphysical worldlessness to an end. To put it simply, the goal of authentic politics is to save the world. The task of the overcoming of metaphysics, however, appears to have been inscribed into two different registers. First, we have the attempt to save the world from technological modernity's onslaught. This position argues against the worldlessness of modernity. This is the political aspect of Heidegger's thought that appealed to a wide variety of people who did not necessary approve of his concrete political decisions. The second register, however, functions as a 'dark' underside of the metaphysical critique of modernity. This darkness is that of the *Black Notebooks* in which the politics of worldlessness finds one of its most significant expressions in Jewish world conspiracy.[13] The precondition for this politics is the historical emergence of what Heidegger calls 'world Judaism' [*Weltjudentum*]. But world Judaism is worldless: 'One of the most hidden figures of the gigantic and perhaps the oldest one is the tenacious skillfulness in reckoning and manipulating and meddling in which the worldlessness of Jewish civilization is grounded' (Heidegger 2014: 97).[14] The Jew becomes worldless precisely at the moment when this figure is identified with the world. The world is now the object of a world-conspiracy of worldlessness. All the theoretical efforts notwithstanding, it appears that the metaphysics of worldlessness needs a concrete agent to represent it in the world. For Heidegger, the metaphysics of technological modernity is embodied in a particular group of people.[15]

The problem with Heidegger's politics of worldlessness, therefore, is that, in the end, he could conceive it only as a historical threat to Dasein even when he imagined it as a structural necessity. This threat was then displaced to a specific historical agent (the worldless Jew). Would it have been possible to avoid this identification? In the spirit of what Walter Benjamin suggests in his 'The Work of Art in the Age of its Technological Reproducibility', we might ask if it would have been possible for Heidegger – or if it is still possible for us today – to produce a concept of the world and that of worldlessness that would have been or would be still 'completely useless for the purposes of fascism' (Benjamin 2003a: 252)?

As a speculative conclusion, we might ask whether there could have been, or still could be, a different politics of the world and a different politics of worldlessness? Can we start with a reversal of the Heideggerian position and ask the following questions: What if it is precisely worldlessness that needs to be saved from the world today, and not the other way around? What if there are things that should not be inscribed in a world? Is it possible that certain things could and should be allowed to persist in their worldlessness? Saving worldlessness, however, does not mean that we must fetishise it. It is not clear that we will have accomplished anything if we simply turn worldlessness into a new world. Rather, the celebration of worldlessness must persist in being worldless to the degree that it refuses to be a world (no matter how small).

How do we oppose the fantasy of the world conspiracy of the worldless Jew? First, we must note that it is not enough to insist that there is no conspiracy. We need to meet Heidegger's 'metaphysical anti-Semitism' on its own grounds and we need to also insist that there is no Jewish world conspiracy because there is no world in the first place. Second, we therefore also need to insist that the point is not to 'reintegrate' the worldless Jew into the world. This world is already metaphysically un-inhabitable for this figure of the Jew. Rather, the point is the opposite: through an analysis of the symptom of the 'worldless Jew' in Heidegger's thought, we should learn to articulate in a positive manner what is attributed to this ideological figure.[16] For it is clear that what the figure of the worldless Jew embodies in Heidegger's thought is something like an inherent limit of his thought. The Jew represents the unavowable possibility of living historically in worldlessness. In this specific context, to learn to live like worldless Jews would simply mean that we would learn to find a liveable community in worldlessness.[17]

It is possible that 'only a god can save us'. But, today, it must save us from the world and not from worldlessness.

Notes

1 'We can formulate these distinctions in the following three theses: [1.] the stone (material object) is *worldless*; [2.] the animal is *poor in world*, [3.] man is *world forming*' (Heidegger 1995: 177).

2 For general discussions of the problem of the world in Heidegger's philosophy, see the following titles: Morriston (1972), Dreyfus (1990), Cerbone (1995), Lafont (2000), Malpas (2006), Gordon (2009), Gaston (2013: 67–98). As these works also demonstrate, much of the critical debate concerning the status of the 'world' in Heidegger's thought focuses on the question of whether Heidegger should be categorised as a realist or as an idealist thinker. Without trying to settle this seemingly interminable debate all too hastily, I merely want to point out here that reintroducing the problem of 'worldlessness' into this debate further complicates the problem. Arguably, while Heidegger's earlier works demonstrate a tendency towards a certain transcendental idealism of worldlessness (since the pure possibility of worldlessness functions here as the condition of establishing Dasein's authentic relation to worldliness), the later works pave the way towards an ontological realism of worldlessness (since in these works the worldlessness of Being is increasingly described independently of the human being).

3 This translation was taken from Krell (2016: 155–6).

4 On the ambiguity of the expression 'feld', see Krell (2016: 155–6).

5 We must, however, also keep in mind the ambiguity of the final sentence of Heidegger's passage. Krell writes the following about this ambiguity: 'The final phrase of the quoted passage, *aus "Welt"*, is difficult to understand: *dann aber vollends gar aus "Welt"*. Is the sense that the stone is to be interpreted "positively" in terms of "earth", which is disclosed to human beings alone, but then "entirely" *excluded from* the concept of world – or, quite the contrary, "entirely" *on the basis of*, or *in terms of* world? The latter would not make a nonsense of the claim that the stone is *weltlos*, although it may seem to; but it would require us to consider once again the final chapters of *Sein*

und Zeit, especially section 80, where "nature" plays a more positive role in the analysis of Dasein than hitherto suspected' (Krell 2016: 156).

6 This critique of Descartes can be extended to the whole of the modern theory of the subject. In fact, Heidegger's other target in this specific context is Kant and what we could call the worldlessness of Idealism. Discussing the spatiality of Dasein, Heidegger writes: '*Space is neither in the subject nor is the world in space*. Rather, space is "in" the world since the being-in-the-world constitutive for Dasein has disclosed space' (Heidegger 2010: 108). In this sense, space shows itself *a priori*: 'This term [the "*a priori*"] does not mean something like belonging beforehand to an initially worldless subject which spins a space out of itself. Here, apriori means the previousness of encountering space (as region) in the actual encountering of things at hand in the surrounding world' (Heidegger 2010: 108). Idealism presupposes a worldless subject only to endow this subject with the power to create the world itself.

7 The well-known historical narrative that Heidegger constructs on the basis of these metaphysical speculations (Western history is the history of the forgetting of being that manifests itself in the rule of science as technology) can now be described as the history of worldlessness. Although the detailed elaboration of the narrative is not part of the argument in *Being and Time*, we find here telling references to how Heidegger imagines the outcome of this story: '*An essential tendency toward nearness lies in Dasein*. All kinds of increasing speed which we are more or less compelled to go along with today push for overcoming distance. With the "radio", for example, Dasein is bringing about today de-distancing of the "world" which is unforseeable in its meaning for Dasein, by way of expanding and destroying the everyday surrounding world' (Heidegger 2010: 103). The worldless being has no history, yet our history is the history of worldlessness.

8 One of the most influential contemporary readings of this aspect of Heidegger's thought can be found in the works of Graham Harman. Harman's argument that tool-being cannot be restricted to a specific type of being and must be interpreted as the general paradigm of all beings is based on the presupposition of the fundamental withdrawal of beings. In other words, in spite of the language that he sometimes uses (which retains the category of the world), we could argue that Harman shows that worldlessness belongs to the very essence of tool-being and that this worldlessness has the possibility of becoming manifest when the tool breaks. For a brief overview of these arguments, see Harman (2011: 35–44). For the argument (partially inspired by Harman's theory of the broken tool) according to which '[i]n

the experience with poetic language there is a temporary suspension of Dasein's entrapment in world', Abbott (2010).

9 For discussions of the idea of 'earth' in Heidegger's though, see the following titles: Oliver (2015: 111–61) and Mitchell (2015).

10 For the argument that there was a significant shift of focus in Heidegger's works from Dasein's world-forming activities to the necessary restraints on Dasein's world-building powers, see Oliver (2015: 130).

11 For discussions of the fourfold, see Young (2001), Harman (2011: 82–94), Mitchell (2015).

12 See note 7 for an earlier discussion of the same type of linguistic ambiguity.

13 For a concise but thorough discussion of the role of the myth of Jewish conspiracy in Heidegger's thought, see Trawny (2015). In addition, see also Mendieta (2017).

14 'Eine der verstecktesten Gestalten des Riesigen und vielleicht die älteste ist die zähe Geschicklichkeit des Rechnens und Schiebens und Durchein-andermischens, wodurch die Weltlosigkeit des Judentums gegründet wird' (Heidegger 2014: 97).

15 Peter Trawny's analysis of Heidegger's 'being-historical anti-Semitism' remains quite relevant here. I would especially call attention to Trawny's analysis of the role of the 'foreign' in Heidegger's thought (Trawny 2015: 47–54). As Trawny puts it, upon first glance, we can distinguish two basic forms of foreignness in Heidegger's reflections on the history of Being: 'To lend the distinction between the two some initial philo-sophical persuasive force, we must distinguish the ontologically foreign from the ontically foreign. There would be, on the one hand, being itself as the foreign itself and, on the other hand, foreign beings that, among other things, could also appear as ethnic foreigners' (Trawny 2015: 51). Being's radical alterity (what we here called the disavowed worldlessness of Being in Heidegger) is opposed to the ontic alterity of specific groups of people. Yet, as Trawny points out, Heidegger quite quickly muddles up these neat distinctions when he tries to associate Being's radical foreignness with Greek and German national identities. This identification leads to a peculiar situation in which the worldlessness of technological modernity is assigned to historical agents like 'Americanism' and 'world Judaism', while the worldlessness of Being, which should remain irreducible to any ontic manifestation, nevertheless enters history through the German people.

16 For a provocative critique of Heidegger in this context, see Emmanuel Lévinas's short essay 'Heidegger, Gagarin, and Us', in which Lévinas identifies the worldlessness of modern technology with the very essence

of Judaism: 'Judaism has not sublimated idols – on the contrary, it has demanded that they be destroyed. Like technology, it has demystified the universe. It has freed Nature from a spell. Because of its abstract universalism, it runs up against imaginations and passions. But it has discovered man in the nudity of his face' (Lévinas 1990: 234).

17 This is what Walter Benjamin suggests in his 'On the Concept of History': 'The themes which monastic discipline assigned to friars for meditation were designed to turn them away from the world and its affairs. The thoughts which we are developing here originate from similar considerations. At a moment when the politicians in whom the opponents of Fascism had placed their hopes are prostrate and confirm their defeat by betraying their own cause, these observations are intended to disentangle the political worldlings from the snares in which the traitors have entrapped them' (Benjamin 2003b: 393). For Benjamin, worldlessness is a tool in the fight against fascism.

2

The Politics of Worldlessness

 Life is worldless. This assumption forms the point of departure for Hannah Arendt's engagements of the problem of worldlessness.[1] Life and world are locked in a supplemental relationship. On the one hand, without life, there is no world. In fact, it is life itself that establishes the conditions of world-formation by producing an excess out of its own essence that takes the human being beyond the needs of mere survival. But there is no world in mere survival itself. The possibility of the world appears on the horizon only when life transcends its biological dimension and becomes more than survival. On the other hand, life represents a constant threat to the world. Nature is something like the enabling condition for the man-made artefact that also threatens the latter with permanent decay and even absolute destruction. Life is what all living beings have in common and, therefore, represents the animality of the human being. The world, however, is the shared human construct that makes the human more than an animal. As a result, life and politics (understood as a communal construction of a world) are constitutively at odds with each other. A term like 'biopolitics' either would have made no sense for Arendt, or it would have had to designate the pseudo-political attempt to eliminate politics itself. Biopolitics is the politics of worldlessness and, as such, no politics at all.

The focus on the worldlessness of life calls attention to Arendt's systematic inversion of the basic Heideggerian thesis on worldlessness that, nevertheless, repeats many of its fundamental assumptions.[2] In opposition to the proposition according to which 'the stone is worldless', Arendt puts forth the argument that it is not the lifeless object but the living subject that is worldless. The inversion affects both terms: the lifeless becomes the living, and the radical objectivity of the stone is replaced by the radical subjectivity of the solipsistic subject. The latter, of course, recalls Heidegger's critique of the worldless subject, but what was a theoretical myth for Heidegger is a historical reality for Arendt. It appears, then, that the lifelessness of the stone is not an important metaphysical problem for Arendt. The fact that the lifeless object is also worldless appears to be an inconsequential fact for her. Worldlessness becomes worthy of our attention not when it happens to the stone but when it happens to the human being. In fact, worldlessness can be applied only to the human being and no other being, since what is at stake in the articulation of the world is the very humanness of this being.

In spite of this inversion, however, Arendt inherits from Heidegger the basic framework within which worldlessness can be articulated as an undesirable condition. On the one hand, her whole thought is oriented by the same rejection of worldlessness that we saw in Heidegger. Politics by definition is the creation of a common world and, therefore, the warding off of worldlessness. In other words, she shares Heidegger's phenomenological investment in the idea (and the experience) of the world. The world must be saved. On the other hand, Arendt also retains the same tension between the historical and structural accounts of worldlessness that, in the end, structured Heidegger's thought. While she agrees that the history of the West is the history of political worldlessness that must be stopped, Arendt also accounts for a structural worldlessness. On a number of occasions, she insists on the fact that the elimination of worldlessness would be just as harmful as the elimination of the world. What can we do with this necessary worldlessness whose very existence seems to go against Arendt's political programme? The urgency of the question is, therefore, rendered even more acute by the fact that Arendt does acknowledge (if ever so grudgingly) the existence of this inalienable form of worldlessness, but then she refrains from exploiting its inherent possibilities.[3]

★ ★ ★

In order to give a schematic shape to our arguments, we could start with the observation that three of Arendt's major books clearly illustrate some of the paradigmatic complications of any politics that defines its own goals in terms of world-formation in opposition to historically produced states of worldlessness. Any such politics will be split between two sets of normative arguments. On the one hand, the politics of worldliness will have to somehow establish the fact that the 'world' represents a positive value that our politics should strive to preserve or bring into being. As a result, a world-politics like this is by definition structured by the conflict between the possibility of worldless-ness and the necessary existence of a world in the general sense. On this level, therefore, we are not talking about concrete worlds but only the mere fact of worldliness or the simple possibility of having-a-world, whatever that world might be like. The crucial point is that the mere having-a-world as a structural possibility already has to be given at least a minimal normative value, since it appears to be unimaginable that worldlessness could have any value whatsoever. The certainty of the undesirability of world-lessness, then, forms the degree zero of any political or even moral judgement in this context.

On the other hand, since not all worlds are created equal, this kind of politics also has to move beyond the structural level and it needs to establish criteria for distinguishing different kinds of worlds from each other. While having a world in general is assumed to be better than not having a world at all, it is never-theless obvious that some worlds might be just about as odious, politically speaking, as some forms of worldlessness. The question, then, emerges whether the political hierarchy of possible worlds could have a foundation other than the structural necessity of worldliness. After professing the moral and political superiority of the fact of worldliness over worldlessness, what criteria can we employ to evaluate the different possible instantiations of this worldliness? How can we move from the minimal value of the mere fact of worldliness to a more complex system of demarca-tions? Can the criteria of these evaluations be strictly speaking worldly (in the sense that they are to be located in specific worlds)? Or do they have to be trans-worldly (in the sense that they apply to all possible worlds)? Or, as an extreme possibility, do they have to be fundamentally non-worldly in nature (in the sense that they have to be irreducible to the problem of worldliness in general)? Regardless of what answers we might give to these questions, it is quite certain that the structural possibility of worldliness might not be able to carry all by itself such an argumentative burden. As a result, it is quite likely that we will need criteria other than worldliness to be able to establish the hierarchy of worlds.

In Arendt's works, the complications of the politics of worldliness play themselves out in terms of a number of possible conflicts between two positive political concepts: the world and freedom.[4] For Arendt, striving for a world is just as desirable as striving for freedom. In fact, the two often mean the exact same thing: in order to inhabit a liveable world, the conditions of political freedom must be present and operative in the human community. But while most of the time the two categories are easy to reconcile with each other, Arendt is also aware of possible conflicts between them. The source of this potential conflict is that freedom remains irreducible to the world. While Arendt starts with the assumption that worldlessness amounts to the absence of freedom (for example, life as the domain of biological necessity cannot give us either a world or freedom), she also discovers through the idea of a necessary form of worldlessness that freedom itself is a worldless agency. This complication leads to a double paradox: 1. Although there is no freedom in worldlessness, without the possibility of worldlessness no world could ever be free. 2. And the source of this worldless freedom from biological necessity is an instant of biological necessity itself: natality.[5] The worldlessness of life produces out of itself both the conditions of world-formation and the conditions of worldless freedom.

In order to illustrate how these theoretical complications play out in Arendt's writings, let us briefly look at three of her best-known works:

1. *The Origins of Totalitarianism* (1951) in effect calls attention to a basic problem of any politics of worldliness: it shows that 'totalitarianism' itself is an extreme possibility of world-politics. In this context, totalitarianism represents the political 'evil' that worldliness might produce out of its own essence. It is important

to keep in mind that, for Arendt, totalitarianism is essentially tied to world-politics in the sense that totalitarianism becomes a real historical possibility only when politics explicitly becomes concerned with the creation of a unified world. The essence of this evil is clearly delineated by Arendt: totalitarianism is the extreme case of world-politics in which the world and world-lessness fully coincide. To put it differently, totalitarianism is so invested in creating a single unified world that it establishes the conditions of a generalised state of worldlessness. In a certain sense, in Arendt's language 'totalitarianism' is the absurd logical conclusion of investing the mere fact of having-a-world with absolute political value.

2. In a similar fashion, *The Human Condition* (1958) calls attention to an inherent complication of any politics that tries to derive the superiority of the world over worldlessness from a philosophical anthropology (that is, from a specific definition of the 'human condition' itself). Here the source of the complication is that the very definition of the human being must establish the criteria for the politics of worldliness. The human being must be defined here as a constitutively world-creating entity that, nevertheless, can be threatened by the spectre of worldlessness. In the end, the central question will concern the human condition's relation to both this constitutive worldliness and what appears to be its necessary counterpart, a constitutive worldlessness. It would certainly be easy to argue that, if world-creation belongs to the very definition of the human being, any politics that promotes this programme is desirable; while any politics that works against this inherent human trait should be rejected. But the moral clarity of this programme can be maintained with such ease only if worldliness alone is a constitutive part of the human being but not worldlessness.

If worldlessness is truly nothing but an external violation of the human being's existential structure, it is easy to claim that all our communal efforts should be directed at rebuffing its assaults. But if worldliness alone is constitutive of the human being (if the human being's historical destiny is truly exhausted by world-creation), it is not entirely clear that we would even need a politics of worldliness, since the fight against worldlessness would be reduced to something like the natural self-defense of the species (not completely unlike putting on a cozy, warm coat in the midst of winter). At the same time, in order to be able to establish the plurality of necessary worlds as a desirable condition (as the very essence of political life itself), we will have to rely on something other than worldliness. The human being cannot, then, be defined merely as a world-creating entity since we still need to account for a structural conflict or antagonism between its possible worlds. In this case, we would have to conclude that the human condition might be accurately described in terms of world-creation only if our definition also makes room for a negative structural principle that works against the very principle of worldliness. One possible solution (and this is the route followed by Arendt in this book) is to argue for the structural necessity of worldlessness. But if both worldliness and worldlessness are structural possibilities, it will take a special effort on our part to establish the fact that only one of them is inherently valuable while the other represents the absolute lack of value. As a result, any politics of worldliness will have to make some room for a politics of worldlessness as well.

3. As a final step, then, *Life of the Mind* (posthumously published in 1978) calls attention to the complications of trying to found a politics in a metaphysics of worldliness. In other words, in this context the political hierarchy of possible worlds should be

based on the inherent structures of Being itself. Arendt's starting point, however, is precisely that there is no hierarchical relation between Being and appearing that could establish the superiority of Being over the world appearances. The worldlessness of Being, therefore, should not be treated as the foundation of an effective politics for the simple reason that there is no political life possible in mere Being. But while political life unfolds in the domain of the commonsense world of appearances, the 'life of the mind' once again takes us back into the domain of worldlessness. Thinking is an essentially worldless activity for Arendt, and it is precisely its worldlessness that turns it into a possible and, depending on the historical context, even necessary political force. To put it differently, the hierarchy of possible worlds is once again disturbed by a necessary worldlessness: while the unliveable nature of the worldlessness of Being establishes the inherent political value of the world of appearances, these worlds themselves threaten to become unliveable without the worldlessness of thinking. It is only the latter that can establish the criteria for distinguishing various possible worlds from each other. The politics of world-formation, therefore, is once again essentially a politics of worldlessness.

At the same time, we can also trace in these three books a philosophical 'deepening' of the problem of worldlessness as we move from historical analysis to a philosophical anthropology and, finally, to a metaphysics of Being itself. On all three levels (history, anthropology and metaphysics), we run into the same set of problems: the politics of world-formation cannot establish its own hierarchical system without reference to necessary moments of worldlessness; but this reference opens up the possibility of a politics beyond these hierarchies. If the world cannot be definitively established as something more valuable than worldlessness, it is possible that politics as such cannot be structurally restricted to the task of world-formation. Even a relatively modest conclusion here would have to concede that, while political activity might certainly manifest itself as world-formation, it must also harbour the possibilities of worldless practices of freedom. But, if that is the case, it might not make sense to try to derive the essence of politics merely from one of its possibilities.

★ ★ ★

First, let us then briefly consider the historical argument as it is presented *The Origins of Totalitarianism*. Upon first glance, the situation appears to be quite clear. For Arendt, totalitarianism represents an especially odious form of the politics of worldlessness. In a certain sense, we could even say that the possibility of worldlessness is the pre-totalitarian 'origin' of totalitarianism. The historical experiences that provided the foundations for the rise of totalitarianism are described in the book with negative terms like homelessness, rightlessness and statelessness – terms that all evoke the idea of worldlessness already in themselves. The inherent possibility of worldlessness functions here as the enabling condition of the birth of totalitarianism, since the latter seeks to exploit this possibility with ruthless consistency.

Arendt's famous formulation of the problem in terms of the 'right to have rights' already indicates that worldlessness is what is at stake here.[6] In fact, the expression 'the right to have rights' refers to the very condition of the politics of worldliness: in order to have a world, one must be enabled to enter this common world in the first place. Therefore, Arendt describes the loss of this right to have rights as 'the deprivation of a place in the world' (Arendt 2004: 376). Those who have lost their right to have rights have lost the world itself: 'Regardless of treatment, independent of liberties or oppression, justice or injustice, they have lost all those parts of the world and all those aspects of human existence which are the result of our common labor, the outcome of the human artifice' (Arendt 2004: 381). The loss of the world, however, is interpreted by Arendt in terms of what might appear to be a paradoxical historical argument. We become aware of the very existence of the right to have rights when people lose this right. As a result, in Arendt's historical account, two opposing tendencies coincide: the absolute unification of the world and the absolute loss of the world. As she puts it:

> We became aware of the existence of a right to have rights (and that means to live in a framework where one is judged by one's actions and opinions) and a right to belong to some kind of organized community, only when millions of people emerged who had lost and could not regain these rights because of the new global political situation. The trouble is that this calamity arose not from any lack of civilization, backwardness, or mere tyranny, but, on the contrary, that it could not be repaired, because there was no longer any 'uncivilized' spot on earth, because whether we like it or not we have really started to live in One World. Only with a completely organized humanity could the loss of home and political status become identical with expulsion from humanity altogether. (Arendt 2004: 376–7)

The historical condition of the loss of the right to have rights is depicted here as the becoming-one of the world. Here we find an early formulation of the thesis that globalisation is worldless. Arendt's argument, however, is that worldlessness manifests itself as the very loss of humanity in an age when humanity becomes conscious of itself as a form of 'concrete universality', as a fully organised global entity. It was the historical birth of the absolute unity of the world that made worldlessness a concrete threat in this specific form as a generalisable condition. If there is only One World, worldlessness is let loose on millions of people who are excluded from this world.

This historical transformation plays itself out in terms of the structural conflict between the singularity of the individual and the universality of the community. Arendt argues that the expulsion from humanity at the heart of this historical form of worldlessness amounts to a full reduction of the individual to the private dimensions of its existence:

> The human being who has lost his place in a community, his political status in the struggle of his time, and the legal personality which makes his actions and part of his destiny a consistent whole, is left with those qualities which usually can become articulate only in the sphere of private life and must remain unqualified, mere existence in all matters of public concern. (Arendt 2004: 382)

This total reduction to the private means that the individual is excluded from the public world of equality and is restricted to the singularity of absolute difference:

> Since the Greeks, we have known that highly developed political life breeds a deep-rooted suspicion of this private sphere, a deep resentment against the disturbing miracle contained in the fact that each of us is made as he is – single, unique, unchangeable. This whole sphere of the merely given, relegated to private life in civilized society, is a permanent threat to the public sphere,

because the public sphere is as consistently based on the law of equality as the private sphere is based on the law of universal difference and differentiation. (Arendt 2004: 382)

The private sphere is depicted here as the zone of existence within which the public tries to contain the ever-present threat of the merely given singularity of the individual. This antagonistic relation between the private and the public (the singular and the universal, difference and equality) is absolutely necessary, although in Arendt's account it is always one side (the public side) that comes out triumphant when it comes to a definition of politics itself.

This formulation of the problem, however, once again shows Arendt's astuteness, since it leads to the introduction of a necessary form of worldlessness: 'No doubt, wherever public life and its law of equality are completely victorious, wherever the civilization succeeds in eliminating or reducing to a minimum the dark background of difference, it will end in complete petrifaction and be punished, so to speak, for having forgotten that man is only the master, not the creator of the world' (Arendt 2004: 383). Although life in the pure privacy of difference is the specific historical threat she examines in her book, the possibility of a public life without the difference of the private (a world without worldlessness) would also lead to catastrophe. It is impossible for Arendt to imagine a full life of worldlessness, since it would imply a stateless, rightless existence fully exposed to the horrors of history. Nevertheless, in the form of the 'private', worldlessness does fulfil a necessary social function. While complete worldlessness leads to a full abandonment by the law, a world without worldlessness gives rise to the totalitarianism of an equality without difference.

★ ★ ★

While Arendt no doubt equates the experience of totalitarianism with a form of worldlessness, upon closer inspection it becomes clear that in the grand historical struggle between the world and worldlessness, totalitarianism represents for her something like a point of indistinction rather than simply the most extreme form of worldlessness. Totalitarianism is the attempt to turn worldlessness into a wholly unified world. This is the inherent contradiction of this political system. But Arendt's argument also reveals the seamy underside of this line of reasoning. If totalitarianism is, in fact, a world of worldlessness, this ambiguity works both ways. The mere existence of totalitarianism already suggests that it might be possible to turn worldlessness into a specific kind of world. At the same time, however, it also suggests that every world is totalitarian in its composition. This latter claim, of course, does not mean that the mere existence of a world will unavoidably lead to the institution of an actual totalitarian political system. It simply means that the permanence of any world is animated by a principle that resists freedom (which always assumes the form of a radical new beginning). This resistance to change is the condition of actual totalitarian systems, but it can have different articulations among which the totalitarian is only one possibility.

At least, this is one of the more challenging arguments of 'Ideology and Terror', the 1953 essay that Arendt eventually decided to add to the second edition of *The Origins of Totalitarianism* in 1958 as a new conclusion to the book. As the title of the essay already suggests, ideology and terror are the two quintessential tools of totalitarianism:

> The compulsion of total terror on one side, which, with its iron band, presses masses of isolated men together *and* supports them in a world which has become a wilderness for them, and the self-coercive force of logical deduction on the other, which prepares each individual in his lonely isolation against all others, correspond to each other and need each other in order to set the terror-ruled movement into motion and keep it moving. Just as terror, even in its pre-total, merely tyrannical form ruins all relationships between men, so the self-compulsion of ideological thinking ruins all relationships with reality. (Arendt 2004: 600)

In this scheme, the function of terror is precisely to destroy the space between human beings that we call the world: 'By pressing men against each other, total terror destroys the space between them' (Arendt 2004: 600). The most important casualty of the elimination of the world is the condition of human plurality itself: 'It substitutes for the boundaries and channels of communication between individual men a band of iron which holds them so tightly together that it is as though their plurality had disappeared into One Man of gigantic dimensions' (Arendt 2004: 600). The abolition of the laws that guarantee proper political distance among individuals leads to the elimination of human plurality. Under totalitarian terror, people become One: the one-ness of this new person is the simple unity of worldlessness, for a man living alone does not live in a world.[7]

Yet, in this reduction of the plurality of human beings to a terrible unity, totalitarianism aims to create a world out of worldlessness. But this is precisely the analysis that eventually puts Arendt on the path to discover (if ever so indirectly) the inverse problem. The inherent totalitarianism of the world first becomes apparent in Arendt's discussions of freedom. Needless to say, totalitarianism is an attempt to eliminate freedom. But freedom is a permanent threat to the world. Freedom is worldless in the sense that it enters the world with the intention of beginning a new world. Although the movement of 'total terror' as the acceleration of the forces of nature and history cannot be stopped, there is nevertheless something that can counteract its seemingly invincible force:

> But it can be slowed down and is slowed down almost inevitably by the freedom of man, which even totalitarian rulers cannot deny, for this freedom – irrelevant and arbitrary as they may deem it – is identical with the fact that men are being born and that therefore each of them is a new beginning, begins, in a sense, the world anew. From the totalitarian point of view, the fact that men are born and die can be only regarded as an annoying interference with higher forces. Terror, therefore, as the obedient servant of natural or historical movement has to eliminate from the process not only freedom in any specific sense, but the very source of freedom which is given with the fact of the birth of man and resides in his capacity to make a new beginning. (Arendt 2004: 601)

Natality (as the cipher of freedom) is a threat for totalitarianism for the simple reason that it is a threat to any already existing world: 'With each new birth, a new beginning is born into the world, a new world has potentially come into being' (Arendt 2004: 599). This constitutive threat of each new beginning is what our positive laws are supposed to contain: 'The laws hedge in each new beginning and at the same time assure its freedom of movement' (Arendt 2004: 600). The law, therefore, plays a double role: it needs to guarantee the freedom of each new beginning; but it must also safeguard the continuity of the common world by counteracting the implicit threat to any permanence that is implied in every new beginning. Only in this restricted sense could we say that the constitution of every world involves a totalitarian dimension that must resist the freedom of new beginnings. But the worldlessness of freedom erupts every time the singularity of the individual makes itself felt in the common world. There is, therefore, an excess of freedom in the world, too many new beginnings, which threatens the permanence of any world. If every new birth in fact led to the creation of a world, no permanence and no world would be possible. The worldlessness of absolute freedom must be contained.

★ ★ ★

The dividing lines between world and worldlessness, totalitarianism and freedom are blurred here to the degree that we need to reckon with a necessary worldlessness: totalitarianism might be an attempt to create a unified world out of worldlessness, but it is only the worldlessness of freedom that can undo this project. The worldlessness of freedom is precisely what we find at the core of Arendt's analysis of the basic experience of totalitarianism. In this context, the radical isolation of the individual functions simultaneously as the condition and the final result of totalitarianism. But, as Arendt explains, this experience is best understood as a fundamentally 'pretotalitarian' (Arendt 2004: 611) structure. In other words, worldlessness might be the enabling condition of totalitarianism as well as its primary result, but in itself worldlessness is not totalitarian for Arendt. In fact, certain forms of worldlessness are necessary both for the constitution of a world as well as for the effective critique of totalitarianism.

One specific location where this point becomes clear is Arendt's distinction between isolation and loneliness:

What we call isolation in the political sphere, is called loneliness in the sphere of social intercourse. Isolation and loneliness are not the same. I can be isolated – that is in a situation in which I cannot act, because there is nobody who will act with me – without being lonely; and I can be lonely – that is in a situation in which I as a person feel myself deserted by all human companionship – without being isolated. Isolation is that impasse into which men are driven when the political sphere of their lives, where they act together in the pursuit of a common concern, is destroyed. (Arendt 2004: 611)

The overlapping fields of isolation and loneliness try to capture two different modalities of the experience of worldlessness: political worldlessness (isolation as the experience of lack of power) and social worldlessness (loneliness as the absence of meaningful social relations). In Arendt's understanding, the experience of totalitarianism implicates both of these fields, even if they are not reducible to the totalitarian experience. To be more precise, the historical specificity of totalitarianism is that it intensifies the experience of worldlessness by combining the two fields into one. In totalitarianism, political isolation is escalated into a generalised state of loneliness. It is this combination that produces the maximal worldlessness of the totalitarian subject.

But, if isolation and loneliness are irreducible to the totalitarian experience, we must also account for the situations in which they produce different kinds of results. For example, Arendt is careful to explain that the general process of production itself needs isolation: 'Yet isolation, though destructive of power and the capacity for action, not only leaves intact but is required for all so-called productive activities of men' (Arendt 2004: 611). As *homo faber*, the human being needs 'to leave temporarily the realm of politics' in order to be able to concentrate on work

(Arendt 2004: 611). Of course, Arendt then also claims that this kind of isolation is never going to be absolute since the individual maintains some kind of a relation to the world. Although work is always performed in isolation, the agent of work nevertheless remains in constant contact with the world since what is at stake in work is precisely the production of an artefact that contributes to the construction of a common world. If the activity of production is deprived of this relation to the produced artefact, it loses its identity as 'work' and becomes mere 'labor'. But when sheer labour begins to dominate all human activities, 'isolation becomes altogether unbearable' (Arendt 2004: 611). In such a situation, nothing remains but the labour of trying to stay alive: 'Under such conditions, only the sheer effort of labor which is the effort to keep alive is left and the relationship with the world as a human artifice is broken. Isolated man who lost his place in the political realm of action is deserted by the world of things as well, if he is no longer recognised as *homo faber* but treated as an *animal laborans* whose necessary "metabolism with nature" is of concern to no one. Isolation then becomes loneliness' (Arendt 2004: 612). Genuine worldlessness arrives only with the shift from work to labour, from isolation to loneliness.

And, yet, the constitutive nature of worldlessness once again complicates the arguments here. As pre-totalitarian experiences that are constitutive of the human condition, isolation and loneliness are nevertheless necessary. The same way that isolation is simply necessary for the production of a common world, loneliness itself is a structural component. Totalitarianism exploits the worldless experience of loneliness: 'But totalitarian domination as a form of government is new in that it is not content with this isolation and destroys private life as well. It bases itself on loneliness, on the experience of not belonging to the world at all, which is among the most radical and desperate experiences of man' (Arendt 2004: 612). The worldlessness of loneliness, therefore, renders the individual uprooted and superfluous: 'To be uprooted means to have no place in the world, recognized and guaranteed by others; to be superfluous means not to belong to the world at all. Uprootedness can be the preliminary condition for superfluousness, just as isolation can (but must not) be the preliminary condition for loneliness' (Arendt 2004: 612). But, in spite of all, this line of argumentation leads Arendt to a strange conclusion: 'Taken in itself, without consideration of its recent historical causes and its new role in politics, loneliness is at the same time contrary to the basic requirements of the human condition *and* one of the fundamental experiences of every human life' (Arendt 2004: 612–13; emphasis in original). Loneliness (as the genuine form of worldlessness) is now simultaneously a constitutive element of human experience and the very negation of the human condition. This conclusion, however, is not necessarily a logical contradiction if we interpret it in terms of an antagonism internal to the human experience: the human condition contains irreconcilable structural possibilities. To put it differently, what is constitutive of the human condition is not worldliness, but a struggle between the forces of worldliness and worldlessness. Totalitarianism is, in a manner of speaking, a short circuit between these irreconcilable structural possibilities, since it makes a world out of worldlessness. But it is precisely the worldless conditions of totalitarianism that have to be mobilised against its absolute rule if we want to welcome freedom into this world.

★ ★ ★

Ideology, the other basic tool of totalitarianism in addition to terror, provides the necessary principle of action for the worldless subjects of totalitarianism but, at the same time, it ruins reality. While terror produces a worldlessness in the form of loneliness, ideology produces worldlessness in the form of the loss of reality. Arendt's definition of ideology, however, is somewhat idiosyncratic. For her, ideology is not 'false consciousness' in general, but a very specific type of misrepresentation of reality that has essential ties to totalitarianism. More precisely, ideology is the application of the logic of an idea to history: 'Ideologies always assume that one idea is sufficient to explain everything in the development from the premise, and that no experience can teach anything because everything is comprehended in this consistent process of logical deduction' (Arendt 2004: 605). So, the danger of ideology is not that it presents an inconsistent or irrational version of history and reality, but that it attributes a logical consistency to them that they do not actually possess. As Arendt argues, then, the three specifically totalitarian elements of ideology are the following: (1) ideology presents a total explanation of history not as what is but what is becoming according to the logic of the idea; (2) ideology is independent of experience and assumes a reality more real than our everyday reality (mostly in the form of conspiracy theories); (3) finally, its methods of demonstration are absolutely logical, even excessively so.

What remains striking in Arendt's descriptions of ideology, however, is that through this analysis the very idea of 'logic' is drawn into the vortex of worldlessness. The structure of ideology reveals that logical deduction is worldless:

> The only capacity of the human mind which needs neither the self nor the other nor the world in order to function safely and

which is as independent of experience as it is of thinking is the ability of logical reasoning whose premise is the self-evident. The elementary rules of cogent evidence, the truism that two and two equals four cannot be perverted even under the conditions of absolute loneliness. It is the only reliable 'truth' human beings can fall back upon once they have lost the mutual guarantee, the common sense, men need in order to experience and live and know their way in a common world. But this 'truth' is empty or rather no truth at all, because it does not reveal anything. (Arendt 2004: 614–15)

Logic simply does not need the world to produce its own truths. This worldlessness is what human beings are thrown back upon when they lose the community of common sense. At the same time, if the loss of the world leads to the total reign of logic, we can also say that the state of worldlessness is not without its own logic. To put it differently, in the state of worldlessness, we are abandoned to pure logic. Worldlessness, for Arendt, is not necessarily an irrational state devoid of any reason but the world of self-evident reason. Arendt, of course, argues that the truths of logic are not really true since they are not political in nature. They are not constructed through the mediation of human plurality but are simply given even to the lonely individual. In this sense, logic has no 'truth', since it does not reveal a world.

Once again, we find that the pre-totalitarian condition of historical totalitarianism is a constitutive element of the human condition. The same way that loneliness is a simple fact of human experience, the worldlessness of logical thought is nothing but a naturally given possibility of human cognition. While the ideal totalitarian subject is the isolated individual who construes historical reality through abstract logical reasoning, of course not every lonely person who happens to think about reality in logical terms (no matter how erroneous they might be) is a ruthless totalitarian leader in the making. Yet, the inherent totalitarianism of the human condition should not be dismissed too quickly here. It calls attention to the fact that, for Arendt, totalitarianism is not just a concrete historical episode but an ever-present possibility of human existence that can manifest itself in different forms and on different scales. Although one tendency of her thinking is to identify worldlessness with totalitarianism and the world with freedom, she herself shows time and again that these four categories (world, worldlessness, totalitarianism and freedom) enter into a dynamic set of relations that are not devoid of chiasmic reversals. While the politics of world-formation inherently contains the possibility of totalitarianism, as we will soon try to show, Arendt herself suggests that worldlessness is itself a precondition of freedom.

★ ★ ★

Of course, with these reflections on the seemingly self-contradictory nature of the human condition, we have already entered the domain of philosophical anthropology. Arendt's most systematic reflection on worldlessness takes place in her second major work *The Human Condition*, where the worldlessness of life is articulated through a whole series of related terms: nature, labour, the social, privacy, the body and even love. What is common to all of these elements is precisely that they represent worldlessness in related but ultimately different registers. In this book, life and the world are defined as conditioning forces of human existence that are somehow at odds with each other. Arendt's list of these conditions runs like this: 'life itself, natality and mortality, worldliness, plurality, and the earth' (Arendt 1998: 11). These conditions are organised around two essential poles: the world and the earth.[8] This opposition of earth and world forms a crucial part of her argument on worldlessness. The earth names the natural conditions of human life, and the world designates the artificial home that humans construct for this life: 'If nature and the earth generally constitute the condition of human *life*, then the world and the things of the world constitute the condition under which this specifically human life can be at home on earth' (Arendt 1998: 134). As a distant echo of Heidegger's essential strife between world and earth in the work of art, Arendt's argument about the mutual dependence on each other of these two conditions concerns the very essence of the human condition:

> Without taking things out of nature's hands and consuming them, and without defending himself against the natural processes of growth and decay, the *animal laborans* could never survive. But without being at home in the midst of things whose durability makes them fit for use and for erecting a world whose very permanence stands in direct contrast to life, this life would never be human. (Arendt 1998: 135)

So, if the world and life are two of the basic conditions of human existence, we need to start with the question: What is a condition? Arendt deploys the idea of the 'human condition' in direct opposition to that of 'human nature'. While there is a natural dimension to human existence, Arendt believes that there is no such thing as 'human nature' – that is, a naturally given essence of humanness. As she puts it, the human being is no doubt a natural living being, but the natural qualities of the human being cannot provide us with a definition of the human being *as* a human being. These natural determinations will never be able to answer the question 'And *who* are we?' (Arendt 1998: 11). As she claims, it is precisely this question that leads to the creation of gods. Philosophical concepts of the divine are often easy to dismiss as mere sacralisations of human capabilities. This insight in itself, however, is not an argument against the existence of God but rather against the existence of human essence.

In opposition to this onto-theology of human nature, therefore, Arendt elaborates the basic terms of a political phenomenology of conditions. The question is, how do these conditions exert their conditioning effects? How do these conditions become manifest in human existence? Arendt's argument is that the human condition is constituted by the fact that the human being is a 'conditioned' being. The human is not simply what it is in accordance with a given essence. Its specific existence is always determined by factors that in the end remain external to any essence. At the same time, however, the human being is also capable of acting on these conditions. Thus, the relationship between the human and its conditions is that of mutual conditioning. On the one hand, humans create the world out of naturally given materials. On the other hand, the world is a conditioning force of human existence:

> The impact of the world's reality upon human existence is felt and received as a conditioning force. The objectivity of the world – its object- or thing-character – and the human condition supplement each other; because human existence is conditioned existence, it would be impossible without things, and things would be a heap of unrelated articles, a non-world, if they were not the conditioners of human existence. (Arendt 1998: 9)

The humanness of the human being is conditioned by the world, which is in turn a creation of the human being itself. The worldliness of the world is a human creation that guarantees the humanness of the human being. The circular relationship between condition and what is conditioned also means that there is no such thing as an absolute condition. In other words, there is no single condition that would condition the human being in an absolute manner. For example, Arendt reminds us that we are all conditioned by earth but, as recent history seems to suggest, 'we are not mere earth-bound creatures' (Arendt 1998: 11). To put it differently, a condition like the earth can change its relation to the human being. The rejection of the very idea of an absolute condition, however, suggests not only that there is no master condition that could determine all other conditions, but also that none of the conditions has an absolute identity in itself. If there is no absolute condition, we must also entertain the idea that there is no self-conditioning condition and that all conditions are themselves conditioned.

This critique of the very idea of human nature shows to what extent Arendt rejects philosophical essentialism. At the same time, however, we can very clearly identify the limits of this criticism, since the rejection of essentialism applies only to the human being:

> It is highly unlikely that we, who can know, determine, and define the natural essences of all things surrounding us, which we are not, should ever be able to do the same for ourselves – this would be like jumping over our own shadows. Moreover, nothing entitles us to assume that man has a nature or essence in the same sense as other things. (Arendt 1998: 10)

This separation of the human being from all other existing entities amounts to an essentialist form of anti-essentialism. If the human being is alone in lacking an essence, it is the unique essence of the human being to be without essence. This anti-essentialism will not be truly anti-essentialist until its scope is expanded beyond the human being to include the world itself. A more consistent anti-essentialism would have to at least admit the speculative possibility that there might be other things that lack essences in addition to the human being. The argument in favour of worldlessness will have to question this limit of her thought. Arendt needs this specific form of essentialism in order to be able to establish the world as an inherently positive category and worldlessness as an inherently negative one. The contradiction is clear: a human being that lacks an essence cannot be tied in an essential way to the experience of the world. There must be forms of being human that are freed from an essential relation to the world. The world is one of the things that conditions the human being, but this condition itself is a conditioned condition. A conditioned condition, however, cannot have an a priori normative value. If there is no human nature, worldlessness must be one of the possible conditions of human existence.

★ ★ ★

But if there is no such thing as human nature and only conditioned conditions exist, what are we left with? Arendt's answer is clear: there are only ways of acting. The human being, in effect, is defined by its actions alone. But this is the point where Arendt's critique of essentialism reaches another curious limit: although the de-essentialised human being is reduced to its actions, Arendt introduces here a hierarchy of possible actions. And the core of this hierarchy is once again the wish to protect the human being from worldlessness. The question for us will be: what justifies the introduction of this hierarchy?

Probably the best-remembered part of Arendt's book is her tripartite typology of human action that distinguishes labour, work and action. These three modes of the *vita activa* are framed by a hierarchical double division. On the one hand, the world is more valuable than worldlessness (a thesis that establishes the centrality of work). On the other hand, there is a similar split within the field of worldlessness itself: the worldlessness of thought (action) is of a higher order than the worldlessness of life (labour). But this hierarchy is defined by an obvious tension between Arendt's descriptive and normative accounts of worldliness: on the level of her purely descriptive analysis, worldlessness time and again emerges in Arendt's account as a necessary structural condition; on the level of her normative arguments, however, worldlessness is obviously a negative category and represents a threat to the politically constructed worlds that human beings inhabit. So, the question is the following: How can Arendt establish a link between the two poles of this tension? How can she establish that the 'world' in itself represents some kind of a value in opposition to the threat of worldlessness?

The problem of worldlessness, therefore, must be mapped onto Arendt's typology of the *vita activa*. The three forms of human activity represent three different ways of relating to the world and, thus, to worldlessness. Labour designates the biological production of life on earth. It guarantees the survival of the individual by producing its necessary means of existence and, thus, ensures the survival of the species. In itself, labour is constitutively worldless, in spite of the fact that it provides the necessary foundations for the construction of the world. It is in this sense that we can justly say that in Arendt's edifice labour represents the necessary worldlessness of the human being. In opposition to the natural dimension, work represents the production of worldliness. Unlike labour, whose products are consumed immediately after they come into being (or they perish by themselves), work introduces permanence and stability to human life. Its products are not consumed but used. Since the products of work are not immediately extinguished in consumption, work creates and preserves the world shared by human beings. Finally, action names the properly political dimension of the human being. Speech and action refer us to the condition of plurality – the existence of others. This is the historical dimension of human existence as it is determined by the condition of new beginnings and, as such, it is the condition of the historicity of the world.

But what is striking here is that in this typology of human actions it is actually worldlessness that dominates the entire field. It appears that both in labour and in action necessary forms of worldlessness determine the human condition. As the creator of a common world, work is inserted between two forms of worldlessness in a desperate attempt to ward off the transience of worldlessness. Labour as a condition of impossibility of the world, appears to be a limit case: while it is worldless, it produces the conditions of a world. But it cannot maintain this world for the simple reason that it produces objects of consumption only incidentally. Its true purpose is not the production of the object but the reproduction of its own process. Thus, if the logic of labour could be totalised (which is the historical tendency behind consumer society), we would find ourselves in a situation in which a world is constantly produced by labour but is immediately destroyed in consumption. This would be a world that flashes up only for a fleeting moment after which it is immediately extinguished. The process of instantaneous creation and immediate destruction enters an endless cycle of repetition. In such a world, the distance between the creation and the eschatological consummation of the world are reduced to an absolute minimum.

Yet, in spite of the fact that action undoubtedly represents a principle higher than labour in Arendt's account, in itself action would be just as worldless as labour. In fact, if we follow Arendt's discussion, we would have to conclude that it is even more worldless than labour. The products of action, speech and thought (which are then significantly different both from consumer goods and useful objects) 'together constitute the fabric of human relationships and affairs' but 'left to themselves, [. . .] they are even less durable and more futile than what we produce for consumption' (Arendt 1998: 95). So, what is their relationship to the world? Arendt writes:

> They themselves do not 'produce', bring forth anything, they are as futile as life itself. In order to become worldly things, that is, deeds and facts and events and patterns of thoughts or ideas, they must first be seen, heard, and remembered and then transformed, reified as it were, into things – into sayings of poetry, the written page or the printed book, into paintings or sculpture, into all sorts of records, documents, and monuments. The whole factual world of human affairs depends for its reality and continued existence, first, upon the presence of others who have seen and heard and will remember, and second, on the transformation of the intangible into the tangibility of things. (Arendt 1998: 95)

This passage makes it clear that the worldlessness of action is constitutive: action is just as worldless as life itself. The problem is that the fundamental conditions of the worldliness of action are external to action itself. Remembrance and reification are themselves not properly speaking actions in the way Arendt wants to define this term. Without these external mediating agents, action, speech and thought would 'lose their reality at the end of each process and disappear as though they never had been' (Arendt 1998: 95). Just like labour, an action instantaneously disappears after it is performed. In this sense, it is even more worldless than labour, since in the case of labour there is at least some distance between the production of an object and its consumption. Action, on the contrary, is instantaneously consummated without producing a tangible object.

Furthermore, labour can produce out of its own process the conditions of world-formation. Since labour can produce more than what is needed for the immediate survival of the individual, it can establish the possibility that some members of the community do not have to spend their lives as slaves to necessity and are free to produce works. Once again, action fails in comparison to labour, since action cannot produce this excess out of itself. It relies on an external set of agents (reification and remembrance) to accomplish this goal. But the logic of this externalisation cannot be derived from action itself. Arendt is clearly aware of this problem when she writes that the 'necessary materialization' of the products of action betrays its essence since it also implies that the 'living spirit' is replaced by the 'dead letter': '[Actions] must pay this price because they themselves are of an entirely unworldly nature and therefore need the help of an activity of an altogether different nature; they depend for their reality and materialization upon the same workmanship that builds the other things in the human artifice' (Arendt 1998: 95). In other words, labour establishes the conditions of work, and work establishes the conditions of action. The worldliness of work is something like the necessary mediator between two forms of worldlessness. But while supposedly the worldlessness of labour reduces us to slaves of necessity, the worldlessness of action elevates us to the domain of freedom.

This is then the central tension that remains unresolved for Arendt: both necessity and freedom (life and thought) are states of worldlessness. The human condition, therefore, is best understood either as a cosmic struggle between two forms of worldlessness or as a struggle within the generalised field of worldlessness itself. The world emerges as a contingent and temporarily limited entity in the internal fissures of this worldlessness. It is neither necessary nor free. It is the prolonged moment when the excess of life over mere survival produces a surface for the reification of thought. The world happens when (as if by mistake yet driven by some inscrutable necessity) worldlessness produces an excess out of itself, and the human spirit captures in this excess the objects of its limited freedom. To put it yet another way: for Arendt, the world is the objectivised difference between the worldlessness of life and the worldlessness of thought. The world as the material difference between two forms of worldlessness is nothing but a kind of 'transcription' of worldlessness. In this sense, at least, in Arendt's thought the world is worldless: it is the reification of worldlessness. The world is simply the way a group of human beings bears witness to the objectification of their essential worldlessness. This world can, therefore, become an object of love (Arendt's *amor mundi*) precisely because under the conditions of human plurality it is imbued, in its very essence, by worldlessness.[9]

★ ★ ★

The anthropological argument put forth in *The Human Condition*, however, is immediately inscribed in a historical narrative. Basically, the entire history of the Western world is depicted by Arendt as the history of worldlessness: Christianity, capitalism and even communism are worldless historical formations.[10] Arendt's critique of Christian worldlessness is focused on two major points: first, Arendt ties worldlessness to Christian eschatology (which is a relation to the world founded upon the ultimate disappearance of the world), but then she argues that it is the Christian concept of 'goodness' (most clearly manifest in the idea of 'good work') that best explains this worldlessness. The problem with Christian eschatology is that it justifies a radical withdrawal from the public sphere. The Christian person is asked to live life as if the world did not exist. But the idea of the end of the world is in direct contrast with the very idea of politics: 'Worldlessness as a political phenomenon is possible only on the assumption that the world will not last; on this assumption, however, it is almost inevitable that worldlessness, in one form or another, will begin to dominate the political scene' (Arendt 1998: 54). It appears, then, that the eschatology of worldlessness has the power to fully contaminate politics. When it appears in politics, it begins to dominate the whole field.

But Arendt also argues that the true foundations of Christian worldlessness emerged only when early Christian eschatological expectations were frustrated by historical events – when the world did not come to an end with the fall of the Roman Empire. Arendt's point is quite clear here: good works represent an extreme case of the early Christian opposition to publicity. Jesus promoted the activity of goodness, which 'obviously harbors a tendency to hide from being seen or heard. Christian hostility toward the public realm [. . .] can also be understood as a self-evident consequence of the devotion to good work' (Arendt 1998: 74). The resistance to publicity is so crucial to the definition of good work that 'the moment good work becomes known and public, it loses its specific character of goodness, of being done for nothing but goodness' sake. When goodness appears openly, it is no longer goodness, though it may still be useful as organized charity or an act of solidarity' (Arendt 1998: 74). In fact, Arendt adds, the goodness of good works must remain hidden to its own author as well. This absolute withdrawal from publicity (according to which the author, the recipient, and the witness of good works must all remain oblivious to the nature of these acts as good works) guarantees the 'curious negative quality of goodness, the lack of outward phenomenal manifestation' (Arendt 1998: 75). In other words, good works must be acts that have no phenomenal manifestations as such in the public or the private domains. They are like the Kantian 'thing-in-itself' of Christian morality: although these acts must completely withdraw from the world of appearances, they nevertheless remain the true essence of moral action within the world.[11]

After this critique of Christianity, then, it is not surprising that Arendt's take on Western modernity relies on a set of similar ideas. At the core of this critique of modernity, we find the diagnosis of what Arendt calls 'the rise of society': 'the emergence of the social realm, which is neither private nor public, strictly speaking, is a relatively new phenomenon whose origin coincided with the emergence of the modern age and which found its political form in the nation-state' (Arendt 1998: 28). While in the ancient city-state the dividing line between the public (*polis*) and the private household (*oikos*) was clear, these lines are blurred for us since the advent of the modern age.

In this original setting, therefore, there was a clear opposition between the political and the social. The household was the site of life and necessity; the polis was the location of political freedom. The specificity of the modern age, then, is marked by the rise of the social as 'a curiously hybrid realm where private interests assume public significance' (Arendt 1998: 35). The rise of society means the rise of *oikos* (economic activity) out of the darkness of the household into the light of the public sphere.

Thus, the emancipation of labour from the private sphere and its inclusion in the public realm led to an 'unnatural growth of the natural', the unstoppable growth of the social realm (Arendt 1998: 47). In a sense, the rise of society means precisely that the natural dimension of the human condition begins to dominate human life with a new intensity: 'it is the life process itself which in one form or another has been channeled into the public realm' (Arendt 1998: 45). But life is the worldless domain of necessity and not that of freedom. Modern society, thus, is a 'society of labourers' in which all members consider what they do to be a means of maintaining their own lives and those of their families: 'Society is the form in which the fact of mutual dependence for the sake of life and nothing else assumes public significance and where the activities connected with sheer survival are permitted to appear in public' (Arendt 1998: 46). Arendt's conclusion is clear: society is worldless.

It is, then, noteworthy that Arendt has to spend quite some time explaining the fact that 'private property' is not entirely worldless. Although its field of origin is the worldlessness of modern privacy and the worldlessness of labour, private property in reality functions as an essential tie to a commonly shared world. It is what anchors the worldless process of labouring to the world of tangible objects. In this sense, private property is not really private but an objective part of the world. To put it differently, private property is the borderline case of privacy as it is the least private part of the private and, as such, it embodies the condition of worldliness within the private. This is why Arendt needs to distinguish property from wealth. While the limited and objective nature of private property functions as a tie between the worldlessness of labour and the public realm, the worldlessness of wealth rests on its nature as a process of infinite accumulation. In this regard, its logic resembles that of labour: wealth does not produce enduring objects, since its true goal is its own consumption and the perpetual reproduction of itself in a process of infinite growth. Thus, the very nature of private property changed under the conditions of capitalism. When private property became privately owned wealth, the private itself ceased to be a worldly phenomenon. The absence of this permanent structure is what renders capitalism worldless.

Finally, Arendt's critique of Marxism and communism also follows a similar logic. Arendt's primary target is Marx's ontology of production that she describes as the 'seemingly blasphemous notion [. . .] that labor (and not God) created man or that labor (and not reason) distinguished man from the other animals' (Arendt 1998: 86). The consequence that follows from this ontology, according to Arendt, is Marx's reduction of everything to production and his reduction of labour to the biological process. Thus, in the end, everything in Marx depends on his definition of life. This is what Arendt calls Marx's 'consistent naturalism': 'The force of life is fertility' (Arendt 1998: 108). Marx's discovery of the 'productivity of labor' is based on the insight that, no matter how futile and non-durable its products might be, labour produces more than what is actually needed for survival. This labour power, therefore, can be channelled in such a way that 'the labor of some suffices for the life of all' (Arendt 1998: 88). Seen from this social viewpoint, 'all laboring is "productive"' (Arendt 1998: 89). But the social viewpoint 'takes nothing into account but the life process of mankind' (Arendt 1998: 89). For a '"completely socialized mankind" whose sole purpose would be the entertaining of the life process' – which is the 'unfortunately unutopian ideal that guides Marx's theories' – 'all work would have become labor because all things would be understood, not in their worldly, objective quality, but as results of living labor power and functions of the life process' (Arendt 1998: 89).

This is where Arendt locates 'the fundamental contradiction which runs like a red thread through the whole of Marx's thought' (Arendt 1998: 104). Marx had an equivocal attitude towards labour: on the one hand, he saw labour as an eternal necessity (in other words, a 'structural' element); on the other hand, he believed that the revolution would emancipate us from labour as such (which is the cornerstone of his historical argument). As she put it: 'The fact remains that in all stages of his work he defines man as *animal laborans* and then leads him into a society in which this greatest and most human power is no longer necessary. We are left with the rather distressing alternative between productive slavery and unproductive freedom' (Arendt 1998: 105). For Arendt, therefore, communism is the dystopia of a world in which everything is reduced to life in a state of absolute worldlessness.

As these three examples illustrate, in the end, even if history is essentially tied to the phenomenon of the world, for Arendt, history is the history of worldlessness. If we follow our own interpretation that in *The Human Condition* the world is the reification of the difference between two forms of worldlessness, we can also see here that history is nothing but the temporal unfolding of this difference. In other words, Arendt's entire argument is based on the implicit assumption that history is the product of the dynamic unfolding of the difference between life and world (the latter understood here as the reification of action under the condition of human plurality). History is the way life, the very condition of worldliness, destroys what it makes possible. Thus, history is the incontrovertible proof of the fact that life is never fully reducible to mere life. Going beyond Arendt's explicit argument, however, we could also say that history as such is a 'moment' in the relentless happening of worldlessness. It is the irreducibility of worldlessness to itself: an internal difference within worldlessness itself that allows the human being to contemplate its own existence in terms of a fate that it cannot ever fully control.

★ ★ ★

Arendt's final writings – the unfinished project of *The Life of the Mind* (1978) – take us back to the metaphysics of worldlessness. Arendt's slightly reconceived metaphysics of the world now starts with the rejection of the classic 'two-world theory' based on the hierarchical dichotomy of true Being and mere appearance (Arendt 1978: 23). The hierarchical relations inherent in these schemes usually suggest that the world of appearances is dependent on something more fundamental, a 'beyond', which is the enabling condition of the world of appearances but itself does not appear. Arendt cites here the Kantian theorem that appearances 'must themselves have grounds which are not appearances' (Arendt 1978: 24). This presupposition of 'the supremacy of the *ground* that does not appear over the surface that does', then, translates into the assumption of the higher rank of the cause over the effects that it produces (Arendt 1978: 25). This presupposition is such a fundamental habit of our thinking that it permeates most of our religious and philosophical schemes and even forms the foundation of modern science.

In order to oppose this metaphysical fallacy, Arendt argues for the reversal of the two-world thesis and asserts that '*Being and Appearing coincide*' (Arendt 1978: 19). It is in this sense that we can talk about the 'primacy, or at least the priority, of appearance' (Arendt 1978: 23). For it remains a fact that for everyday life appearances always come first and all metaphysical speculations on the invisible grounds of these experiences are at best entertaining if not outright laughable. This is why Arendt's point is that the inherent worldlessness of Being in relation to the world of appearances that it makes possible needs to be rethought. Even if the worldlessness of Being enjoys a higher ontological rank in our metaphysical speculations, the fact is that one cannot live in this kind of worldlessness:

> No man, it has turned out, can live among 'causes' or give full account in normal human language of a Being whose truth can be scientifically demonstrated in the laboratory and tested practically in the real world through technology. It does look as though Being, once made manifest, overruled appearances – except that nobody so far has succeeded in *living* in a world that does not manifest itself of its own accord. (Arendt 1978: 26)

This, then, is a basic contradiction of the two-world theory: its metaphysics is the metaphysics of worldlessness that assumes that the enabling cause of the world is something in itself worldless; but this higher ground is irreconcilable with life itself. There is no life in worldlessness.

From our perspective, the most important difference between *The Human Condition* and *The Life of the Mind* is that in the latter life is no longer simply worldless but, in a sense, is coextensive with the world itself. While in the earlier work biological life was the fundamental paradigm of worldlessness, in the later work both animal and human life contain the conditions of worldly appearance. In this new context, the very principle of life includes a certain 'urge toward self-display': 'In contrast to the inorganic thereness of lifeless matter, living beings are not mere appearances. To be alive means to be possessed by an urge towards self-display which answers the fact of one's own appearingness. Living things make their appearance like actors on a stage set for them' (Arendt 1978: 21). These words evoke the Heideggerian thesis of the worldlessness of the stone and suggest that life can now be easily reconciled with the world. The natural dimension of the human condition is no longer simply a threat to the man-made world of artefacts. These connections between life and the world are made even clearer when she writes:

> The urge toward self-display – to respond by showing to the overwhelming effect of being shown – seems to be common to men and animals. And just as the actor depends upon stage, fellow-actors, and spectators, to make his entrance, every living thing depends upon a world that solidly appears as the location for its own appearance, on fellow-creatures to play with, and on spectators to acknowledge and recognize its existence. (Arendt 1978: 21–2)

The world is now primarily interpreted from the perspective of human (and animal) plurality rather than the objective in-between that simultaneously connects and distances human beings from each other. The focus is now on the act of self-display shared by all living beings.[12]

In fact, the very title of the book, *The Life of the Mind*, suggests that we are possibly talking about a different kind of life when we move from the *vita activa* to the contemplative life. While in these late works, biological life is less worldless, the new idea of the 'life of the mind' once again shows the necessity of worldlessness. To put it differently, the inherent worldlessness of life has been transferred from biological life to the life of the mind:

> Since plurality is one of the basic existential conditions of human life on earth [. . .] to be by myself and to have intercourse with myself is the outstanding characteristic of the life of the mind. The mind can be said to have a life of its own only to the extent that it actualizes this intercourse in which, existentially speaking, plurality is reduced to the duality already implied in the fact and word 'consciousness', or *syneidenai* – to know with myself. (Arendt 1978: 74)

The life of the mind is predicated upon the radical reduction of human plurality to its absolute minimum. In mental activities, human plurality is reduced to the minimal requirement of any plurality as duality (at least two partners are needed for there to be a world), and it is internalised in an act of turning away from the outer world of appearances. This is a worldlessness that has already internalised the minimal structure of the world. Thus, the worldlessness of the life of the mind is not the worldlessness of solipsism, since it simply shows that plurality is the general condition of life on earth – even the solitary life of the mind is modelled on the principle of plurality (Arendt 1978: 46).

★ ★ ★

It is in this context that the term 'withdrawal' takes on a new technical meaning in Arendt's argument. Withdrawal becomes something like the enabling condition of all mental activities. Thinking, willing and judging are different forms of withdrawal from the world of appearances:

> The primacy of appearance for all living creatures to whom the world appears in the mode of an it-seems-to-me is of great relevance to the topic we are going to deal with – those mental activities by which we distinguish ourselves from other animal species. For although there are great differences among these activities, they all have in common a *withdrawal* from the world as it appears and a bending back toward the self. (Arendt 1978: 22)

This time around the positive capacity for worldlessness (the capacity to withdraw from the world and to bend back towards the self) is what constitutes the human being. Worldlessness is no longer the mark of the inhuman condition, but the constitutive act of the human being.

What renders thinking the most radical of the three mental activities is that it is the only one that presupposes an almost complete withdrawal from the world. Willing and judging – which to a certain degree presuppose thought's turning away from the world – withdraw from the world only temporarily (Arendt 1978: 92). While thinking is concerned with truly invisible entities that are not part of the world of appearances, willing and judging will need concrete and particular objects that are always part of our worlds. The worldlessness of thinking, therefore, is the crucial problem that we need to account for:

> While thinking I am not where I actually am; I am surrounded not by sense-objects but by images that are invisible to everybody else. It is as though I had withdrawn into some

never-never land, the land of invisibles, of which I would know
nothing had I not this faculty of remembering and imagining.
Thinking annihilates temporal as well as spatial distances.
(Arendt 1978: 85)

The full meaning of this description emerges only when we
consider thinking in opposition to 'common sense, this sixth
sense that fits our five senses into a common world' (Arendt
1978: 81). In fact, Arendt defines the specificity of the human
condition as well as the history of philosophy in terms of the
'intramural warfare' between the worldliness of common sense
and the worldlessness of thinking (Arendt 1978: 81).

Arendt summarises the 'outstanding characteristics of the
thinking activity' by reference to the following points: 'its
withdrawal from the common-sense world of appearances, its
self-destructive tendency with regard to its own results, its re-
flexivity, and the awareness of sheer activity that accompanies
it, plus the weird fact that I know of my mind's faculties only
so long as the activity lasts' and adds that this state of affairs also
means that 'thinking itself can never be solidly established as one
and even the highest property of the human species' (Arendt
1978: 88). What is striking in this list of properties is that they
provide only negative criteria: it is as if, reading these words,
thinking itself disappeared right in front of our eyes. Thinking
is a self-reflexive process concerned only with itself that lacks
any permanence as it simultaneously negates the world (withdrawal) and itself (self-destruction). Its worldlessness consists of
this ephemeral negativity: everything that is solid melts into air.

The nothingness of thinking is clearly articulated in the conclusion of the book, where Arendt tries to answer the question
'Where are we when we think?' (Arendt 1978: 195). The answer
is clear: nowhere. To be more precise, Arendt's argument is that

121

first thinking is everywhere. This omnipresence, however, is based on the generalisation inherent in every thought. Thinking leaves behind the world of the particular in its quest for 'essences' that cannot be localised. These generalised essences are then applicable everywhere, but 'this "everywhere" that bestows on thought its specific weight is spatially speaking a "nowhere"' (Arendt 1978: 199). Somewhat later, Arendt adds: 'And since this nowhere is by no means the twofold nowhere from which we suddenly appear at birth and into which almost as suddenly we disappear in death, it might be conceived only as the Void' (Arendt 1978: 200). For Arendt, this nothingness is the very mark of human finitude.

Thus, it is the self-consuming negativity of thinking that once again introduces the idea of death into Arendt's argument:

> Because of thinking's need to transcend [the world of appearances], we have turned away; in a metaphorical sense, we have *dis*appeared from this world, and this can be understood – from the perspective of our natural and of our common-sense reasoning – as the anticipation of our final departure, that is, our death. (Arendt 1978: 83)

In fact, this relationship is best described according to Arendt as a metaphorical reversal of common-sense priorities. In thinking, life is death and the absent is present: 'Seen from the perspective of thinking, life in its sheer thereness is meaningless; seen from the perspective of the immediacy of life and the world given to the senses, thinking is, as Plato indicated, a living death' (Arendt 1978: 87). At the same time, for the philosopher, who lives the life of the mind, 'a life without meaning *is* a kind of living death' (Arendt 1978: 87; emphasis in original). Thus, seen from either side, the inherent antagonism between common sense and thinking manifests itself here in the metaphor of 'living death', a life that is no life at all. The crucial point about this metaphor is that it articulates a limit case that does not fully belong to either of the two extreme positions. Neither life nor death, thinking is worldlessness as it appears in the world ('the paradoxical condition of a living being that, though itself part of the world of appearances, is in possession of a faculty, the ability to think, that permits the mind to withdraw from the world without ever being able to leave it or transcend it') (Arendt 1978: 45). Common sense, however, as the world without worldlessness, is life not worth living.

It is this conclusion that suggests that in the end there is no absolute worldlessness for Arendt. Even thinking is only relative in its worldlessness as it is simply more worldless than the other mental activities. In fact, it is Arendt's theory of metaphor itself that establishes this conclusion. For Arendt, the function of metaphor is to connect the invisible contents of the mind with concrete sensible experiences. We could paraphrase this definition by saying that metaphor always ties the worldlessness of thought to worldly appearances. But this does not mean that sense experience is secondary in relation to thought. To the contrary, Arendt argues that language is the only possible medium for the manifestation of thought both for the outside world and to the thinking ego itself (Arendt 1978: 102). As a result, the relationship of the mind and the world is defined by a certain irreversibility based on the absolute necessity of appearances: 'There is, finally, the fact of the irreversibility of the relationship expressed in metaphor; it indicates in its own manner the absolute primacy of the world of appearances and thus provides additional evidence of the extraordinary quality of thinking, of its being always out of order' (Arendt 1978:

109). The most important conclusion that follows from the fact that 'the thinking ego obviously never leaves the world of appearances altogether' is that 'there are no two worlds because metaphor unites them' (Arendt 1978: 110). As the cipher for the absolute necessity of appearance, metaphor is the name of the primacy of the world over worldlessness.

★ ★ ★

While in the previous chapter, discussing Heidegger, we moved from metaphysics to politics, in the case of Arendt we moved from politics to metaphysics. This is why it might be necessary to point out that even in *The Life of the Mind* thinking and the politics of worldlessness are inherently tied together. Once again, the starting point is the living death of thinking:

> Thinking accompanies life and is itself the de-materialized quintessence of being alive; and since life is a process, its quintessence can only lie in the actual thinking process and not in any solid results or specific thoughts. A life without thinking is quite possible; it then fails to develop its own essence – it is not merely meaningless; it is not fully alive. Unthinking men are like sleepwalkers. (Arendt 1978: 191)

Here the very essence of life is identified with thinking, and this identification is what takes us back to the politics of worldlessness.

As a first step, Arendt insists on the social uselessness of thinking. Even its moral byproduct, conscience, is really only a secondary consideration with regard to the actual activity of thinking. As a result, thinking in itself appears to be wholly alien to politics: 'And it has no political relevance unless special circumstances arise' (Arendt 1978: 192). Following Karl Jaspers, Arendt calls these special circumstances 'boundary situations' (Arendt 1978: 192). Life is a 'boundary affair' in the sense that worldly existence unavoidably forces us to transcend the boundaries of our individual lives when we must confront a past that preceded us and a future that awaits us. These moments of transcendence are the instances when thinking ceases to be a 'politically marginal activity', since in situations of 'political emergencies' we will be called upon to pass judgement on the past and form projects of the will for the future. The point is that in times when thoughtlessness prevails and everyone 'is swept away unthinkingly by what everybody else does and believes in, those who think are drawn out of hiding because their refusal to join in is conspicuous and thereby becomes a kind of action. In such emergencies, it turns out that the purging component of thinking [. . .] is political by nature' (Arendt 1978: 192). The negative world-destroying essence of thinking constitutes its inherent political dimension. Although, in one sense, politics for Arendt is always a politics of worldliness, what these thoughts reveal here is that the politics of worldlessness is after all the positive enabling condition of freedom. As Arendt's critique of Eichmann also demonstrates, the only ally we have in the fight against the thoughtlessness of the world today is the worldlessness of thinking itself.

Thus, Arendt's reflections on thoughtlessness also demonstrate that the concept of worldlessness carries an additional argumentative burden in her writings. Simply put, worldlessness functions as the structural agency that is supposed to guarantee the smooth transition between her descriptive and normative accounts of the human being, as well as between the ontological and moral registers. The mere description of the human condition leads to the conclusion that the worldlessness of thinking is the very condition of morality.

Notes

1 For the argument that the category of 'life' (especially as it relates to that of 'thought') constitutes the central theme of Arendt's entire work, see Kristeva (2001).

2 Arendt's relation to Heidegger (both in a personal and in a philosophical sense) is virtually an omnipresent topic of discussion in the secondary literature on Arendt. From the perspective of our analysis of worldlessness, however, a few of these titles might be worth mentioning here. For a systematic overview of this philosophical relationship, see Villa (1996). In addition, Elisabeth Young-Bruehl argued in *Why Arendt Matters* that what Arendt found objectionable in Heidegger's philosophy was the fundamentally 'unworldly' nature of his thought (Young-Bruehl 2006). In a similar fashion, Svetlana Boym (also implicating Giorgio Agamben in this critique) argued that Arendt developed her theory of worldliness as a rejection of Heidegger's philosophy (Boym 2009).

3 It is worth noting here that Judith Butler's recent work also directly addresses the Arendtian critique of worldlessness. Butler's position demonstrates a common duality. On the one hand, Butler is a champion of the critique of worldlessness. On this level, she accepts the general outline of Arendt's argument. On the other hand, she offers an astute critique of the Arendtian politics of worldliness. Butler argues that the Arendtian definition of politics as a 'space of appearance' cannot account for those who fall outside this field. In other words, Arendt cannot account for the ontological status of the destitute. Since it is obvious that those outside the field of appearance do not simply cease to exist, Butler shows that this state of worldlessness is still defined by the possibilities of acting together: human worldlessness is a terrain of acting in concert and not the radical absence of the possibility of communal action (Butler 2015: 80–1). In addition, see also her interview with Stephanie Berbec (Butler 2017).

4 For a classic analysis of the role of freedom in Arendt, see Kateb (1984).

5 In this sense, the concept of 'natality' functions as the paradoxical limit concept that allows Arendt to inscribe worldlessness at the very heart of worldliness. For useful discussions of this concept in Arendt, see Birmingham (2006: 4–34), O'Byrne (2010), Diprose and Ziarek (2018).

6 While the idea of the 'right to have rights' has already garnered a lot of attention in Arendt criticism, I would like to refer here briefly only to Werner Hamacher's recent provocative rereading of this concept. Hamacher's conclusion that 'the right to have rights was never a right to

be had' implicitly also establishes the foundations of a reconceptualisation of the law from the perspective of worldlessness as it suggests that the law is always based on specific non-possessive relation to alterity (Hamacher 2017).

7 For a useful set of discussions of totalitarianism and terror in Arendt's works, see Villa (2001).

8 For an overview of Arendt's use of earth and world as complementary categories, see Oliver (2015: 71–110).

9 While traditional interpretations of the role of the world in Arendt's thought all tend to recognise the world's essential fragility, instability and ephemeral nature, these accounts usually still miss the significance of worldlessness for this theory. What my interpretation suggests is that the reason why the world can become an object of a desire is precisely that the world does not exist for Arendt (in the sense that it lacks ontological consistency or guarantees). The world might be real, but its existence is not an unquestionable necessity for Arendt. This is why we could also argue (contrary to these traditional interpretations) that Arendt's theory of worldliness includes this concept in that of worldlessness: Arendtian worldliness is a specific mode of human worldlessness. For discussions of this Arendtian love of the world, see Bernauer (1987).

10 For a well-known critique of Arendt's descriptions of modern worldlessness as 'a continuation of Christianity by other means', see Blumenberg (1983: 8). For discussions of Blumenberg's readings of Arendt, see Brient (2000) and Bajohr (2015).

11 We should also briefly mention here that Arendt finds the extreme case of Christian political experimentation in the monastic orders. As political experiments, however, these orders led to the 'establishment of a kind of counterworld, a public realm within the orders themselves' (54). In other words, they were political only in the sense that within the confines of the order they produced a limited public space. Her negative political judgement is in stark contrast with Giorgio Agamben's work on monasticism in *The Highest Poverty* (Agamben 2013).

12 In this expansion of the concept of life to include the very problem of appearance (and, thus, potentially worldliness itself), we can detect at least the possibility of extending Arendt's conception of plurality beyond the human being. For a critique of Arendt's definition of plurality from the perspective of biodiversity, see Oliver (2015: 33, 72).

3

The Science of Worldlessness

The unconscious is worldless. This is the fundamental lesson of Freud's most discomforting metapsychological speculations. In fact, we could even say that the ultimate discovery of psychoanalysis, the existence of the unconscious, is a discovery of the primacy of worldlessness. Thus, the idea of the Freudian unconscious immediately juxtaposes the worldlessness of life and the worldlessness of thought. The hypothesis of the fundamental worldlessness of life leads us to the theory of the (death) drive, which in turn becomes the foundation of the worldlessness of thought. In fact, we could argue that the hypothesis of the worldlessness of life functions as the generative matrix of Freud's metapsychological speculations. It is the mythical and historical starting point from which most of the central psychoanalytic concepts (the drive, the wish, the dream, the libido, schizophrenia, narcissism, masochism, etc.) are derived. We could go even further and claim that worldlessness functions as the very condition of psychoanalytic conceptuality as such – it also accounts for the very possibility of the kind of conceptual thinking that is materialised in scientific discourse.

While the term 'worldlessness' never appears explicitly as an operative concept in Freud's writings, his definition of life is nevertheless based on a specific movement that is best described as a turning away from the world. The essence of life is that it encounters external reality only tangentially, only to move away from it towards a self-defined homeostasis. In this sense, the special theoretical burden that the idea of worldlessness carries in Freud's writings is precisely that it is responsible for establishing a link between the biological (life) and the psychic (thought). To the degree that life is essentially worldless, thought emerges out of this life as a function of life's worldlessness. Thus, thought is not a tool for constituting the world or knowing the world, but a way of ensuring that life accomplishes its goal in spite of the persistence of an often hostile reality.

In this context, what sets Freud apart both from Heidegger and Arendt is his unwavering attachment to the ideal of science. While for Heidegger and Arendt modern science is precisely an unwitting agent of worldlessness that must be criticised, Freud repeatedly insists that psychoanalysis is a science. No doubt, it is an unusual science that expands its field to phenomena that were earlier thought to be simply incompatible with scientific thought (dreams, jokes, symptoms, etc.). Freud seemed to believe, however, that this expansion constitutes an application of the logic of science that is more consistent than what the natural sciences boast of. In other words, Freud's point appears to be that science cannot be merely the science of the world. It has to become also the science of worldlessness.

Thus, in a direct reversal of Heidegger's and Arendt's critique of the Cartesian subject, Freud forces us to ponder the primacy of worldlessness over the experience of the world. As we have seen, Heidegger and Arendt both rejected the Cartesian pre-supposition of a mythical worldless subject as the necessary starting point for the theorisation of the subject's relation to the world.[1] The phenomenological position is that Dasein is always already worldly – otherwise, it would not be Dasein. Freud's intervention, however, is best understood in this context as a simultaneous critique of Heidegger's and Descartes' take on worldlessness. In other words, unlike Heidegger, Freud insists on the primacy of worldlessness over worldliness; on the other hand, unlike for Descartes, this primary worldlessness is nevertheless a historical problem for Freud. To put it differently, for psychoanalysis, worldlessness represents a historical origin both phylogenetically and ontogenetically. As such an origin, it functions as an enabling condition that persists or, more precisely, insists as a permanent presence in the form of a memory. But, and this is the other side of the psychoanalytic encounter with worldlessness, as such a permanent presence, it is not simply a memory but a structural condition. At the same time, in addition to being an enabling condition, it also represents a possible threat to the ego. Although psychoanalysis also pathologises certain forms of worldlessness (psychosis, schizophrenia, narcissism), its goal is not simply to do away with worldlessness. What is pathological is not worldlessness as such, but specific relations to this primary fact. Consequently, the cure does not consist of the eradication of worldlessness from the psychic apparatus.

This last point is crucial for a contemporary theory of worldlessness because it suggests that psychoanalysis offers us something very different from dominant interpretations of the worldlessness of modernity. The mental suffering caused by the modern age is often treated as a sure sign that what modernity produces in its subjects could be grasped as a generalised state of psychosis or schizophrenia (or any number of related pathologies). This chapter will, therefore, first examine some of Freud's reflections on the unconscious, the death drive and pathological formations like schizophrenia in order to demonstrate to what degree psychoanalysis was organised by the thought of world-lessness already at the moment of its inception in such a way that it could be best described as the science of worldlessness. After these discussions of Freud, the second half of the chapter will turn to Lacan's theories of the signifier, psychosis and anxiety, in order to show that Lacanian psychoanalysis actually fully reverses the common understanding of worldlessness as a pathological formation that has increasingly dominated modernity. Contrary to these widely accepted accounts, psychoanalysis as the science of worldlessness proves that what is pathological about the modern age is not the simple fact of the loss of the world but precisely modernity's unrelenting fetishistic investment in the category of the world.

* * *

The idea of the worldlessness of life was already one of the fundamental organising principles of Freud's earliest psycho-analytic writings. In Freud's theory of the dream, for example, the historical emergence of thought in the form of the so-called 'secondary processes' is described as a necessary modification of the hallucinatory wish-fulfilment of the 'primary processes'. According to the well-known definition provided in *The Inter-pretation of Dreams*, the dream performs a double function: on the one hand, the dream is a wish-fulfilment; on the other hand, it is the guardian of sleep. On both counts, it is in an essential relation to a state of worldlessness: the wish is an attempt to return to a 'structural' form of worldlessness that persists in the form of a historical memory; while sleep is an attempt to suspend the ego's relations to the external world which, in effect, functions as a repetition of a primary state of worldlessness.

The problem of wish fulfilment clearly shows how Freud aims to derive the worldlessness of thought from an inherent function of life. When Freud speculates about the origins of the dream, he has to start with the hypothesis (or even 'fiction' [Freud 2010: 594]) that the psychical apparatus was fundamentally worldless in its primitive stages. The dream is a byproduct of this originary state of worldlessness. This hypothesis, as Freud puts it, holds that 'at first the apparatus's efforts were directed towards keeping itself so far as possible free from stimuli' (Freud 2010: 564–55). The fulfilment of this original programme (the maintenance of an essentially worldless state), however, is frustrated by 'the exigencies of life' (Freud 2010: 565). Various internal (somatic) needs arise that demand satisfaction. The memory of the eventual satisfaction of such a need is, then, linked to the memory of the internal excitation:

> As a result of the link that has thus been established, next time this need arises a psychical impulse will at once emerge which will seek to re-cathect the mnemic image of the perception and to re-evoke the perception itself, that is to say, to re-establish the situation of the original satisfaction. An impulse of this kind is what we call a wish. (Freud 2010: 656)

This derivation of the historical emergence of the 'wish' in the psychic apparatus shows to what extent the very concept of the wish is now tied to the hypothesis of worldlessness. The problem, however, is that at this primitive stage of development, the psychic apparatus finds a shortcut to accomplish this regression: it hallucinates the fulfilment it wishes for. The structural possibility of this hallucination highlights the fact that the worldlessness of the primary processes is so dominant that they are perfectly capable of finding a means of sealing themselves off from external reality.

The problem with a hallucinated satisfaction, however, is obvious. The need is not truly fulfilled and, therefore, it persists. As a result, the apparatus is in search of a 'more efficient expenditure of psychical force' (Freud 2010: 566), which consists of bringing this regression to a halt right before it culminates in the hallucinated satisfaction. This strategy will allow the apparatus to seek out other solutions 'which lead eventually to the desired perceptual identity being established from the direction of the external world' (Freud 2010: 566). This is the process that Freud will eventually call 'reality-testing'. A new system must be put to work here whose task is to control the voluntary movements of the organism 'for purposes remembered in advance' (Freud 2010: 566). In other words, at this stage, a new kind of 'thought-activity' has to be initiated that allows the apparatus to establish a perceptual identity between the mnemic image of satisfaction and a piece of external reality. In the end, however, such thought activity is nothing but a form of wish-fulfilment: 'Thought is after all nothing but a substitute for a hallucinatory wish; and it is self-evident that dreams must be wish-fulfilments, since nothing but a wish can set our mental apparatus at work' (Freud 2010: 566). The worldliness of thought (its essential relation to the external world in the function of reality-testing) appears here as a mere substitute for the worldlessness of the original wish-fulfilment. Dreams, therefore, retain this function at their core: in them, some kind of a regression to an original state of worldlessness becomes possible again. But this, in the end, is the decisive difference between sleep and psychosis. In sleep, even though the unconscious is given considerably more freedom, no motor activity is possible. Therefore, the unconscious cannot take over our relations to the external world. In the case of psychosis, however, this suspension of motor activities is lacking, and hallucinatory regression becomes the means through which the individual relates to external reality.

But the dream serves two masters simultaneously: the unconscious and the preconscious systems. On the one hand, the dream is a fulfilment of an unconscious wish; on the other hand, it is the fulfilment of the preconscious wish to prolong sleep (Freud 2010: 570). In most cases, a compromise between the two demands is possible. To use Freud's words, this is then the actual 'function of the dream': 'it discharges the *Ucs.* excitation, serves it as a safety valve and at the same time preserves the sleep of the preconscious in return for a small expenditure of waking activity' (Freud 2010: 577). If a compromise between the two systems is not possible, we awaken. But even when the dream acts as a 'disturber' rather than the 'guardian' of sleep, its true usefulness resides in fulfilling its double function (Freud 2010: 578). This is why Freud suggests that in reality all dreams are 'dreams of convenience' – that is, dreams that try to preserve sleep by incorporating disturbing sensations emanating from the external world into the story of the dream (Freud 2010: 570). The dream is, therefore, quite capable of absorbing the stimuli of the external world in order to isolate the apparatus from this external world. The dream's dual function, thus, calls attention to an interesting fact. The unconscious is the way an originary form of worldlessness persists; the preconscious, whose energies are often directed at resisting this unconscious, however, responds to this persistence by relying on another form of worldlessness. The preconscious wishes to sleep. But sleep, in Freud's definition, is yet another form of worldlessness.

In one of Freud's final unfinished texts published under the title *An Outline of Psycho-Analysis* (1938), he repeats the same ideas with a new intensity. The dream combines two forms of worldlessness. On the one hand, the dream is a form of psychosis; on the other hand, sleep is once again described as a form of worldlessness. Relying on the language of the second topography, Freud describes the mechanism of dream formation with the following words:

> The ego gives evidence of its original derivation from the id by occasionally ceasing its functions and allowing a reversion to an earlier state of things. This is logically brought about by its breaking off its relations with the external world and withdrawing its cathexes from the sense organs. We are justified in saying that there arises at birth an instinct to return to the intra-uterine life that has been abandoned – an instinct to sleep. Sleep is a return of this kind to the womb. (Freud 1989: 40)

Although the conflict is no longer described in terms of the tension between the unconscious and the preconscious systems but that between the ego and the id, the argument remains essentially the same: 'We shall be taking every experience into account if we say that a dream is invariably an *attempt* to get rid of a disturbance of sleep by means of a wish–fulfilment, so that the dream is a guardian of sleep' (Freud 1989: 46). If dreams are, in fact, worldless on both of these counts (since the wish has its roots in the organism's original worldlessness and the function of sleep is to block out the external world), we can say that dreams are guardians of not only sleep but also of worldlessness.

★ ★ ★

135

This derivation of the emergence of thought from the world-lessness of life, however, also shows us to what extent the very field of the Freudian unconscious is divided between life and thought. The most striking thing about Freud's early writings on the unconscious is the essentially Kantian framework within which he chose to address the problem.[2] The reference to Kant allows Freud to frame the problem of the unconscious by way of a threefold division of experience: the external world, the internal world and the third element that withdraws from the phenomenal representation by consciousness. This third entity is constituted when the radical withdrawal of life from consciousness (in the form of drives), nevertheless, gains some access to phenomenal representation (in the form of the ideational representatives of the drives) by way of the repression of these thoughts (what we can properly call the unconscious). Thus, the Freudian unconscious is born when the worldless-ness of life enters the field of representation without entering consciousness.

The distance from the Heideggerian paradigm of worldless-ness is quite clear. For Freud, it is not the lifeless stone that is worldless but the unconscious itself – to the degree that it has the structure of a thing-in-itself. Thus, the reference to Kant establishes a recurrent pattern in psychoanalytic literature: the unconscious cannot be reduced to the Kantian problematic of the transcendental aesthetic. Space and time, as the very conditions of the appearance of phenomena, do not apply to the unconscious the same way as they do to objects of representation, since the unconscious is located in 'another scene' and is 'timeless'. This is one of the basic meanings of the proposition that the unconscious is worldless. Even though it maintains a relation to the field of representation, in an essential way its existence remains alien to the phenomenal world. As a result, the very existence of the unconscious is proof that something other than the world exists.

The essence of this Kantian framing of the problem of the unconscious is to establish a link between the unconscious and the thing-in-itself. As a first step, we get a simple equation: the unconscious is just as worldless as the thing-in-itself. Upon a first reading, this proposition means that the unconscious must be characterised by a radical withdrawal from consciousness. The methodological problem is quite clear: Freud has to explain how it is possible to have an idea of something like the unconscious. If the unconscious is truly unconscious, it represents a radical alterity in relation to consciousness (just like the thing-in-itself). Following this logic, we would have to conclude that there is no way the unconscious could ever make an appearance in consciousness. Freud, aware of this Kantian problem, has to go out of his way to legitimise the very hypothesis of the unconscious: he has to argue that the assumption of the unconscious is '*necessary* and *legitimate*' (Freud 1957b: 166, emphasis in original).

The legitimacy of the assumption of the unconscious depends on the inference of its very existence based on the phenomenology of intersubjective communication. First, based on our interactions with others, we infer that other people also possess a consciousness like we do. In a second step, this inference is then generalised in the form of an animism that assumes that every existing thing possesses consciousness. But this assumption increasingly appears to consciousness as mere mysticism. Thus, as a third and final step, the inference is internalised. We encounter events in the life of the mind that appear to us as if they belonged to other people: 'they are to be explained by a mental life ascribed to this other person' (Freud 1957b: 169).

Applied to the self, the inference of another consciousness at first leads to the assumption of a 'second consciousness' in the mind (Freud 1957b: 170). But what psychoanalysis discovers is the existence of latent mental processes that seem 'alien' to us and do not seem to have the characteristics of a consciousness at all. As a result, psychoanalysis will show that we are not talking about a second 'consciousness' at all: 'what is proved is not the existence of a second consciousness in us, but the existence of psychical acts which lack consciousness' (Freud 1957b: 170).

This 'metaphysical deduction' of the unconscious, however, leads to the conclusion that the unconscious is, after all, not quite like the thing-in-itself. The worldlessness of the unconscious is of a different nature from the worldlessness of the thing (since it derives from the worldlessness of life):

In psycho-analysis there is no choice for us but to assert that mental processes are in themselves unconscious, and to liken the perception of them by means of consciousness to the perception of the external world by means of the sense-organs. We can even hope to gain fresh knowledge from the comparison. The psychoanalytic assumption of unconscious mental activity appears to us, on the one hand, as a further expansion of the primitive animism which caused us to see copies of our own consciousness all around us, and, on the other hand, as an extension of the corrections undertaken by Kant of our views on external perception. Just as Kant warned us not to overlook the fact that our perceptions are subjectively conditioned and must not be regarded as identical with what is perceived though unknowable, so psycho-analysis warns us not to equate perceptions by means of consciousness with the unconscious mental processes which are their object. Like the physical, the psychical is not necessarily in reality what it appears to us to be. We shall be glad to learn, however, that the correction of internal perception will turn out not to offer such great difficulties as the correction of external perception – that internal objects are less unknowable than the external world. (Freud 1957b: 171)

Neither the external nor the internal world are what they appear to be. If mental processes are in themselves unconscious, as far as the life of the mind is concerned, the unconscious represents the norm and consciousness is the exception. Consciousness emerges as a result of perceptions. The perception of the internal world is what is at stake here in this paradoxical 'Kantian animism'. Thus, the unconscious is the rather unusual thing-in-itself about which we can, after all, know something. The aspect of this thing that is actually knowable is the ideational representative of the drives: 'An instinct can never become an object of consciousness – only the idea that represents the instinct can' (Freud 1957b: 177). The drives are so alien to consciousness that the very opposition of unconscious and conscious states breaks down in their domain. They are in themselves unknowable, but the ideas and affects that are attached to them can become part of the conscious/unconscious dialectic. As Freud explains, we talk about 'repressed instinctual impulses' precisely when the idea attached to the drive is repressed (Freud 1957b: 177). This also means that the field of the unconscious is split between two regions: the region of the unrepresentable drives and the repressed unconscious ideas. The link between the two is precisely where the mystery of the unconscious is located since this interval constitutes the domain that appears to account for the very possibility of representability as such. The possibility of assigning ideational representatives to unrepresentable drives is the very condition of thought itself.

The worldlessness of the unconscious, therefore, is structurally similar to the thing-in-itself in that they are both defined by a radical withdrawal from human consciousness. In this sense, they are not fully present in the world of phenomena that constitutes the world of our daily experiences. But, as Freud suggests, the unconscious is a different kind of entity since it is already constituted by a specific set of representations. To put it differently, while there are no representations in the Kantian thing, the unconscious is always already constituted by representations. To be more precise, we see here how the field of the unconscious is split between the worldlessness of life and the worldlessness of thought. Freud's argument is that the drives represent the radically worldless aspect of life that are properly speaking 'not even' unconscious. They become unconscious only when they attach themselves to an idea that is repressed. The unconscious, then, is the way that the radical worldlessness of life manifests itself through the worldlessness of thought.[3]

* * *

Up to this point, we have briefly examined only the way the transition from the worldlessness of life to the domain of thought takes place through the establishment of the unconscious: it is the worldlessness of life that establishes the necessity and possibility of representation (first, through the institution of memory in the emergence of the wish and, then, through the institution of thought as a substitute for the wish); but when the radical worldlessness of life, nevertheless, gains access to representation, it splits the domain of thought into two irreconcilable fields. In other words, we have traced the existence of what we could call the 'structural' worldlessness of the unconscious (since this kind of worldlessness is constitutive of the human psyche). But the practical question that will eventually come to dominate psychoanalytic discourse concerns the pathological manifestations of worldlessness. How does a constitutive factor manifest itself in the form of pathological formations?

So, it is important for us to note that the problem of unconscious representations leads Freud to a discussion of the worldlessness of schizophrenia. In fact, we could say that Freud's definition of schizophrenia suggests that it is something like a paradigmatic case of the pathological form of worldlessness:

> In the case of schizophrenia, on the other hand, we have been driven to the assumption that after the process of repression the libido that has been withdrawn does not seek a new object, but retreats into the ego; that is to say, that here the object-cathexes are given up and a primitive objectless condition of narcissism is re-established. The incapacity of these patients for transference (so far as the pathological process extends), their consequent inaccessibility to therapeutic efforts, their characteristic repudiation of the external world, the appearance of signs of a hypercathexis of their own ego, the final outcome in complete apathy – all these clinical features seem to agree excellently with the assumption that their object-cathexes have been given up. (Freud 1957b: 196–7)

Schizophrenia, as a primitive form of objectless narcissism, involves giving up the external world in an apathetic retreat into the ego. It produces the basic list of symptoms that we often associate with the negative effects of worldlessness in general. But it is not simply an excessive form of egotism that we are dealing with here. Rather, Freud's point is that schizophrenia makes something important visible about the unconscious. The analysis of the schizophrenic's speech – what Freud calls 'organ speech' (Freud 1957b: 199) – allows Freud to distinguish between the different kinds of representations that exist in the human mind. The first thing we must notice about schizophrenic discourse is that it introduces a significant gap between things and words. Analytic experience shows that schizophrenics treat words differently: 'In schizophrenia words are subjected to the same process as that which makes the dream images out of latent dream-thoughts – to what we have called the primary psychical process' (Freud 1957b: 199).

It is this state of affairs that, in the end, leads Freud to the well-known conclusion that we need to distinguish word-presentations (*Wortvorstellung*) from thing-presentations (*Sachvorstellung*): 'If now we put this finding alongside the hypothesis that in schizophrenia object-cathexes are given up, we shall be obliged to modify the hypothesis by adding that the cathexis of the word-presentations of objects is retained' (Freud 1957b: 200). All of a sudden, the worldlessness of schizophrenia appears in a new light. At the same time that the schizophrenic withdraws into a narcissistic state of worldlessness by giving up object cathexes, he also ends up hypercathecting words. Schizophrenia appears to be a narcissistic state of purely linguistic relation to reality. It is defined by the worldlessness of words that no longer have direct ties to objects.

At this point, we can clearly formulate the difference between Freud's descriptions of schizophrenia and his definition of the unconscious. On the one hand, we have the *word*lessness of the unconscious. As we have just seen, in the unconscious, there are only object cathexes. In order for something to become conscious, the object needs to be hypercathected by way of a corresponding word-presentation. On the other hand, we have the *world*lessness of schizophrenia. In schizophrenic discourse, there are only words. It is as if in schizophrenia we encounter an inside-out version of the unconscious. The very mechanisms that constitute the unconscious (the so-called 'primary processes') are applied to precisely that piece of reality (words) which is absent from the unconscious. In schizophrenia, the word/thing relation is reversed in this regard: primary processes are applied to words, not things. In this sense, the worldlessness of schizophrenia is the strange entryway through which a negative image of the unconscious is put on display and is allowed to enter the world. While in the unconscious we encounter things without a world, in schizophrenia we encounter a supposedly purely linguistically constructed world without things.

But schizophrenia is more than just a pathology. It is also something that can account for the psychic conditions of the science of psychoanalysis itself. In a certain sense, abstract thought itself constitutes a schizophrenic discourse:

> When we think in abstractions there is a danger that we may neglect the relations of words to unconscious thing-presentations, and it must be confessed that the expression and content of our philosophizing then begins to acquire an unwelcome resemblance to the mode of operation of schizophrenics. We may, on the other hand, attempt a characterization of the schizophrenic's mode of thought by saying that he treats concrete things as though they were abstract. (Freud 1957b: 204)

If theoretical language as such is schizophrenic since it produces word-presentations without corresponding object-presentations, schizophrenia is the psychic condition of pure conceptuality as such. To the degree that psychoanalysis is also a theoretical practice, from time to time it relies on the pure language of schizophrenic discourse. Schizophrenia now appears to be the precondition of a specific type of scientific thought, which in the end might be the science of worldlessness.

★ ★ ★

This discussion of schizophrenia already makes it clear that one of the most important theoretical tools psychoanalysis provided for the analysis of worldlessness was the concept of narcissism. To be more precise, it is the idea of 'primary narcissism' that takes the topic of worldlessness to a new dimension. For in the case of this primary narcissism we are dealing with a kind of structural worldlessness that is simultaneously a historical reality (both phylogenetically and ontogenetically) and permanent structural possibility. It is through this concept that Freud tackled the possibility of necessary worldlessness that is in itself not a pathological deviation from the normal development of the individual but an enabling condition of psychic development as such.[4]

Freud, therefore, argues that narcissism is not simply a perversion but part of the 'regular course of human sexual development' (Freud 1957a: 73). In fact, he goes even further and claims that it might designate 'the libidinal complement to the egoism of the instinct of self-preservation, a measure of which may justifiably be attributed to every living creature' (Freud 1957a: 73–4). The constitutive narcissism of life came to the surface as part of the analysis of the worldlessness of schizophrenia (or, as Freud prefers to refer to it here, 'paraphrenia'). The crucial difference between the worldlessness of neurosis and the worldlessness of schizophrenia, however, is that, although both are defined by a renunciation of the external world (people and things), the neurotic still retains his erotic attachment to the world in phantasy: 'he has, on the one hand, substituted for real objects imaginary ones from his memory, or has mixed the latter with the former; and on the other hand, he has renounced the initiation of motor activities for the attainment of his aims in connection with those objects' (Freud 1957a: 74).

While the neurotic, therefore, retains the phantasy of his relation to the world (but refuses to do anything about this erotic attachment), the schizophrenic withdraws from the world without replacing this relation with a phantasy. The libidinal attachment to the world is now completely directed towards the ego. The resulting 'megalomania' of the schizophrenic, however, is not a new creation but the intensification of a condition that existed even before the onset of the illness. It is this assumption, then, that necessitates the distinction between primary and secondary narcissism (Freud 1957a: 75). Freud conceives of this theoretical breakthrough as a necessary extension of his libido theory, which now needs to distinguish object-libido from ego-libido. This clear-cut division, however, is immediately complicated by the following evocative image: 'Thus we form the idea of there being an original libidinal cathexis of the ego, from which some is later given off to objects, but which fundamentally persists and is related to the object-cathexes much as the body of an amoeba is related to the pseudopodia which it puts out' (Freud 1957a: 75). The object-libido appears to be something like a specific extension of the original libidinal cathexis of the ego. This difficulty of maintaining a clear distinction between the two (which is, nevertheless, very important for Freud's theoretical struggle against Jung) accounts for the fact that the phenomenon of 'primary narcissism' is not directly accessible to us. It is available to us only through inference.

So, the problem of primary narcissism concerns the psychosexual development of the individual and raises the question of the first object choice of an infant (Freud 1957a: 87). What is the first object? Freud argues that there are two options: 'We say that a human being has originally two sexual objects – himself and the woman who nurses him – and in doing so we are postulating a primary narcissism in everyone, which may in some cases manifest itself in a dominating fashion in his object-choice' (Freud 1957a: 88). This is where, as Freud argues, the paradigmatic (although not universally valid) difference between male and female object choices can be articulated. Men tend to be attached to their object-choice: the child's original narcissism is transferred to the sexual object. In the case of women, however, we get an 'intensification of the original narcissism' without a genuine object-choice (Freud 1957a: 88). The worldlessness of woman manifests itself in this excessive narcissism. Female narcissism, however, performs a special role for the 'erotic life of mankind' (Freud 1957a: 89): 'For it seems very evident that another person's narcissism has a great attraction for those who have renounced part of their own narcissism and are in search of object-love' (Freud 1957a: 89). These speculations suggest that, for Freud, female sexuality is a privileged domain for the phenomenology of primary narcissism – the original libidinal investment of the ego and a decisive turning away from the external world. The dialectic of the world and worldlessness receives a special spin here: masculine worldliness is sustained by the worldlessness of woman.

★ ★ ★

But it is *Beyond the Pleasure Principle* (1920) that offers us some of the most memorable reflections on the worldlessness of the unconscious. The very hypothesis of the death drive is based on the assumption that life is essentially worldless. At every crucial moment of Freud's argument, we find that life turns away from the world. It is certainly aware of the existence of an external reality, but this awareness does not amount to a knowledge of the world. In Freud's account, as is well-known, life emerges in the inorganic world as a specific type of energy, a tension, whose basic principle is self-cancellation (Freud 1989a: 46). Initially, life was nothing but the instantaneous emergence and self-negation of this energy. Like a series of electric discharges, at its origin, life was a myriad randomly induced self-extinguishing sparks until external factors intervened to prolong the journey that takes life from its emergence to its self-cancellation. As Freud puts it, first death was 'an easy matter' for a living substance (Freud 1989a: 46), but then external influences forced it to take 'ever more complicated *détours* before reaching its aim of death' (Freud 1989a: 46). Life, then, is a 'circuitous path to death' (Freud 1989a: 46). The drive is precisely this tendency that forces life to be this perpetual act of self-cancellation. Contrary to common belief, Freud claims, the 'first instinct' is not the instinct of self-preservation but its opposite, 'the instinct to return to the inanimate state' (Freud 1989a: 46).

Hence the famous definition of the drive: '*an instinct is an urge inherent in organic life to restore an earlier state of things* which the living entity has been obliged to abandon under the pressure of external disturbing forces' (Freud 1989a: 43, emphasis in original). But if 'all the organic instincts are conservative, are acquired historically and tend towards the restoration of an earlier state of things' (Freud 1989a: 45), the function of external reality in the development of life is reduced to a mere obstacle. What we perceive as organic development is merely the result of external disturbing forces. It might have the deceptive appearance of progress, but its true aim is to restore the initial state of things from which the living organism emerged. As we know it from Freud, 'everything living dies for *internal* reasons' (Freud 1989a: 46), since 'the organism wishes to die only in its own fashion' (Freud 1989a: 47). This is the meaning of the world then. As far as life is concerned, the external world first emerges as an interruption of the programme of the drive. In other words, external reality forces its way into life through the unwelcome disturbance of the inherent worldlessness of the drive: 'what has left its mark on the development of organisms must be the history of the earth we live in and of its relation to the sun' (Freud 1989a: 45). Such are the cosmic effects of external reality on the elementary living entity. The cosmos is inscribed in the history of life, but this life itself resists the cosmos. The world is a significant detour in the long history of the worldlessness of life.

Once again, the worldlessness of thought is discussed in *Beyond the Pleasure Principle* in reference to Kant:

> As a result of certain psycho-analytic discoveries, we are today in a position to embark on a discussion of the Kantian theorem that time and space are 'necessary forms of thought'. We have learnt that unconscious mental processes are in themselves 'timeless'. This means in the first place that they are not ordered temporally, that time does not change them in any way and that the idea of time cannot be applied to them. These are negative characteristics which can only be clearly understood if a comparison is made with conscious mental processes. On the other hand, our abstract idea of time seems to be wholly derived from the method of working of the system Pcpt.-Cs. and to correspond to a perception on its own part of that method of working. This mode of functioning may perhaps constitute another way of providing a shield against stimuli. (Freud 1989a: 31–2)

Freud suggests here that psychoanalysis has reached a point in its development that enables it to engage the Kantian argument that space and time are 'necessary forms of thought'. For Kant, let us recall, time is the form of internal experience and space is the form of external experience. In other words, time and space are not qualities of objects themselves, since they constitute the subjective conditions of sensibility. But Freud reminds us that the unconscious is timeless, which implies that there is something in the internal world itself that escapes time. This appears to be a significant deviation from the Kantian definition of time as 'internal sense'. Time as we know it, then, is in fact a defense mechanism against the stimuli that would disturb the homeostasis of the living organism. What is not entirely clear in the passage is whether Freud is talking about external or internal stimuli or both. If the conscious representation of time is a defense against internal stimuli, we could say that time functions as a protective shield against the timelessness of the unconscious. If it is a defense against external stimuli, time serves as a way of warding off the traumatic excesses of the external world. In this latter sense, time is not simply an insufficient means of accessing reality in itself. It is, in fact, an active way of protecting us from the noumenal world of the thing-in-itself. The fact that we do not know anything about the thing-in-itself, therefore, is not just an unfortunate accident or a lamentable tragedy. According to Freud, it belongs to the very essence of life that it does not want to know the noumenal world. What experience teaches us is that the limited encounter with the phenomenal world is sufficient to fulfil the programme of the death drive. The possibility emerges here that the conscious constitution of the 'world' is but a defense mechanism designed to protect us from the traumas of worldlessness.

★ ★ ★

These discussions already call attention to the fact that one of the most consistent aspects of Freudian thought – a common thread of his writings that stretches from his earliest to his final texts – is the systematic distinction between the 'external world' and the 'internal world' of the psychic apparatus. Time and again, Freud returns to this opposition as a fundamental presupposition of his metapsychology. At first, this structuring principle of his thought appears to be a prime example of what Arendt called a 'two world theory'. But, in reality, in Freud's case we are dealing with a specific subversion of the kind of theories that posit the existence of a world that is more real than the world of our experiences. In Freud's writings, the two worlds are on the same ontological level. We cannot identify one of the worlds with true Being and the other with mere appearance. In fact, the crucial point is that both of these worlds are real. No doubt, the external world is the location of empirical reality, and the world of the human psyche is the source of mere appearances (in the form of hallucinations). But Freud's point is neither that the mind creates the world, nor that the world is the only thing real (and the mind is nothing but the source of mere appearances). These forms of vulgar idealism and vulgar materialism are both alien to his thought. Yet, in Freud's insistence on the distinction between the external and internal worlds, we do encounter a metaphysical limit of his thinking. The nature of this limit could be grasped in terms of an ambiguity that makes it difficult to separate the meanings of the operative terms 'reality' and 'world' in Freud's texts. While some of Freud's arguments effectively show that a reality is not necessarily a world, on a number of other occasions he treats these ideas as if they were simply equivalent.

The clearest formulation of this subversion of the two-world thesis can be found in *An Outline of Psycho-Analysis*, a text that was written with the intention of summarising the most significant findings of psychoanalysis in a dogmatic and concise form. After the general description of the most important concepts and a brief explanation of the clinical practices of psychoanalysis, the short book ends with a section that aims to survey 'the theoretical yield' of analytic work — in other words, it tries to identify the contributions of psychoanalysis to human knowledge in general. Quite significantly, this conclusion is broken down into two chapters that bear the titles 'The Psychical Apparatus and the External World' and 'The Internal World'. It is in the context of this separation of the two worlds from each other that we gain an important insight into the role of worldlessness in the Freudian system:

> The core of our being, then, is formed by the obscure *id*, which has no direct communication with the external world and is accessible even to our own knowledge only through the medium of another agency. Within this id the organic *instincts* operate, which are themselves compounded of fusions of two primal forces (Eros and destructiveness) in varying proportions and are differentiated from one another by their relations to organs or systems of organs. The one and only urge of these instincts is towards satisfaction, which is expected to arise from certain changes in the organs with the help of objects in the external world. But immediate and unheeding satisfaction of the instincts, such as the id demands, would often lead to perilous conflicts with the external world and to extinction. The id knows no solicitude about ensuring survival and no anxiety; or it would perhaps be more correct to say that, though it can generate the sensory elements of anxiety, it cannot make use of them. The processes which are possible in and between the assumed psychical elements of the id (the *primary process*) differ

widely from those which are familiar to us through conscious perception in our intellectual and emotional life; nor are they subject to the critical restrictions of logic, which repudiates some of these processes as invalid and seeks to undo them. (Freud 1989b: 84–5)

All of our central concerns are discussed in this passage: 1. The core of our being is a form of worldlessness; 2. Yet the satisfaction of the drives involves some kind of a relation to the external world; 3. But this relation to the external world is not defined by the ultimate goal of survival; 4. As a result, the id knows nothing about anxiety; 5. And the laws that govern its operations cannot be captured by formal logic. To paraphrase, the id does not care for the world, survival, anxiety or logic. Its worldlessness is also a form of disregard for life (its own life) and thought (in the form of logic).

Of course, we can speak about the worldlessness of the id only in the sense that it does not concern itself too much with the external world. It maintains an indirect relation to this world, but the latter in itself is all but irrelevant for it. The id's primary concern is itself:

The id, cut off from the external world, has a world of perception of its own. It detects with extraordinary acuteness certain changes in its interior, especially oscillations in the tension of its instinctual needs, and these changes become conscious as feelings in the pleasure-unpleasure series. It is hard to say, to be sure, by what means and with the help of what sensory terminal organs these perceptions come about. But it is an established fact that self-perceptions – coenaesthetic feelings and feelings of pleasure-unpleasure – govern the passage of events in the id with despotic force. The id obeys the inexorable pleasure principle. But not the id alone. (Freud 1989b: 85)

As we can see, within the Freudian framework, it might be misleading to speak about the worldlessness of the id since its separation from the external world is, nevertheless, modelled on the basis of the creation of another 'internal' world. The world of the id, however, is based on self-perception. As a result, the id functions here as a paradoxical world onto itself: a world of the one. As such, it is a world without a world.

★ ★ ★

The worldlessness of the id, then, becomes the foundation of Freud's definition of the pathological formations of the ego. According to one of Freud's often repeated theses, the id is the core of our being not only in the topological but also in the phylogenetic sense. In the beginning, there was the id. As far as we are concerned, this claim also means that in the beginning there was worldlessness. The mythical origin of life and the human being is a specific form of 'energy' that becomes capable of auto-affection. The ego and the superego are later developments that, historically speaking, have their origins in the id itself. So, when in light of this definition of the worldless world of the id Freud proceeds to a description of the ego, he quite systematically follows the same path that he did with the id but inverts the id's most salient characteristics (Freud 1989b: 85–6). Unlike the id, the ego is tied to the external world: 'Starting from conscious perception it has subjected to its influence ever larger regions and deeper strata of the id, and, in the persistence with which it maintains its dependence on the external world, it bears the indelible stamp of its origin (as it might be "Made in Germany")' (Freud 1989b: 86). Unlike the id, the ego is dominated by the reality principle: 'Just as the id is directed exclusively to obtaining pleasure, so the ego is governed by the considerations of safety' (Freud 1989b: 86). As a result, unlike for the id, life and survival are crucial problems for the ego: 'The ego has set itself the task of self-preservation, which the id appears to neglect' (Freud 1989b: 86). Consequently, anxiety also fulfils an important function for the ego as it gives 'warning of dangers that threaten its integrity' (Freud 1989b: 86).

In this situation, therefore, it is understandable that one of the most important activities of the ego is reality testing. While the id does not care about the reality of the objects that provide it with satisfaction, the ego needs to be sure of the reality of the threats that face it. It is the question of reality, then, that takes us to the problem of the different pathologies that torment the ego:

> We have repeatedly had to insist on the fact that the ego owes its origin as well as the most important of its acquired charac-teristics to its relation to the real external world. We are thus prepared to assume that the ego's pathological states, in which it most approximates once again to the id, are founded on a cessation or slackening of that relation to the external world. (Freud 1989b: 89)

The pathological states of the ego are defined here in terms of a withdrawal from the external world and an approximation of the original worldlessness of the id. Freud suggests here that this paradigm can be generalised, and all the basic diagnostic categories of psychoanalysis can be described in terms of world-lessness. In its most extreme form, this turning away from the world leads to psychosis, which now appears to be the most radical form of worldlessness that one can experience. But, as Freud tries to show, we find the same problem at the core of all forms of neurosis as well. Thus, we can already see that we are not merely talking about the general pathologisation of world-lessness here. The point appears to be rather that the very notion of pathology is defined in relation to worldlessness. The issue is not that worldlessness as such is pathological but that every pathological formation can be understood as a specific relation to worldlessness.

Yet, the source of the problem is precisely that this renunci-ation of the external world is never quite successful. Even psychosis is only a partial rather than an absolute withdrawal from the external world:

> The problem of psychoses would be simple and perspicuous if the ego's detachment from reality could be carried through completely. But that seems to happen only rarely or perhaps never. Even in a state so far removed from the reality of the external world as one of hallucinatory confusion, one learns from patients after their recovery that at the time in some corner of their mind (as they put it) there was a normal person hidden, who, like a detached spectator, watched the hubbub of illness go past him. (Freud 1989b: 89–90)

Thus, the pathologies of the ego are best described in terms of this failed or incomplete worldlessness that produces a 'psychical split' between the detachment from the external world and a persistent attachment to reality: 'Two psychical attitudes have been formed instead of a single one – one, the normal one, which takes account of reality, and another which under the influence of the instincts detaches the ego from reality' (Freud 1989b: 90). But the splitting of the ego, as the general paradigm of all mental illnesses, does not simply designate here an empty formal structure (as if any kind of split could lead to a patho-logical mental state). The interesting point is that this split also comes with a specific content: it is a struggle (or, to use one of Freud's metaphors, a 'civil war') between the world and world-lessness. Accordingly, then, we have to assume that at the core of all pathological formations we can eventually identify a failed state of worldlessness. To put it differently, what is pathological is not worldlessness itself but the specific modality of the failure to fully withdraw from the world.

Freud uses the example of fetishism to illustrate the point that this splitting of the ego is not restricted to psychosis alone. At the heart of fetishism, we find the split between a disavowal of the external world and a correct recognition of reality. Once again, this duality shows us that the withdrawal from the world is never quite complete: 'In fetishists, therefore, the detachment of the ego from the reality of the external world has never succeeded completely' (Freud 1989b: 92). In spite of the disavowal that forms its essence, fetishism remains a way of existing in relation to the world. This paradigm, therefore, can be defined as a 'universal characteristic of neuroses' (Freud 1989b: 92): 'two different attitudes, contrary to each other and independent of each other. In the case of neuroses, however, one of these attitudes belongs to the ego and the contrary one, which is repressed, belongs to the id' (Freud 1989b: 93). As a result, the ego is constantly caught between two worlds:

> Whatever the ego does in its efforts of defence, whether it seeks to disavow a portion of the real external world or whether it seeks to reject an instinctual demand from the internal world, its success is never complete and unqualified. The outcome always lies in two contrary attitudes, of which the defeated, weaker one, no less than the other, leads to psychical complications. (Freud 1989b: 93)

The ego's defense mechanisms are always defenses against a world (either the internal or the external world): as a result, we can say that the ego maintains itself as an intermediary agency between two worlds by mechanisms of worldlessness. But this turning away from the world is never complete: the facticity of the ego is always a form of failed worldlessness.

To complete the picture, we could recast here Freud's entire second topology in terms of worldlessness. First, the ego functions as a mediating agency between the worldless id and the external world. But the emergence of the superego introduces a split into this ego: 'A portion of the external world has, at least partially, been abandoned as an object and has instead, by identification, been taken into the ego and thus become an integral part of the internal world' (Freud 1989b: 94). This way the superego becomes the agent of a double inversion, a spatial and a temporal reversal: in the superego, the outside becomes inside and the present becomes past. As far as the topology of the division between an external and internal world is concerned, the superego marks the beginning of the breakdown of this neat distinction: 'the super-ego continues to play the part of an external world for the ego, although it has become a portion of the internal world' (Freud 1989b: 95–6). The temporal inversion follows directly from the spatial. While the ego dwells in its present relation to the external world, the id represents the organic past and the superego the cultural past:

> Thus the super-ego takes up a kind of intermediate position between the id and the external world; it unites in itself the influences of the present and the past. In the establishment of the super-ego we have before us, as it were, an example of the way in which the present is changed into the past. (Freud 1989b: 97)

While the ego is a mediating agency between worldlessness and the world in the sense that it is the location of a compromise, the superego is an active mediator that transforms the external world into an internal agency. Freud's conclusion, therefore, appears to be that a neat separation of these two worlds is, strictly speaking, impossible. The ego's attempts to mediate between the worldless id and the world of external reality lead to an internal split of the ego itself. As a result, the internal world is never fully 'internal' (as it includes the external world in the form of the superego), and neither is it fully a 'world' (as it is determined by the world-lessness of the id).

★ ★ ★

In light of these discussions, then, Freud's claim that psycho-analysis is not a *Weltanschauung* takes on a special significance. In a typical move of Freud's argument, the question of *Weltanschau-ung* once again pits science against religion:

> In my opinion, then, a *Weltanschauung* is an intellectual construc-tion which solves all the problems of our existence uniformly on the basis of one overriding hypothesis, which, accordingly, leaves no question unanswered and in which everything that interests us finds its fixed place. It will be understood that the possession of a *Weltanschauung* of this kind is among the ideal wishes of human beings. (Freud 1989c: 195–6)

Based on this definition, we have to consider the paradoxical conclusion that, according to Freud, the function of a *Weltan-schauung* is actually to distance us from the reality of the external world. In other words, a *Weltanschauung* will give us precisely what is not in the world: it unifies the world under one idea. In this sense, the possession of a *Weltanschauung* allows us to hide the inherent inconsistency of the world, the very worldlessness of reality. By looking at reality as if it were a world, we constitute this world through an act of wish-fulfilment.

This is, then, what we could call the two worlds of religion according to Freud: 'Religion is an attempt to master the sensory world in which we are situated by means of the wishful world which we have developed within us as a result of biological and psychological necessities' (Freud 1989c: 207). Although the necessity of the wishful world is not denied here, Freud's argument is that the creation of this wishful world by religion will eventually block access to the sensory world in which we actually exist. Science, on the other hand, tries to lead us back to the reality of the external world: 'Its endeavor is to arrive at correspondence with reality – that is to say, with what exists outside us and independently of us and, as experience has taught us, is decisive for the fulfilment or disappointment of our wishes. This correspondence with the real external world we call "truth"' (Freud 1989c: 211).

Psychoanalysis is a science. What follows from this statement for Freud is that psychoanalysis does not have a *Weltanschauung* of its own. It shares the scientific *Weltanschauung*. But, as we have already seen, the expression 'scientific *Weltanschauung*' now appears to be a contradiction in terms. No doubt, science itself aims at a general explanation of the world. But the scientific *Weltanschauung*, as Freud remarks, does not fit Freud's own definition of what constitutes a *Weltanschauung* for two major reasons. First, Freud calls attention to the fact that science is an unfinished project: 'It is true that [science] too assumes the *uniformity* of the explanation of the universe; but it does so only as a programme, the fulfilment of which is relegated to the future' (Freud 1989c: 196). What kind of a future is this? Freud is not likely to believe in an infinite postponement of this scientific truth. Since he defines truth as the correspondence of knowledge to reality, he believes that the time of scientific truths will come. This future is a real future, not the perpetual present of an infinite postponement. At the same time, there is a limit for him to the self-cancelling nature of science. As he puts it, the provisional nature of scientific truth is exaggerated: 'there is even today a solid ground-work' (Freud 1989c: 216). So, the 'present incompleteness' of science is a disturbing fact, but this is the only realistic solution at our disposal since 'nothing can take its place' (Freud 1989c: 216). Given this state of affairs, our only hope is a 'dictatorship of the intellect' (Freud 1989c: 212).

The second major difference is that science is 'marked by negative characteristics' (Freud 1989c: 196), since it sets absolute limits to what is possible and rejects revelation, intuition, divination. But science appears to occupy a strangely paradoxical or liminal position. As has been made clear, science is the opposite of a genuine *Weltanschauung* (exemplified by religion). At the same time, as a negative *Weltanschauung*, it fulfils the essence of a *Weltanschauung* even better than a regular one. It is the only genuine *Weltanschauung* that provides access to reality and the world. On the one hand, a *Weltanschauung* is worldless in the sense that it constitutes a wishful world that denies us access to reality. On the other hand, the negative *Weltanschauung* of science is the only one that is not worldless but gives us access to the world.

It is in this sense that we can speak of psychoanalysis as the science of worldlessness. As Freud explains, we can distinguish two sciences: 'Strictly speaking there are only two sciences:

psychology, pure and applied, and natural science' (Freud 1989c: 222). One of the sciences is the science of the external world; the other science, psychology, deals with the internal world. Psychoanalysis, therefore, is a specific form of this second science: 'As a specialist science, a branch of psychology – a depth-psychology or psychology of the unconscious – it is quite unfit to construct a *Weltanschauung* of its own: it must accept the scientific one' (Freud 1989c: 196). So, it first appears that science is by definition the science of the world (the real external world). But now we see that the external world is the specific domain of the natural sciences. Psychoanalysis, however, claims to have an object other than this external world: it is the science of the internal world and, as a form of 'depth-psychology', it is actually the science of the unconscious. However, the unconscious and the world are at odds with each other in Freudian thought. They both belong to science, but as we have seen in itself the unconscious does not form a part of the sensible world. Thus, we could go even further than the proposition according to which psychoanalysis does not have its own worldview. Psychoanalysis is not a worldview, but not because it does not have a 'view', but because in the unconscious there is no 'world' to view in the first place.

★ ★ ★

In the end, however, it was Lacan who eventually explicitly articulated the status of psychoanalysis as the science of worldlessness.[5] The introduction of the signifier as the core question of psychoanalysis reorients Lacanian ontology along two axes: the axis of an ontological difference (the difference between being — ?

and non-being) and the axis of sexual difference (the difference between masculine and feminine sexuality).[6] Thus, the fact that the signifier is at the centre of this ontology guarantees that we are, in effect, talking about an ontology of worldlessness.[7] In the case of ontological difference, Lacan reasserts the primacy of non-being in relation to the world. In the case of sexual difference, Lacan argues that the world will always be divided against itself. Two of Lacan's better-known statements clearly illustrate these points: 'the unconscious is structured like a language' suggests that the worldlessness of thought is far from some kind of a primordial chaos and must be treated as a structured entity; while the proposition according to which 'there is no sexual relation' indicates that sexual difference will produce irreducible effects that remove human relations from the field of meaningful communication.

We should start here by briefly revisiting the quasi-mythical scene of the birth of the signifier in Lacan's so-called Rome Discourse ('The Function and Field of Speech and Language in Psychoanalysis' from 1953), which is often treated as an early programmatic statement for Lacanian psychoanalysis. As Lacan tells this story, historically speaking, first there was the symbolic object of exchange, the gift. This gift is not a signifier yet, as it is not part of a properly formulated language. Nevertheless, the symbolic object is something like the worldly and historical condition of signification itself and functions as the foundation of law and language (since the law for Lacan is the law of language: 'the law of man has been the law of language since the first words of recognition presided over the first gifts' [Lacan 2006a: 225]). In order for the symbolic object to become a word, 'something else' (Lacan 2006a: 228) is still necessary – the presence of an absence.

The symbolic object itself is produced by way of a transformation from a different kind of being: the useful tool. When the useful tool becomes the object of exchange, it loses its earlier function. In its new position as a useless tool, the object now takes on an entirely different possibility as it can become the site of an unworldly manifestation. After losing its practical function in the world, however, the useless object still needs to lose its very being to become a proper word. For what distinguishes a word from an object is not simply the mode of its material presence (one is a solid object, while the other is a verbal utterance) but precisely the way it relates to an absence: the word makes an absence present. Yet, in this sense, the identity of the word itself is split between the 'sonorous quality of its matter' (its *hic et nunc* as its worldly dimension) and its vanishing being (the worldless dimension of thought), since the concept permanently withdraws from the sensuous world (Lacan 2006a: 228).

This definition of the word, however, leads to a complete reversal of perspective. As Lacan puts it, with the birth of the word, 'absence itself comes to be named in an original moment' (Lacan 2006a: 228). What is at stake here, therefore, is not simply naming a specific absence (which is always only one dimension of signification) but naming absence itself. The very possibility of absence has to be accounted for. This step is essential since, in this genetic narrative, it marks the advent of the very first articulated couple: presence/absence. The primary act of symbolisation constituted by the presence/absence dyad is going to be the condition of possibility for the emergence of the differential system of any later signification.

The true meaning of the reversal becomes obvious when we understand that the point is not simply to argue that absence is a secondary modification of the full presence of being. Rather,

Lacan's point is that there is no world before absence enters the field of being. The world is born only after absence has been marked in the flesh of being. This is why Lacan suggests here that from the presence/absence dyad 'a language's [*langue*] world of meaning is born, in which the world of things will situate itself' (Lacan 2006a: 228). Just to make sure that we do not misunderstand this claim as a reference to a simple relation of complementarity between two worlds (the world of language and the world of things) that need to be put in a relation of correspondence with each other by way of the signifier, Lacan immediately provides an even clearer formulation of the problem when he says that 'concepts [. . .] engender things' (Lacan 2006a: 228) – that is to say, the world of things does not exist independently or before the world of language.

It is this final step that turns things upside down in a fashion that is not quite the typical form of linguistic idealism.[8] Lacan's point is not that the subject creates the world (which would not exist without the synthesising agency of the subject), but that language as an asubjective agency does. The subject and the world are both effects of the signifier, whose primary function is to introduce a certain type of nothingness into the midst of beings. As Lacan puts it just a few lines later:

> It is the world of words that creates the world of things – things which at first run together in the *hic et nunc* of the all in the process of becoming – by giving its concrete being to their essence, and its ubiquity to what has always been: κτῆμα ἐς ἀεί. (Lacan 2006a: 229)

The word gives concrete being to the essence of the undifferentiated whole of being that exists in a state of eternal becoming as it provides a place of appearance for what has always been. And what counts for Lacan is that this production of the world has its own logic. As he observes, a 'logic of combinations' is at work in the creation of this world: 'the law of numbers – that is, of the most highly purified of all symbols – prove to be immanent in the original symbolism' (Lacan 2006a: 229). The primordial Law, as he puts it, is 'identical to a language order' (Lacan 2006a: 229).

Thus, the birth of the signifier will have to account for the creation of the world. There would be no world without the signifier, even if the signifier itself does not quite conform to our common understanding of what constitutes a world. We could argue here that this story is about the primacy of worldlessness in relation to the world in at least two senses. If we recreate the logical sequence of events described by Lacan, we find that we start with the undifferentiated whole of beings which, we assume, exists in a state of worldlessness. The world will emerge from this ontologically primary domain of worldlessness by way of the symbolic object. One being in this undifferentiated whole must distinguish itself by bearing the mark of something that appears to be alien to being in its primary state: absence. With the introduction of the absence/presence duality, the world of language enters the scene. Finally, the world of things (which is now different from the undifferentiated whole of beings) emerges as the retroactive effect of the world of language. But this does not mean that worldlessness has disappeared from the stage, since this last logical step of the creation of the world of things takes place by way of the word 'giving its concrete being to their essence'. The original ontological worldlessness of being (which remains inaccessible to us) is reproduced in the form of an absence made present in the signifier. The worldliness of the word must be understood in relation to this secondary world-lessness that makes the signifier into a 'trace of nothingness'

(Lacan 2006a: 228). The signifier is the agency that constitutes the world but which, in its very being, is essentially the worldly manifestation of something non-worldly.

★ ★ ★

The conditions of the emergence of the signifier must be present in the perpetual becoming of being. There must be something else in being that is not simply the self-presence of this becoming. This something else is nothing, taken in the sense of something other than being. The fact that being also includes the possibility of non-being must be the ontological ground for the emergence of the presence/absence dyad and, thus, for the birth of the signifier. Still speaking an ontological language that is not entirely alien to Lacan's thought, this would mean that the signifier is the being in which non-being comes into being. The Heideggerian overtones of this argument are not accidental, as Lacan himself admits when he concludes 'The Instance of the Letter in the Unconscious' with the following reference: 'When I speak of Heidegger, or rather when I translate him, I strive to preserve the sovereign signifierness of the speech he proffers' (Lacan 2006b: 438). As these words already suggest, just as he did with Freud, Lacan rereads (or translates) Heidegger from the perspective of the signifier.[9] In this regard, one of Lacan's most instructive encounters with Heidegger takes place in *Seminar VII*, in the session that bears the title 'On creation *ex nihilo*'.

Lacan returns here to Heidegger's essay 'The Thing', only to show that Heidegger's jug (or, in Lacan's text, the potter's vase) is certainly a thing but only to the degree that it is a signifier. The introduction of the signifier in this context, however, breaks the intimate link Heidegger established between the thing and the world. The proximity of the thing to the world no longer applies. For Heidegger, as we have seen in Chapter 1, the function of the thing is to stay the world and, through the gathering and unification of the fourfold, to make the worlding of the world possible for us. This worlding of the world is what the worldlessness of modernity makes impossible for us as it reduces all things to mere objects of representation. While Lacan distances himself from the historical aspect of this argument when he says that 'I will not be concerned here with the function of *Das Ding* in Heidegger's approach to the contemporary revelation of what he calls Being and that is linked to the end of metaphysics,' he is clearly following the general outline of Heidegger's argument in terms of the structure of the thing (Lacan 1992: 120). But what Lacan argues here, against Heidegger, is that the thing will always refer us to the ruin of the world and establishes a direct link between the thing and worldlessness (rather than the world).

The Heideggerian concern with earth and sky is, then, reformulated here in terms of the problem of the primordial symbolisation of presence and absence that functions in Lacan as the condition of signification. Speaking of the vase as simultaneously a useful utensil and a signifier, Lacan maps the earth/sky distinction onto the problem of signification: 'If it really is a signifier, and the first of such signifiers fashioned by human hand, it is in its signifying essence a signifier of nothing other than of signifying as such or, in other words, of no particular signified' (Lacan 1992: 120). The crucial point here is that Lacan reformulates the Heideggerian terminology around the minimal dyad of absence/presence: earth stands for presence, the sky for the absence of gods. The vase unites 'celestial and terrestrial powers' (Lacan 1992: 120) because it introduces the void into a world that was completely oblivious to its possibility. The question of the fullness or emptiness of the vase is the way presence and absence first appear to us: 'It creates the void and thereby introduces the possibility of filling it. Emptiness and fullness are introduced into a world that by itself knows not of them' (Lacan 1992: 120).

Phenomenologically speaking, then, the signifier is responsible for introducing the void into the world – even if the world itself would not be able to exist without the signifier. Lacan, then, immediately indicates that what is at stake in this argument is precisely the existence of the world – and the sad state in which it finds itself:

> The example of [. . .] the vase allows us to introduce that around which the central problem of the Thing has revolved, to the extent that it is the central problem of ethics, namely, if a reasonable power created the world, if God created the world, how is it that whatever we do or don't do, the world is in such bad shape? (Lacan 1992: 121)

The unsettling experience that the world is not what it is supposed to be has long been at the heart of our reflections on worldlessness. But as Lacan argues here, in their symmetrical opposition, both creationist mythology and ancient philosophy miss a crucial point. What is masked by the first 'is the fact that the vase is made from matter. Nothing is made from nothing' (Lacan 1992: 121). And this is precisely the fundamental presupposition of the latter: 'matter is eternal, and that nothing is made from nothing' (Lacan 1992: 121). What ancient philosophy misses is the dimension of the signifier. Even for an Aristotle, the world (in its interhuman dimension as well) is reduced to mere nature, a plenitude without the void of the signifier. The psychoanalytic view, however, displaces these two extreme positions by introducing the problem of the signifier in the middle. The vase is made from matter and not from nothing, but the creation of the signifier is the construction of nothingness in the midst of being. This is why, as Lacan says, 'the fashioning of the signifier and the introduction of a gap of a hole in the real is identical' (Lacan 1992: 121). The signifier is worldless in the sense that it creates the nothingness from which the world emerges.

The surprising conclusion that Lacan draws from this insight concerns the very status of modern science. While it might appear that modern science is Aristotelian in its ontology, in reality, science needs the idea of creation *ex nihilo*, which remains simultaneously its historical origin and its telos. As Lacan puts it, modern science could develop only out of 'biblical or Judaic ideology, and not our ancient philosophy or the Aristotelian tradition' (Lacan 1992: 122). Since the essence of this science is a certain 'symbolic mastery' over the domain of being, its history is defined by a crucial tension between, on the one hand, the 'free reign to the signifier' which guarantees that the laws of science develop in the direction of an increasingly coherent whole and, on the other hand, the fundamental view that it holds with regard to the contingency of being (Lacan 1992: 122). To paraphrase, science provides an increasingly more and more systematic description of existence in its totality but cannot justify existence itself.

In fact, Lacan claims that science produces a concept of existence that undermines our traditional understanding of that term: 'the vault of the heavens no longer exists, and all the celestial bodies [. . .] appear as if they could just as well not be there. Their reality, as existentialism puts it, is essentially characterized by facticity; they are fundamentally contingent' (Lacan

1992: 122). The idea of the contingency of being, however, undermines the phenomenological certainty with which we approach the world of our experiences: 'what is expressed for us in the energy/matter equivalence is that one final day we may find that the whole texture of appearance has been rent apart, starting from the gap we have introduced there; the whole thing might just disappear' (Lacan 1992: 122). The metaphysics of modern science is essentially an ontology of worldlessness, since what appears to us to be the permanence of the natural world is merely the symbolic coherence of scientific explanations. In reality, however, the world might just disappear at any moment and without any reason whatsoever.[10] Yet, according to Lacan, it belongs to the very essence of modern science to protect us from the consequences of this insight.

★ ★ ★

This focus on the signifier also explains the importance of psychosis for the early Lacan.[11] Of course, psychosis is only one of the diagnostic categories of Lacanian psychoanalysis, but it also designates an important limit to analysis as it is not entirely clear what analysis can do with a psychotic. Psychosis is, therefore, either a potential stumbling block for analytic practice or a testing ground for analytic theory. From a theoretical perspective, then, the significance of psychosis for Lacan is easy to explain: it is a special case study because it allows us to thematise the subject's relation to the signifier in its purest form. Since at the core of psychosis we find the foreclosure of the signifier, it allows us to raise the question of the subject in relation to signification as such.

Thus, 'On a Question Prior to Any Possible Treatment of Psychosis' (written in 1957 right after the completion of his seminars on psychosis) stages the problem of psychosis in terms of a conflict between phenomenology and structural analysis. It is the latter that will show us the crucial problem: 'The relation between the signifier and the subject that this analysis uncovers can be found [. . .] in the very appearance of the phenomena' (Lacan 2006c: 449). This structural analysis of psychosis, therefore, shows that what is at stake in the relation between the subject and the signifier is the problem of appearance as such. Psychosis poses a challenge to phenomenology because it is the structure that most clearly highlights the function of the signifier in the very constitution of what appears.

It is, then, not surprising that Lacan once again takes up the problem of psychosis in relation to the question of being: psychosis is construed here in terms of the question of the subject's existence. Lacan argues that what is at work in psychosis is not projection, not the loss of reality, not regression, not even the repression of homosexual desire, but a specific relation to the Other. What takes place in the locus of the Other is articulated there as a discourse whose syntax will define the way the question of the subject's existence emerges for this subject:

> For it is an experiential truth for psychoanalysis that the question of the subject's existence arises for him, not in the kind of anxiety it provokes at the level of the ego, which is only one element of his cortege, but as an articulated question – 'What am I there'? – about his sex and his contingency in being: namely, that on the one hand he is a man or a woman, and on the other that he might not be, the two conjugating their mystery and knotting it in symbols of procreation and death. (Lacan 2006c: 459)

The important point is that the two axes of the ontology of the subject (the contingency of being on the one hand, and sexual difference on the other) are articulated around the problem of the signifier. The question of the subject is actually a calling into question that is already articulated in the unconscious: 'this question is a calling into question there – that is, prior to any analysis this question is articulated there in discrete elements' (Lacan 2006c: 459). These elements are signifiers 'grasped here functioning in their purest form' (Lacan 2006c: 459).

The presence of the signifier in the unconscious (indeed, the very fact that the unconscious is structured like a language) here implies that it is the location of this calling into question whose scope eventually extends to the entire world. First, it might appear that the signifier simply follows the routes provided to it by the structures of the 'real world', and in this sense it is derivative of the signified (Lacan 2006c: 459–60). But Lacan's point is precisely to reassert the primacy of the signifier over the signified. And the primacy of the signifier means that everything that exists will have to be determined by something that does not exist:

> But this is not the case at the level of the calling into question, not of the subject's place in the world, but of his existence as a subject, a calling into question which, starting with him, will extend to his within-the-world relation to objects, and to the existence of the world, insofar as its existence, too, can be called into question beyond its order. (Lacan 2006c: 460)

The signifier is the agency behind the constitution of the world – but this constitution takes place by the introduction to being the possibility of non-being. As a result, the subject and the world exist only on condition of the possibility of their non-existence.

This possibility manifests itself in the experience of the calling into question of the subject's existence, which leads to the calling into question of the existence of world. Under the sway of the signifier, the subject's exposure to the possibility of worldlessness is constitutive.

★ ★ ★

At this point, it might be worth restating a basic Lacanian idea about psychosis that could be useful for any theory of worldlessness: psychosis is a structure. Lacan rejects the idea that the loss of reality would be the constitutive factor of psychosis.[12] While the common understanding of psychosis as the 'twilight of the world' (le crépuscule du monde) is certainly useful in accounting for some of the phenomena one encounters in psychosis, Lacan suggests that this identification is misleading, since it implies that psychosis is an unstructured state. Lacan distances himself from the expression 'twilight of the world' for two reasons. First, because it is an eschatological fantasy that is produced by the psychotic's discourse itself. In this context, it is worth pointing out that the expression Weltuntergang is borrowed from Schreber's memoirs.[13] Lacan describes Schreber's relation to God in terms of a redemption fantasy: 'this fantasy parodies the last surviving couple, who following some human catastrophe, would find themselves confronted with what is total in the act of animal re-production, holding as they would the power to repopulate the earth' (Lacan 2006c: 476–7). The motive of the loss of the world is internal to the psychotic's discourse, where it functions as the precondition of the creation of a new world. It should also be noted that the creation of the new world proceeds from a sexual relation (between the subject and the Other, between Schreber and God) that is unhampered by the usual complications.

The second reason why Lacan is suspicious of this category is that it implies a therapeutic teleology that resembles the structure of the psychotic fantasy. In the clinical setting, the expression 'the twilight of the world' refers to a preliminary stage before a psychotic break that is characterised by confusion, disorientation and even a loss of the sense of reality. In his seminar, Lacan described this state with the following words:

> From the phenomenological point of view, and remaining cautious, we can admit that there is a state here that can be described as the twilight of the world. [Schreber] is no longer amongst real beings – this *being no longer amongst* is typical, for he is amongst other much more burdensome elements. (Lacan 1993: 107; emphasis in original)

The assumption is that the period of the twilight of the world is followed by the construction of a new unreal world constituted by the delusional metaphor. As Lacan puts it: 'There is [. . .] a decline, a twilight of the world, and at one point a quasi-confusional disorder of the apprehensions of reality, only because the world has to be recreated' (Lacan 1993: 314). But this scheme of the loss and the subsequent recreation of the world 'introduces, at the most profound stage of the mental confusion, a sort of teleology' (Lacan 1993: 314). The psychotic loses the world only so that he can recreate it.

But what would happen to psychosis if we approached it without the eschatological fantasy or the theoretical teleology? It would emerge as a structure that could be properly formalised. Commenting on the so-called I-schema that claims to achieve precisely this goal, Lacan writes: 'The schema shows that the final state of the psychosis does not represent the frozen chaos encountered in the aftermath of an earthquake, but rather the bringing to light of lines of efficiency that makes people talk when it is a problem with an elegant solution' (Lacan 2006c: 477). If we abandon the reference to a catastrophic collapse of the world and the subsequent chaos, psychosis shows itself to be the site of 'lines of efficiency' that are determined by 'the only organicity that is essentially involved in this process: the organicity that motivates the structure of signification' (Lacan 2006c: 477). The dissolution of the world remains an integral part of the process, but its function and meaning change. It is now best understood as the effect of the signifier within the imaginary register: 'Condensed in the form of this schema, the relations emerge by which the signifier's induction effects, impacting the imaginary, bring about the upheaval in the subject that clinicians refer to as the "twilight of the world", necessitating new signifying effects in response' (Lacan 2006c: 477).

The objective of these responses to the twilight of the world is to restore order in the subject. But reality is restored to the psychotic subject (who becomes here 'a sort of island') at the cost of the 'eccentric reshapings of the imaginary, I, and of the symbolic, S, which reduce reality to the field of the skew between them' (Lacan 2006c: 478). And Lacan makes it quite clear what we should learn from this conclusion: 'The subordinate conception that we must have of the function of reality in the [psychotic] process, in both its cause and effects, is what is important here' (Lacan 2006c: 478). The loss and the restoration of reality are, in this sense, secondary manifestations of what is truly at work in psychotic process – 'man's relation to the signifier' (Lacan 2006c: 479). If we focus on what really takes place in the process (which can be understood by reference to the mechanism of foreclosure as the failure of the paternal metaphor), we discover in psychosis something different from a state of chaos – a system of logical functions and relations. In spite of all the suffering it entails, as Lacan notes in one of his remarks, psychosis does not preclude the possibility of imaginary relations: 'the relation to the other qua relation to one's semblable, and even a relation as elevated as that of friendship in the sense in which Aristotle makes it the essence of the conjugal link, are perfectly compatible with the skewing of the relation to the Other with a capital O and all the radical anomalies it brings with it' (Lacan 2006c: 478). It is possible that psychosis involves the loss of the world, but even psychotics can have friends.

★ ★ ★

Following a pattern that we have already seen repeated several times, Lacan's conclusions here bear on the scientific status of psychoanalysis. The same way that Freud's analysis of schizophrenia led him to an insight into the schizophrenic nature of psychoanalytic discourse itself, Lacan concludes his essay on psychosis with a reflection on the psychotic discourse of modern science. To be more precise, Lacan suggests that the very discourse of modernity is structured by a delusion, and science partakes of this delusion in a way that renders it complicit in a collective psychosis.[14] Speaking of a 'false modesty' (Lacan 2006c: 480) that defines scientific pedantry, Lacan suggests that science 'evokes the ineffability of lived experience' (Lacan 2006c: 480) in order to exclude the unconscious from its domain. But, as psychoanalysis makes clear, 'it is not ineffable precisely because it [ça] speaks' (Lacan 2006c: 480). The latter ('it speaks') is, of course, Lacan's formula for the ontological status of the unconscious as an entity structured like a language and whose proper locus is the discourse of the Other. The point is that given this structural definition of the unconscious, the most intimate part of what appears to be ineffable personal experience (the 'true structure' of subjectivity [Lacan 2006c: 480]) is in fact possible to describe in an act of scientific formalisation (which is, nevertheless, not without its limits).

The kind of science that does not want to know about the unconscious, therefore, becomes an important cultural means of avoiding the unconscious. By declaring the intimacy of personal experience to be beyond scientific description, such a science in effect maintains a structural similarity with the delusional subjectivity:

> Thus from the same vantage point to which delusional subjectivity has brought us, I will turn to scientific subjectivity: I mean the subjectivity that the scientist at work in science shares with the man of the civilization that supports it. I will not deny that I have seen enough on this score in our time to wonder about the criteria by which this man —with a discourse on freedom that must certainly be called delusional (I devoted one of my seminars to it), with a concept of the real in which determinism is no more than an alibi that quickly becomes anxiety provoking when one tries to extend its field to chance (I had my audience experience this in a preliminary experiment), and with a belief that unites men, half the universe at least, under the symbol of Father Christmas (which no one can overlook) – would stop me from situating him, by legitimate analogy, in the category of social psychosis which, if I am not mistaken, Pascal established before me. (Lacan 2006c: 480)

The dominant mode of subjectivity produced by modernity is supported by a delusional discourse on freedom (politics), a concept of reality that is torn between the two extremes of absolute determinism and radical contingency (ontology), and the persistence of religious faith (religion). And Lacan hastens to add: 'There is no doubt but that such a psychosis may turn out to be compatible with what is called an orderly state of affairs' (Lacan 2006c: 480). The mass psychosis of modernity, in other words, is not a form of chaos, but precisely a way of relating to an order that we often take for granted as what is naturally given to us. But the compatibility of this mass psychosis with what we consider to be the natural order of things 'does not authorize the psychiatrist, even if he is a psychoanalyst, to trust in his own compatibility with this orderly state to believe that he is in possession of an adequate idea of the *reality* to which his patient supposedly proves to be unequal' (Lacan 2006c: 480).

If what one could consider to be the 'normal' state of affairs in the age of modernity is a form of social psychosis, and if modern science contributes to this state of affairs by legitimising the avoidance of the unconscious, psychoanalysis fulfils its function as the science of the unconscious by assuming the role of a witness to its discourse. This is why Lacan speaks of the 'endorsement' that psychoanalysis gives to the psychotic's delusion, since 'it legitimates it in the same sphere as the one in which analytic experience normally operates and because it rediscovers in his discourse what it usually discovers as the discourse of the unconscious' (Lacan 1993: 132). In a memorable phrase, Lacan calls the psychotic 'a martyr of the unconscious' (Lacan 1993: 132) in the sense that the psychotic bears witness to the unconscious:

> It's an open testimony. The neurotic is also a witness to the existence of the unconscious, he gives a closed testimony that has to be deciphered. The psychotic, in the sense in which he is

in a first approximation an open witness, seems arrested, immobilized, in a position that leaves him incapable of authentically restoring the sense of what he witnesses and sharing it in the discourse of others. (Lacan 1993: 132)

Lacan's critique of the psychoanalytic *status quo* with regard to psychosis could be then described as a revaluation of the function of worldlessness in the psychotic process. The common understanding of the worldlessness of psychosis holds that the process consists of two major steps in this regard. As a preliminary step to the actual psychotic break, the dissolution of the imaginary produces a state of worldlessness in the form of the twilight of the world. But, in a second step, this loss of the world leads to the creation of a new world that allows the subject to restore its internal order. This new delusional order, however, constitutes an idiosyncratic world, a state worthy of the name 'world' only in the sense that it bears all the formal characteristics of a world (it is a closed whole with differentiated identities). Psychosis, in this sense, is an attempt to install the unconscious itself as if it were a world (rather than use the world as a defense against it). Consequently, this new order lacks a crucial aspect of what we often expect from a world: it does not provide the psychotic with a liveable community. In fact, this new world isolates the psychotic from his surroundings by imprisoning him in a singular world. The Lacanian definition of psychosis, however, argues that even when the psychotic loses the world, he is not simply let loose in the vast ocean of beings without a few signs to orient his comportment. The psychotic is not simply abandoned in the midst of being without anything to hold on to, as he stays in a specific relation to the signifier. The nature of this relation implies that the worldlessness of psychosis is not a state of chaos but a structured state.

In many respects, then, Lacan reverses the terms of the common association of worldlessness with psychosis and other pathological formations. Lacan's point is not that a life in worldlessness would be nothing more than a state of permanent psychosis, an endless and hopeless delusional suffering without a world. What is pathological is not the mere exposure to world-lessness but precisely the persistent delusion of the world. The problem with psychosis is that it is structured by the inexorable rhythm of the complete loss and the delusional rebirth of the world. The generalised psychosis of Western modernity is, therefore, not (as the Heideggerian thesis would have it) an ir-reversible decline that takes the form of a progressive exposure to a technologically induced state of worldlessness, but precisely an intransigent belief in the world supported by the discourses of science, politics and religion. To put it differently, what is psychotic about modernity is its delusional investment in the category of the world itself that persists in it in spite of the fact that it also sets its subjects on a path towards an arduous discovery of the simple fact of worldlessness.

★ ★ ★

In light of this critique of modernity, it is now possible for us to clearly articulate what Lacan means by the suggestion that psychoanalysis is the science of worldlessness. In Lacan's account, under the sway of this modern psychosis, the subject's relation to worldlessness becomes legible in an experience we tend to consider more 'normal' than that of psychosis: the certainty of anxiety. In the case of anxiety, we come face to face with a 'signal' that might in the end refer us to a kind of worldlessness that is altogether different from the catastrophic collapse of the imaginary. And it is precisely anxiety that leads us to the question: What does the *object a* have to do with the world?

The theory of the *object a* is based on a new topology that explicitly breaks with the Freudian metaphysical distinction between an internal and an external world. This is the ultimate lesson of Lacan's critique of the Freudian theory of anxiety as a signal of an internal danger for the ego: 'there is no internal danger' (Lacan 2014: 152). The anatomical and historical foundation of this topology is Lacan's critique of the idea of 'birth anxiety'. In opposition to Freud, Lacan insists that the structuring of the phenomenon of anxiety cannot be reduced to the moment of birth: 'It is impossible to locate such a complex relationship between anxiety and ego right back at the start' (Lacan 2014: 121). Although Freud was correct to locate the origin of anxiety at a pre-specular level, this stage cannot be identified with birth. The intermediary agency between the specular object (the object constituted on the level of the imaginary in the form of an image) and the *object a* is indeed a cut, but this separation is not the separation from the mother. Our entry into the world, as the separation from the mother, is not what defines the logic of anxiety. Lacan pushes this origin back further before the moment of birth when he discusses the 'egg's relation to the mother's body in mammals' (Lacan 2014: 121). Lacan, however, evokes the parasitic relation between the embryo and the mother's body not in order to locate this cut between mother and infant, but to identify it as an operation internal to the development of the embryo. The decisive cut takes place not when the child 'falls into the world', but when the embryo separates from the embryonic envelopes (Lacan 2014: 121).

Although Lacan speaks of the relation between what is 'detached from these envelopes with the cut of the embryo' (Lacan 2014: 122) and the separation that produces the *object a* only in terms of an analogy, it is clear that his point is to locate a specific topology at the origin of life that breaks with the simple inside/outside distinction. This suggests that unlike in Freud, for Lacan the original moment is not the turning back of life on itself towards death, but the constitution of the Möbius-strip-like surface that will serve as the foundation of the new metaphysics of the worldlessness of life: 'the Möbius strip is a surface that has just one face and a surface with just one face cannot be turned inside out. If you turn it over, it will still be identical to itself. This is what I call *not having a specular image*' (Lacan 2014: 96). Lacan uses the example of the cross-cap (a topological structure that can be produced from a self-intersecting Möbius strip) to illustrate the ontological status of the *a*. Lacan's point is that if you slice the cross-cap, the residual part itself will have the structure of a Möbius strip. This leftover is what Lacan calls the *a*, an entity without a specular image (Lacan 2014: 97).

As Lacan explains, what is at stake here is the function of the mirror stage in the 'general institution of the field of the object' (Lacan 2014: 90). This process can be broken down into three steps. The first step is the subject's identification with the specular image. The second step is the constitution of the imaginary other (his *semblable*) by another act of identification that shows to what extent the subject's identity is caught up in that of the imaginary other. The third step consists of the introduction of a mediating object between the subject and his *semblable* (Lacan 2014: 91). This object, however, raises the question of belonging: who does it belong to? To me or to the other? The problem is that not every object can be shared and, therefore, we need to distinguish on this level two kinds of objects: objects of exchange and objects that cannot be shared (Lacan 2014: 91). We experience anxiety when these unshareable objects emerge in the form of so-called partial objects (of which Lacan identifies five basic types: the oral, the anal, the phallic, the scopic and the vocal object) (Lacan 2014: 91). Anxiety, therefore, tells us that the object *a* precedes the imaginary constitution of the field of objectivity. In this priority, it represents a special relation to an originary state of primary narcissism:

> Prior to the mirror stage, that which will be *i(a)* lies in the disorder of the objects *a* in the plural and it is not yet a question of having them or not. This is the true meaning, the deepest meaning, to be given to the term *autoeroticism* – one lacks any self, as it were, completely and utterly. It is not the outside world that one lacks, as it is quite wrongly expressed, it is oneself. (Lacan 2014: 118–19)

In the beginning, before the world of objects, there was no self, only objects *a*. As far as the ontology of the object *a* is concerned, then, Lacan makes it clear that it is only metaphorically speaking an object, since it remains irreducible to the field of objectivity: 'the object we have to speak about under the term of *a* is precisely an object that is external to any possible definition of objectivity' (Lacan 2014: 86). As a result, it is the kind of entity that by definition escapes the logic of the Kantian transcendental aesthetic (Lacan 2014: 87). It remains irreducible to the space and time understood as the pure forms of intuition. Lacan's point is that 'no intuition [. . .] that is founded purely and simply upon the intuition of consciousness can be held to be origina-tive, or valid, and thus it cannot constitute the starting point of any transcendental aesthetic' (Lacan 2014: 87). The intuition of consciousness cannot be originary, since the subject is 'primordially' unconscious. At the originary constitution of the subject, we find not the intuition of consciousness but the signifier.

★ ★ ★

What follows from this last point is that, moving beyond the imaginary register, we also have to examine the object *a*'s relation to the symbolic order and the signifier. Reflecting on the 'function of the lack in its originative structure' (Lacan 2014: 136), Lacan once again evokes the Möbius strip for the sake of what he calls a little 'tale' that functions here as the quintessential Lacanian allegory of worldlessness:

> If the insect that wanders along the surface of the Möbius strip forms a representation of the fact that it is a surface, he can believe from one moment to the next that there is another face that he hasn't explored, the face that is always on the back of the face along which he is walking. He can believe in this other side, even though there isn't one, as you know. Without knowing it, he is exploring the only face there is, and yet, from one moment to the next, it does indeed have a back. [. . .] Is the matter settled because we are describing this little missing piece, the *a* on this occasion, with this paradigmatic shape? Absolutely not, because the very fact that it is missing is what forms the reality of the world the insect is walking about in. The little interior eight is well and truly irreducible. In other words, it is a lack for which the symbol cannot compensate. This is not an absence that the symbol can counter. (Lacan 2014: 136)

What the insect of the tale lacks is an access to worldlessness. In this new topology, we can distinguish two major ontological domains: on the one hand, we have the Möbius strip that constitutes the continuous surface of the inside and outside worlds; on the other hand, we have the worldless *a* whose lack is constitutive of the lived reality of the world and remains impossible to symbolise.

This is where we can locate Lacan's contribution to the Freudian theory of the worldlessness of life and the worldlessness of thought. The late Lacan's concern with the limits of symbolisation designates the object *a* as an entity beyond signification. What concerns Lacan now is the unsymbolisable remainder. The starting point for the early (structuralist) Lacan was that the signifier constitutes a world by retroactively structuring the world of things. But the constitution of the world of language consists of the introduction of a hole into being. In this sense, the signifier is a worldless agency that nevertheless functions as the means of constituting the world out of this nothingness. The most radical form of worldlessness in this context would be a state of being without the signifier. The assumption that worldlessness amounts to the lack of the signifier explains the central position of psychosis as the exemplary limit case. To the degree that psychosis is constituted by the foreclosure of the signifier, it is a state which is not absolutely without a signifier but reduces the subject's relation to it to a pure minimum. Psychosis manifests what is knowable for us of worldlessness. The psychotic bears witness to the unconscious with a directness that makes it exemplary. Beyond this point, however, we would have nothing to talk about.

The late Lacan's argument, however, is that there is always something beyond the signifier that constitutes the world for us: a worldless entity that is only metaphorically an object. According to this new topology, the world can no longer be divided into an 'inner' and an 'outer' world. In place of this duality, we get a continuous surface. If we are in the world, we can assume that there is another world attached to this world (as if it were the other side of the surface). But we know that this other side simply does not exist: once under the sway of the signifier, the subject's 'inner' world (constituted by the imaginary and symbolic registers) cannot be simply separated from the 'outer' world of reality. And yet, there is something other than the world. This is the radical lack that forms the reality of the world and remains forever alien to the symbol. This irreducibility, however, does not mean that we do not know anything about it. Anxiety is the most reliable proof we have of the fact that something other than the world exists.[15]

★ ★ ★

To illustrate the underlying dialectic of this logic, early on in his anxiety seminar Lacan distinguishes the world from the stage. This demonstration – whose goal is to clarify the relations between the imaginary and symbolic registers and which is offered in the context of a critique of Lévi-Strauss – proceeds in three steps that could be briefly described in the following terms: first, we have the world of things which is, in a second step, disturbed by the entry of the signifier, which in turn will refer us to the order of the objects of desire. In slightly different terms, this means that we move from epistemological objects, by way of the signifier, to objects of desire. In the end, this means for us that we move from the world, through the signifier, to a reflection on worldlessness.

   1. *First phase*: 'I shall say that the first phase is as follows – there is *the world*' (Lacan 2014: 33, emphasis in original). Lacan

186

makes it clear that our phenomenological starting point is the self-evidence of the world of intuition. But, as he immediately adds, we do not know what the simple presence of the world means. As a result, Lacan calls the kind of thinking that insists on the primacy and homogeneity of this world 'primary materialism' (which is '*materialist* in the eighteenth-century sense') (Lacan 2014: 33). This kind of materialism reduces the play of structure to the structures of the brain and, in the end, to the structures of matter itself and, therefore, cannot properly articulate the function of structure.

2. *Second phase*: 'So, first phase, *the world*. Second phase, *the stage*. The stage is the dimension of history' (Lacan 2014: 33, emphasis in original). By instituting a separation between the locus of the spectator and the stage, this phase creates the impression that there is a radical divide between the world and the signifier — as if the laws of the signifier were incompatible with the laws of the world. But the introduction of the stage ultimately leads to the reversal of the logic that seeks to assert the primacy of the material world in relation to the signifier:

> Once the stage has come to the fore, what happens is that the whole world is put upon it, and with Descartes one can say, *Onto the world's stage go I*, as befits, *larvatus, masked*. From this point on, the question may be posed as to what the world, what at the start we quite innocently called the world, owes to what has come back down to it from this stage. Everything that throughout the course of history we have called *the world* has left behind superimposed residues that accumulate without the faintest care for contradiction. What culture transports to us in the guise of the world is a stack, a shop crammed full of the flotsam and jetsam of worlds that have followed one after the other, and which, of all their incompatibility, don't get on any the worse with each other within every single one of us. (Lacan 2014: 34)

The world no longer exists in its existential purity, since it is overwritten by sedimented layers of meaning inscribed on it throughout history. What we perceive in cultural transmission to be the world is, in fact, a complex overdetermined historical construct that lacks the kind of consistency we tend to attribute to a closed order. As far as Lacan is concerned, what follows from this reversal is quite clear: 'as soon as we start making reference to the stage, nothing is more legitimate than to call into question what the world of cosmism is in the real' (Lacan 2014: 34). The path towards worldlessness has been opened. The staging of the world points in the direction of an acosmic real.

3. *Third phase*: 'the third phase, namely, the stage on the stage, shows us where our questioning ought to be directed' (Lacan 2014: 37). Lacan introduces this final phase with reference to Hamlet's staging of the *Mouse-trap*, the play within the play that is supposed to reveal Claudius's guilty conscience. Lacan argues that in Hamlet's story we find two kinds of imaginary identification: one with the specular image, the other with the object *a* that is always beyond the specular object. On the one hand, by staging the play, Hamlet puts on display a specular image with which he identifies (by assuming the very crime for which he is seeking revenge). On the other hand, at the decisive moment, Hamlet's behaviour is determined by another kind of identification, what Lacan calls his 'identification with Ophelia' (Lacan 2014: 36). This latter move, modelled on Freud's definition of mourning, could be defined as an identification with the object – to be more precise, an identification with the object of desire as *a*. Quite significantly, it is this second identification that will make it possible for Hamlet to abandon his strategies of evasion and to do what needs to be done.

The third phase of the dialectic of the world, therefore, leads to one of the most compelling formulations ever provided by Lacan of the status of psychoanalysis as the science of worldlessness:

> At any rate, this object of desire oughtn't to be confused with the object defined by epistemology. The advent of the object of our science is very specifically defined by a particular discovery of the efficacy of the signifying operation as such. This means that what is specific to our science, I'm saying to the science that has been in existence at our side for two centuries now, leaves open the question of what earlier I called the cosmism of the object. Whether or not there is a cosmos is uncertain, and our science advances precisely to the extent that it's given up maintaining any cosmic or cosmizing presuppositions. (Lacan 2014: 37)

Psychoanalysis avoids the traps of 'assured cosmism' and 'historical pathos' precisely by moving beyond the first two stages of this dialectic (Lacan 2014: 38). The first phase implies an incorrigible faith in the simple givenness of the world; the second phase leads to a historicism that believes that there is no real world, only historical constructions of worlds. The third phase displaces both of these extremes: it assures us of the existence of a real worldlessness.[16]

Notes

1   In his Cartesian critique of Heidegger, Slavoj Žižek provided the following definition of the worldlessness of the Freudian unconscious: 'Heidegger's notion of "being-in-the-world" points towards our irreducible and unsurpassable "embeddedness" in a concrete and ultimately contingent life-world: we are always-already in the world, engaged in an existential

189

project within a background which eludes our grasp and forever remains the opaque horizon into which we are "thrown" as finite beings. [. . .] Lacan, however, in an unheard-of gesture, claims the exact opposite: the Freudian "unconscious" [. . .] stands for the rational subject insofar as it is originally "out of joint", in discord with its contextualized situation: the "unconscious" is the crack on account of which the subject's primordial stance is not that of "being-in-the-world"' (Žižek 2008: 71–2).

2 For discussions of Freud's references to Kant, see Tauber (2010: 116–45) and Grigg (2009: 95–108).

3 Arguably, we can find a distant echo of this Freudian argument in Catherine Malabou's reflections on plasticity, when Malabou calls for a 'reasonable materialism' that 'would posit that the natural contradicts itself and that thought is the fruit of this contradiction' (Malabou 2008: 82). Furthermore, we should also note here what role the category of the 'world' plays in Malabou's arguments that are based on a strategic opposition of neoliberal 'flexibility' and cerebral 'plasticity'. On the one hand, Malabou observes that 'the plasticity of the brain is the real image of the world' (Malabou 2008: 39). In other words, plasticity assumes the role of an ontological category that simultaneously accounts for the 'working' of the brain and the construction of the world. On the other hand, she clearly formulates a political programme based on this ontological assumption: 'not to replicate the [neoliberal] caricature of the world: this is what we should do with our brain' (Malabou 2008: 78). According to this argument, the contemporary state of generalized worldlessness should be opposed by way of a new consciousness of the brain's plasticity. This is how the 'biological alter-globalism' of plasticity becomes for Malabou 'the form of another possible world' (Malabou 2008: 80).

4 For the argument that the contemporary state of worldlessness should be opposed by way of our recovery of a 'primordial narcissism', see Stiegler (2009).

5 We should, of course, keep in mind Adrian Johnston's point that 'Lacan's attitudes toward the notion of scientificity undergo major changes during the course of his intellectual itinerary. To get a sense of this arc of alterations, one finds, in the 1950s, statements such as "our discourse should be a scientific discourse" [. . .] By the 1970s, [. . .] this ambition is abandoned and repudiated' (Johnston 2013: 58). For useful discussions of Lacan's views on science, see the essays collected in Glynos and Stavrakakis (2002), as well as Fink (1995: 138–45); Milner (1991, 2000); Morel (2000); Cutrofello (2002); Johnston (2013: 39–58).

6 This chapter focuses exclusively on the early Lacan and follows his teaching only up to the mid-sixties because its primary goal is to examine the effects on the phenomenological tradition of the introduction of the signifier. For systematic attempts to develop an ontology of worldlessness based on the works of the late Lacan, see Bryant (2011: 245–93) and Johnston (2013).

7 Even if they did not always explicitly speak the language of worldlessness, Lacan's followers have long recognised the fact that his 'ontology' should be interpreted in related terms. For example, Joan Copjec has argued that Lacanian ethics 'takes off from the proposal that being is not-all or there is no whole of being' (Copjec 2004: 6). Reflecting on the subject's position in relation to the world, Copjec writes: 'If the subject is able to envision for herself this admittedly supernumerary place in the world, this is because she locates in the world an empty place, one occupied by precisely nothing. The surplus of the subject requires this deficit of the world, which, by this very incompleteness, is revealed to be incapable of realizing itself on its own' (Copjec 2004: 173). In a similar fashion, in his reflections on 'weak nature', Adrian Johnston identifies 'the later Lacan of the nonexistent big other [. . .], the psychoanalytic thinker of the not-All [. . .] and a detotalized Real' as the ontological inspiration behind a truly contemporary materialism (Johnston 2013: 3).

8 The question concerning Lacan's supposed idealism or materialism has been at the centre of a number of contemporary debates. At the core of these discussions, we often find Alain Badiou's critique of Lacan's linguistic idealism in *Theory of the Subject*: 'Language = structure: such is the constituent statement [. . .] Even so, to the extent that it claims to expand all the way to the thesis: the world is discourse, this argument in contemporary philosophy would deserve to be rebaptized: "idealinuistery"' (Badiou 2009b: 188). For the argument that the idealism/materialism opposition is insufficient to interpret Lacan's positions, see Johnston (2009: 119–24) and Eyers (2012: 121–64).

9 For discussions of Lacan's relations to Heidegger, see Balmès (1999), Badiou (2006b) and Žižek (2009). In his introduction to the second edition of *The Ticklish Subject*, which bears the title 'Why Lacan is not a Heideggerian', Žižek argues that while the earlier Lacan accepted the Heideggerian critique of Descartes, in the later Lacan we witness a paradoxical return to Descartes since, at this point, Lacan embraces the cogito as the subject of the unconscious (Žižek 2008: xx). The crucial point raised by Žižek here is that the Lacanian 'real of jouissance' must be located beyond the domain of being and, therefore, beyond the domain of Heideggerian ontology.

10 This is the thesis that was worked out in much more detail in Quentin Meillassoux's *After Finitude* (Meillassoux 2010).

11 In the context of our own argument, we should point out that arguably psychosis marks a crucial point of disagreement between Lacan and Heidegger. As Žižek puts it, 'Lacan's implicit clinical reproach to Heidegger's existential analytic of *Dasein* as "being-toward-death" is that it is appropriate only for neurotics and fails to account for psychotics: a psychotic subject occupies an existential position for which there is no place in Heidegger's mapping' (Žižek 2008: xvii).

12 Insisting on the fact that the psychotic is not simply outside language (but represents a specific relation to the signifier that takes shape already within the symbolic order), Žižek claims: 'To put it in Heidegger's terms, the psychotic is not *welt-los*, deprived of the world: he already dwells in the opening of Being' (Žižek 2008: x).

13 Schreber's term *Weltuntergang* was translated into English as the 'end of the world' (Schreber 2000: 75).

14 For example, Andrew Cutrofello argued that, although the subject of modern science is constitutively worldless, modern metaphysics has tried to compensate for this loss by way of an anxiety-inducing reconstitution of the world: 'The Cartesian subject "loses its world" when it discovers itself qua cogito or subject of the signifier in the second Meditation, but it attempts to reestablish that world, rather in the manner that Freud describes the psychotic's attempt to recreate reality' (Cutrofello 2002: 154).

15 As Cutrofello put it, in the context of a confrontation between Lacan and Heidegger, 'it is the difference between a discourse that sees in anxiety the mark of the subject's being-in-the-world and a discourse that sees in anxiety the mark of the subject's not-being-in-the-world' (Cutrofello 2002: 157).

16 Discussing Lacan's understanding of Heidegger, François Balmès observes: 'Le monde, pour Lacan, n'est en aucun cas le réel; dès l'origine l'idée de monde est dépréciée, rejetée du côté de l'illusoire totalisation imaginaire' (Balmès 1999: 59).

4

The Phenomenology of Worldlessness

Différance is worldless. Not in the sense that deconstruction would offer nothing more than the nihilistic undoing of all possible worlds only to render life completely meaningless. Différance is worldless because it is older than the world, in fact, older than any dialectic of the world and its negation. It precedes this dialectic and makes it possible in the first place only to displace it whenever the occasion arises. Différance could be a name for the kind of non-privative worldlessness that precedes the very possibility of the loss of the world. It is 'more originary' than our common understanding of worldlessness because it has never known a world. In Derrida's early writings, différance indicates the impossible starting point for deconstruction – the moment of strategic intervention that must derive its authority from itself. As such, it is certainly only a provisional and an inadequate name for something that is definitely not a thing and yet functions simultaneously as the enabling condition and internal limit of deconstruction itself. Neither a word, nor a concept, it never appears as such: 'There is no essence of *différance*; it (is) that which not only could never be appropriated in the *as such* of its name or its appearing, but also that which threatens the authority of the *as such* in general, of the presence of the thing itself in its essence' (Derrida 1982: 25). This undermining of the 'as such' is precisely what ties its thematic to the problem of the world. For what Derrida's readings of Heidegger will never cease to question is precisely the status of the phenomenological 'as such' that supposedly accounts for the phenomenon of the world itself.[1]

But as Derrida put it, 'the thematic of *différance* may very well, indeed must, one day be superseded, lending itself if not to its own replacement, at least to enmeshing itself in a chain that in truth it never will have governed' (Derrida 1982: 7). This necessity stems from the fact that *différance* – which is '"older" than Being itself' (Derrida 1982: 25) – remains a metaphysical name for something that is essentially unnameable (Derrida 1982: 26). Whether the time has come for an overcoming of this thematic might be debated, but what Derrida's final seminars suggest is that this chain of terminological substitutions that started with différance ends (even if only provisionally) with the deconstructive quasi-concept of worldlessness. Looking back from the end of Derrida's oeuvre, it now appears that the necessity of affirming the undeconstructible condition of deconstruction has remained a permanent concern that accompanied all of Derrida's reflections regardless of the concrete topics that formed the occasions for their unfolding. And the crucial point is that there is a deconstructive concept of worldlessness that must be located on the level of this undeconstructible condition. The unconditional affirmation of this worldlessness might be one of the critical contemporary historical tasks of deconstruction.

And yet, under the sway of différance, neither life nor thought is strictly speaking worldless for Derrida. Unlike for Arendt and for Freud, for Derrida life is tied in an essential manner to the idea of the world.[2] In fact, the task of deconstructive thought is to trace the difference between the worldlessness of différance and the worldliness of life. There is no life *in* worldlessness. Life in the Derridean sense appears on the scene only when the worldlessness of différance produces an unconditional affirmation of itself in thought. But in this affirmation, it ceases to be fully worldless. In fact, the very term 'hauntology' is an emblematic expression of the philosophical predicament of our times: while worldlessness is the only defensible ontological assumption, the spectre must nevertheless appear. For Derrida, the ontological impossibility of the world is immediately tied to the phenomenological necessity of worlds in such a way that this link becomes the foundation of the only imaginable deconstructive ethics (and politics).[3] In order to establish this last point, in what follows, I will first examine Derrida's critique of phenomenological worldlessness in Husserl's writings, and then I will discuss Derrida's critique of the ontology of Dasein's worldliness in Heidegger's thought. The point of these parallel readings is to show that although the 'method' of deconstruction consists of a demonstration of the mutual contamination of being and appearance, worldliness and worldlessness, in the end in his final seminars Derrida does end up choosing the world over worldlessness. In other words, in his final texts we can trace the consequences of a theoretical decision in favour of the world that does not necessarily follow from the logic of his aporetic method.

★ ★ ★

Derrida's critique of Husserl immediately locates the problem of worldlessness at the heart of the phenomenological project. In fact, the deconstruction of phenomenology is, in an essential way, the critique of the phenomenological conception of worldlessness. According to this critique, phenomenology remains blind to the fact that its notion of worldlessness is based on a metaphysical definition of worldlessness. The philosophical problem is that phenomenology conceives of both the world and worldlessness based on the scheme of the self-presence of the living present. If we follow the logic of this criticism, then, we could argue that in its original conception, at the very beginning of its historical journey, deconstruction was the attempt to formulate a non-metaphysical approach to worldlessness. If phenomenology is indeed founded on and, in an emphatic sense, is a metaphysics of worldlessness, and if deconstruction is an episode or even a scandal in the history of this phenomenology, then the entire project of deconstruction could be described in terms of a phenomenology of worldlessness.[4]

What could a 'phenomenology of worldlessness' designate? Immediately, it raises the phantasmatic possibility of a phenomenology that is not concerned with the way the 'world' is constituted as the ultimate horizon of phenomenological experience. Rather, such an unusual phenomenology would have to be focused on the moments when this ultimate horizon, the world itself, ceases to fulfil its supposedly constitutive function. These are the moments when, phenomenologically speaking, the world ceases to exist. Thus, in a certain sense, it would have to be an apocalyptic phenomenology of the end of the world that, nevertheless, does without any eschatological framework. But, in order to account for the originality of deconstruction, we have to insist that the phenomenology of worldlessness cannot simply be an old phenomenology with a new object. The goal is not simply to expand the phenomenological machine's field of operation in order to account for a specific kind of human experience that might have been neglected or marginalised by earlier thinkers. A more disturbing programme for phenomenology would be to simply do without the very idea of a world and still embark upon a philosophical description of human experience. The point, therefore, is that such a reorientation of phenomenology would necessarily affect its very methodology. It is not only that the object of phenomenology changes from the world to worldlessness; its basic conceptual network itself has to be transformed.

This critique is outlined in a programmatic manner in *Voice and Phenomenon* (1967), where Derrida starts his engagement of phenomenology with a move that is by now quite familiar to us: he charges that the phenomenological critique of metaphysics is based on metaphysical presuppositions. Derrida claims that the ultimate goal of Husserl's critique of metaphysical speculation was not to simply do away with metaphysics but, by eliminating its historical aberrations, 'to restore an authentic metaphysics' (Derrida 2011b: 5). As Derrida recounts here, Husserl argues that the failure of this perverted metaphysics was that it remained blind to the phenomenological problem of authentic 'ideality': 'that which *is*, which can be *repeated* indefinitely in the *identity* of its *presence* because of the very fact that it *does not exist*' (Derrida 2011b: 5, emphasis in original). It is this description of the iterability of the ideal object (as that which 'is' but 'does not exist') that takes us to the problem of worldlessness under the name of 'non-mundanity', for it is this specific definition of ideality that 'will allow us to speak of the non-reality and of the necessity of essence, of the noema, of the intelligible object and of non-mundanity in general. This non-mundanity, not being another mundanity, this ideality not being an existent that comes down from the sky, will always have its origins in the possibility of the repetition of the act that produces it' (Derrida 2011b: 6). According to the critique put forth by Husserl himself, traditional metaphysical thought was too 'worldly' in the sense that it could not account for the worldlessness of ideality. As Derrida's words suggest, at best, classic metaphysics conceived of worldlessness as 'another mundanity' that comes down to us from the skies. In this sense, it was not properly speaking a thought of worldlessness that oriented its thinking, since the idea of worldlessness was always tied to the idea of another world (a world that is unlike our world but is, nevertheless, still a world). Phenomenology attempts to correct this situation by building its whole theoretical edifice around the insight into the essential nature of the ideal object. 'Authentic metaphysics' is by definition the metaphysics of authentic worldlessness.

★ ★ ★

According to phenomenological thought, how can we then imagine the relationship of the world to this essential non-mundanity? In order to articulate this question as precisely as possible, Derrida focuses on Husserl's insistence on the difference between phenomenological psychology and transcendental phenomenology (Derrida 2011b: 9). The specific nature of this difference is the key to this metaphysics of worldlessness since it refers us to the very difference between the transcendental domain and that of mundanity. The central question here concerns the way the transcendental ego manifests itself. How can we tell the difference between the everyday psychic experience of the mind (which remains essentially empirical and, therefore, worldly) and the constitutive domain of the transcendental ego (which is essentially worldless)? The source of the theoretical problem is that Husserl simultaneously asserts the full coincidence of the two fields and their radical difference. How can two fields (that of the world and of worldlessness) fully coincide and, at the same time, remain radically heterogeneous? The difference between the psychical and transcendental consciousness falls within lived experience and is, therefore, a paradoxical difference that does not distinguish anything:

> This is a difference which in fact distinguishes nothing, a difference which separates no being, no lived-experience, no determinate signification. This is a difference however which, without altering anything, changes all the signs, and it is a difference in which alone the possibility of a transcendental question holds, that is, the possibility of freedom itself. This is, therefore, the fundamental difference without which no other difference in the world would make sense or even have a chance of appearing *as such*. (Derrida 2011b: 10)

The transcendental ego is radically different from the natural self, but this difference in itself is nothing. To put it differently, the transcendental ego is distinguished from the psychological ego by nothing that could be understood through classic conceptions of difference. As Derrida puts it, 'the (transcendental) I is not an other' (Derrida 2011b: 10). As a result of this strange difference that cannot be conceptualised as a difference, 'truly, no language is equal to this operation by which the transcendental ego constitutes and opposes its own mundane self, that is, opposes its soul, by reflecting itself in a *verweltlichende Selbstapperzeption*' (Derrida 2011b: 10). Thus, the transcendental ego is best defined by a set of tensions between worldlessness and the world: on the one hand, it is the worldless subject that objectivises itself in a worldly self (and, thereby, constitutes this worldly self in the first place); on the other hand, the worldless ego exists in a permanent opposition to its own worldly manifestations, even if this 'self-objectivation' might be conceived of as the externalisation of its own essence (its own soul).

The task of phenomenology is, therefore, to make this nothing appear that separates the worldless from the worldly. This is the method of transcendental reduction, which now appears in a new light. The transcendental reduction is not simply a methodology of reducing the world and making the transcendental ego appear. It is the precise point where worldlessness is not simply an object of phenomenology but a constitutive factor of its very methodology. The transcendental dimension, in other words, is not only an object of phenomenology as it is its very enabling condition. Derrida writes:

> This *nothing* that distinguishes the parallels, this nothing without which no explication, that is, no language, would be able to develop freely in the truth without being distorted by some real milieu, this nothing without which no transcendental, that is, philosophical, question would be able to take a breath, this nothing arises, if we can say this, when the *totality* of the world is neutralized in its existence and reduced to its phenomenon. *This operation is that of the transcendental reduction.* (Derrida 2011b: 11, emphasis in original)

It is precisely the purity of this transcendental reduction (the reduction of the world to its pure phenomenon) that deconstruction will set out to question. Husserl calls the fatal confusion of these two parallel domains 'transcendental psychologism', an error that consists of the elimination of the nothing of this peculiar difference. Husserl insists that we must struggle against this confusion, and we must maintain the nothingness of this fundamental difference between the world and worldlessness.

As Derrida reminds us, Husserl finds the model of this necessary articulation in the act of 'nuancing': 'we have to practice at all costs "Nuancierung" which distinguishes the parallels, one of which is in the world and the other is outside the world without being in another world, that is, without stopping to be, *like every parallel, alongside* and *right next to the other*' (Derrida 2011b: 12, emphasis in original). Transcendental psychologism does not understand that 'if the world needs a *supplement of soul,* the soul, which is in the world, needs this *supplementary nothing* that is the transcendental and without which no world would appear' (Derrida 2011b: 12). The logic of supplementarity introduces two divisions: on the one hand, the world needs the soul; on the other hand, the soul needs the nothing of an internal differ-ence that becomes the condition of the world itself. The circle is closed: the supplementary nothing to the soul is actually the condition of the world itself. Derrida, therefore, suggests that (according to Husserl) the difference between the world and the worldlessness of the transcendental is this supplementary nothing. This is the starting point for the deconstruction of phe-nomenological worldlessness: the nothingness of the difference between the world and worldlessness is différance itself. The vicious circle of the world and worldlessness must be broken.

★ ★ ★

The ideal object and the transcendental ego, therefore, meet in the dimension of phenomenological worldlessness. But where is this dimension? Or, better yet, how is this dimension of world-lessness constituted? The answer to this question will take us to the core of Derrida's critique of Husserl. Derrida's answer is quite clear: it is the medium of the 'voice' – or, as he refers to it, 'the phenomenological voice' – that carries the theoretical burden in Husserl's writings to account for the constitution of the ideal object by a transcendental consciousness that intends this object:

> The ideal object is the most objective of objects; it is in-dependent of the *hic et nunc* of events and of the acts of the empirical subjectivity who intends it. [. . .] But its ideal-being is *nothing* outside of the world; it must be constituted, repeated and expressed in a medium that does not impair the presence and the self-presence of the acts that intend it: a medium that preserves at once the *presence of the object* in front of the intuition and the *presence to oneself*, the absolute proximity of the acts to themselves. Since the ideality of the object is only its being-for a non-empirical consciousness, it can be expressed only in an element whose phenomenality does not have the form of mundanity. *The voice is the name of this element. The voice hears itself.* (Derrida 2011b: 65, emphases in original)

Since the ideality of the ideal object exists only for a non-empirical consciousness, the medium itself in which the object can be constituted and expressed must also be worldless. This worldless medium is the voice that makes a worldless object present for a worldless subject. In order to account for the world-lessness of this phenomenological voice that hears itself, we have to emphasise that we are not talking about the mundane sonority of speech. To the contrary, the voice refers to a very specific type of speech that manages to do without the external detour of the world: the silent, internal monologue of the self that Husserl calls the 'solitary life of the soul' (Derrida 2011b: 34).

Derrida's point, therefore, is to show that this supposedly worldless internal monologue cannot be construed as the location of a simple self-presence without the detour of différance. Husserl needs the hypothesis of an original, silent, 'pre-expressive' layer of lived-experience in order to be able to maintain a systematic difference between two kinds of signification, 'expression' (*Ausdruck*) and 'indication' (*Anzeichen*). While an expressive sign always carries a meaning (*Bedeutung*), a mere indicative sign is strictly speaking meaningless, although it is not without signification. As Derrida argues here, it is clear that for Husserl the indicative sign is secondary in relation to the expressive sign for the simple reason that it is only the latter that intends an ideal object while the former remains purely empirical. Thus, the special position of expression in relation to indication is explained by the fact that it has an intentional structure and, as such, it is in a special relation with the domain of ideality. What, therefore, must be excluded from the domain of pure expression and meaning is 'the totality of the visible as such and of the spatial as such' (Derrida 2011b: 29). The purity of pure expressivity is the worldlessness of ideality:

> Pure expressivity will be the pure active intention (spirit, psyche, life, will) of a *bedeuten* that is animating a discourse whose content (*Bedeutung*) will be present. [. . .] Therefore, this is *self-present* in the life of a present that has still not exited from itself into the world, into space, into nature. (Derrida 2011b: 34)

But, as we can see, expressivity as pure intentionality can be worldless only on condition of its self-presence in the living present. Once this temporal condition is disturbed, once its self-presence is contaminated by difference, its worldlessness will no longer be possible to maintain in its ideal purity. It is in this sense that the interior monologue of consciousness emerges in

Husserl's account to prove the existence of pure expressivity. For Husserl's goal is to show that 'indication no longer functions in the solitary life of the soul' (Derrida 2011b: 36). In other words, Husserl's objective is to show that ideal subjectivity does not need indication to constitute its own self-relation. In this context, then, the worldlessness of the phenomenological voice (the medium that allows for the constitution of the ideal object and the transcendental ego) is tied to the worldlessness of the sign. The idea of pure expressivity (signification without indication) is based on the assumption that the sign is not entirely in this world.

★ ★ ★

The task set forth by Derrida, therefore, consists of the deconstruction of the transcendence of the voice. As he puts it, 'this transcendence is only apparent' (Derrida 2011b: 66), but this appearance is constitutive of consciousness and the truth/appearance distinction. The foundation of this apparent transcendence, then, is the ideality or the worldlessness of the sign. The signifier, the signified and the object all have an ideal form: 'But this ideality, which is only the name of the permanence of the same and the possibility of its repetition, does not *exist* in the world and it does not come from another world' (Derrida 2011b: 45, emphasis in original). The signified (in the sense of the expressed *Bedeutung*) is 'always essentially ideal' and, as such, 'immediately present to the act of expression' (Derrida 2011b: 66). But the foundation of this immediate presence is actually that the signifier itself is ideal: 'the phenomenological body of the signifier seems to erase itself the moment it is produced'

(Derrida 2011b: 66). In fact, the worldless ideality of the signifier (the fact that the signifier itself can remain the same in spite of its different empirical manifestations) is the very form in which the signified appears to be directly accessible for consciousness: 'This erasure of the sensible body and of its exteriority is *for consciousness* the very form of the immediate presence of the signified' (Derrida 2011b: 66).

The worldlessness of the sign, however, is never quite pure. As we have seen, the interiority of the subject is the product of the interior monologue of the phenomenological voice, and the transcendence of the phenomenological voice is the product of the ideality of signification. Thus, the problem of the pure ideality of signification occupies a special position in this argument, since it eventually undermines the thesis of the worldlessness of the phenomenological voice:

> Someone will object perhaps that this interiority belongs to the phenomenological and ideal side of every signifier. For example, the ideal form of a written signifier is not in the world, and the distinction between grapheme and the empirical body of the corresponding graphic sign separates an inside of phenomenological consciousness and an outside of the world. And that is true of every visible or spatial signifier. Of course. Nevertheless, every non-phonetic signifier involves, right within its 'phenomenon', within the (non-mundane) phenomenological sphere of experience in which it is given, a spatial reference; the sense of 'outside', 'in the world' is an essential component of its phenomenon. In appearance, there is nothing like that in the phenomenon of the voice. (Derrida 2011b: 65)

First it appears to us that the physical sign is necessarily worldly, while its ideal form is worldless. The phenomenological voice would then be tied to the ideality of the sign. But signification cannot be reduced to this simple scheme, as there are signs that undermine the inside/outside distinction that it is based on. Some signs already include in their supposedly worldless phenomenon a direct reference to the world. This internalisation of the world in phenomenological worldlessness implies that the phenomenological voice cannot be reduced to the ideality of signification in general. There are signs that must be excluded from the phenomenological voice in order to secure the pure interiority of subjectivity. The very distinction between inside and outside, subject and world, is made possible and, at the same time, disturbed by signification. To put it differently, Derrida accepts that the worldlessness of the sign is a necessary enabling condition of signification. But his critique here also suggests that phenomenological worldlessness is always contaminated by the world. Phonetic signs might be maintained in this rigorous isolation of an ideal worldlessness, but non-phonetic signs disturb this neat distinction. Being non-phonetic signs, they lack the 'acoustic image' and fall outside of the phenomenological voice. The phenomenological voice cannot 'speak' them, so they are not part of the subject's interiority. They point towards an irreducible outside. Thus, the discovery of the irreducible contamination of the worldless ideality of the sign by an outside world is the first crucial step in the deconstruction of the transcendence of the voice.

* * *

Ultimately, the deconstruction of the phenomenological voice concerns a specific figure of worldlessness: pure auto-affection. Derrida suggests that the entire phenomenological edifice is sustained by the fiction of a pure self-relation that dispenses with the other and avoids the detour of the world. Husserl has to posit this pure self-relation in the mode of an absolute self-presence in order to establish both the autonomy of the transcendental subject and the efficacy of the phenomenological reduction. It is because of the absolute self-relation of the transcendental phenomenological voice that the method of phenomenology consists of the suspension of the world and the subsequent thematisation of a constitutive dimension of worldlessness. The phenomenological reduction reduces the world only to discover the non-worldly conditions of the emergence of the world itself.

Derrida's critique, then, concerns the transcendence of this phenomenological voice through an analysis of the structure of speech. What exactly is the relation of this pure voice to speech? As we all know, it belongs to the very structure of speech that when I speak, '*I hear myself during the time* that I speak' (Derrida 2011b: 66, emphasis in original). In this hearing-oneself-speak, the speaker experiences the absolute proximity of the signifier to the intention of signification. This intimacy of the signifier and meaning in the living act that animates the signifier suggests that the 'soul of language' exists independently of its exteriorisation in the signifier: 'The soul of language does not risk death in the body of a signifier abandoned to the world and to the visibility of space' (Derrida 2011b: 67). The soul can 'show' the ideal object or ideal meaning without exiting ideality in 'the interiority of life present to itself' (Derrida 2011b: 67). This 'intimacy of life to itself' (Derrida 2011b: 67) guarantees that it is 'implied in the very structure of speech that the speaker *hear himself*' (Derrida 2011b: 67; emphasis in original). As Derrida puts it: 'Considered from a purely phenomenological viewpoint, within the reduction, the process of speech has the originality of being already delivered as a pure phenomenon, having already suspended the natural attitude and the existential thesis of the world' (Derrida 2011b: 67). Unlike other phenomena that one encounters in everyday experience, in the living act of hearing oneself speak the speaker simultaneously perceives the sensible form of the signifier and understands his own intention of expression. In the act of speech, the world is already suspended, since the pure phenomenon of intended meaning is already given to the speaker. As a result of this hearing-oneself-speak, phenomenologically speaking, speech is always already worldless.

This is why hearing-oneself-speak is a unique type of auto-affection: it is worldless both on the level of the signified and that of the signifier. On the one hand, the signifieds that appear in it are pure idealities. On the other hand, the very signifiers at work in it are purely ideal: 'the subject is able to hear himself or speak to himself, is able to let himself be affected by the signifier that he produces without any detour through the agency of exteriority, of the world, or of the non-proper in general' (Derrida 2011b: 67). Hearing-oneself-speak, therefore, is not just any kind of auto-affection but the auto-affection that functions in the medium of pure ideality. This is why it is different from other forms of auto-affection (for example, seeing or touching oneself), since it can maintain itself in this purity: 'Every other form of auto-affection must either pass through the non-proper or renounce universality' (Derrida 2011b: 67).

We can speak of a 'pure' auto-affection here in the sense that hearing-oneself-speak reduces even the interiority of one's own body. Not even the internal sensations of the body can be this pure, since they still involve a minimal form of exteriority. As a result, we have to conclude that 'hearing-oneself-speak is lived as absolutely pure auto-affection, in a proximity to self which would be nothing other than the absolute reduction of space in general' (Derrida 2011b: 68). This absolute purity, however, is not a simple negation or withdrawal from the world, but a topologically much more complex structure:

> Requiring the intervention of no determinate surface in the world, *producing itself in the world as an auto-affection* that is pure, [the voice] is an absolutely available signifying substance. For the voice encounters no obstacle to its emission in the world precisely insofar as it produces itself there *as pure auto-affection.* Undoubtedly this auto-affection is the possibility of what we call *subjectivity* or the *for-itself*, but without it no world would appear *as such*. For, in its depth, the voice assumes the unity of sound (which is in the world) and the *phone* (in the phenomenological sense). An objective 'mundane' science can surely teach us nothing about the essence of the voice. But the unity of the sound and the voice, which allows the voice to produce itself in the world as pure auto-affection, is the unique instance that escapes from the distinction between intramundanity and transcendentality; and by the same token, it makes this distinction possible. (Derrida 2011b: 68, emphases in original)

Although it does not require a specific surface in the world, this absolute auto-affection nevertheless produces itself as pure signifying substance in the world. It is a form of worldlessness that produces itself inside a world. At the same time, this worldly worldlessness must also be understood as the very condition of the phenomenological emergence of any world whatsoever. The unity of sound and voice (voice as pure auto-affection within the world) is the condition of the very distinction between the world and worldless transcendentality, but itself cannot be captured by either of these categories. It is neither worldly nor worldless (in the phenomenological sense) and, as such, it makes the very distinction impossible.

A deconstructive reading of Husserl, therefore, shows that the phenomenological voice as absolute auto-affection functions as the condition of impossibility of phenomenology itself. On the one hand, it provides the foundation of the entire Husserlian system in that the hypothesis of the voice allows the phenomenologist to isolate the transcendental dimension in its purity. On the other hand, Derrida's reading shows that this purity is impossible to maintain with absolute consistency. It is precisely the voice that undermines the foundational distinctions of phenomenology itself. The voice is posited as the necessary instance of worldlessness that is simultaneously the condition for the emergence of any world and that nevertheless still appears in this world.

Différance, therefore, haunts the Husserlian system, since it introduces the possibility and even the necessity of an originary non-presence into auto-affection. In opposition to the phenomenological idea of pure auto-affection, différance could be described as a deconstructive mode of auto-affection in the mode of pure difference. Derrida calls attention to the fact that any consistent conceptualisation of auto-affection will have to proceed by a reconceptualisation of what the self of this self-relation consists of: 'Auto-affection as the operation of the voice assumed that a pure difference came to divide self-presence. The possibility of everything that we believe we are able to exclude from auto-affection is enrooted in this pure difference: space, the outside, the world, the body, etc.' (Derrida 2011b: 70). Auto-affection, therefore, cannot be the absolute proximity of the self to itself in the intimacy of life. To the degree that it involves a relation of the self to itself, it must introduce a minimal distance that will function as the opening of the self to alterity. It is possible that a self-relation constitutes the self, but in this relationality difference is also established in the heart of the same:

> This movement of différance does not supervene upon a transcendental subject. The movement of différance produces the transcendental subject. Auto-affection is not a modality of experience that characterizes a being that would already be itself (*autos*). Auto-affection produces the same as the self-relation in the difference with itself, the same as the non-identical. (Derrida 2011b: 71)

Différance is not the secondary deconstruction of a transcendental subject that would already be itself before the intervention of the operation of deconstruction, but the originary condition of the very constitution of the transcendental subject as something that is not identical to itself. And the consequences of this objection are far reaching for phenomenology:

> As soon as we admit that auto-affection is the condition of self-presence, no pure transcendental reduction is possible. But it is necessary to pass through the reduction in order to recapture the difference in closest proximity to itself: not to its identity, nor its purity, nor its origin. It has none of these. But in closest proximity to the movement of différance. (Derrida 2011b: 71)

The phenomenological method itself undergoes a transformation here. In the light or shadow of différance, the transcendental reduction becomes impossible but necessary. Its original goals are impossible to maintain: the phenomenological reduction cannot give us the transcendental subject in its pure identity as self-presence. But it is possible that it can give us something else if we are careful enough with its application: the originary non-presence of différance. It is in this sense that we could say that deconstruction is a phenomenology of différance, the absolute difference that is older than the world itself.

We could, then, summarise Derrida's critique of Husserl as a rejection of the supposed transcendental purity of the phenomenological concept of worldlessness. This kind of worldlessness is always contaminated by the world, as it is always in some kind of a relation to worldliness. The world remains irreducible. One of the most speculative aspects of this argument concerns the very definition of time and the relation of time and space. For Derrida's point is that the theme of auto-affection should not be reduced to an analysis of the structure of speech. In fact, the originality of speech comes from the fact that, in Husserl's writings, ideality is identified with pure temporality. The 'omnitemporality of ideal objects' means that even before it is expressed, sense is temporal. But the temporality of sense is only one possible mode of temporality that should be distinguished from the movement of temporalisation itself, and it is this movement that introduces the problem of auto-affection.

When Husserl tries to account for the origins of the movement of temporalisation, he has to posit a 'source-point' for this movement (Derrida 2011b: 71). The question is: How can this movement of temporalisation start in the first place? Husserl's answer is that 'an originary impression [. . .] engenders itself' (Derrida 2011b: 71). The absolute beginning for the continuous production of new 'nows' is not itself a product but an act of spontaneous self-generation. But Derrida's point is that the process by which the living now produces itself in a spontaneous generation is already pure auto-affection 'in which the same is the same only by affecting itself with an other, by becoming the other of the same' (Derrida 2011b: 73). As a result of this self-generation through auto-affection, we have to conclude that 'the living present arises on the basis of its non-self-identity, and on the basis of the retentional trace. It is always already trace' (Derrida 2011b: 73).

So, Husserl's definition of the transcendental posits a worldless dimension as purely temporal without the space or spatiality of the world. But if this supposedly pure temporality is constituted by an act of auto-affection, it is always contaminated by what had to be excluded from its identity. Time is always disturbed by an original spacing that introduces an interval, a distance, a difference, at the heart of its identity. As a result, the temporality of sense cannot be reduced to the absolute interiority of a worldless transcendence: 'Since the trace is the relation of intimacy of the living present to its outside, the openness to exteriority in general, to the non-proper, etc., *the temporalization of sense is from the very beginning "spacing"*' (Derrida 2011b: 73). The movement of temporalisation is auto-affection but, precisely because it is a self-relation, it already includes in itself the opening to the world: 'Even the exiting "into the world" is also originarily implied by the movement of temporalization' (Derrida 2011b: 74). Once again, it is this originary openness to the world that renders the phenomenological project impossible: 'temporalization is at once the very power and the very limit of the phenomenological reduction. Hearing-oneself-speak is not the interiority of an inside closed in upon itself. It is the irreducible openness in the inside, the eye and the world in speech. The phenomenological reduction is a scene' (Derrida 2011b: 74).

★ ★ ★

Early texts like *Voice and Phenomena*, therefore, clearly show that at its historical origin the programme of deconstruction was formulated as an encounter with phenomenology and the problem of worldlessness. We could say that this programme was first articulated in terms of a philosophical desire for another phenomenology of a different kind of worldlessness. In light of this opening, then, it is not surprising that Derrida's lifelong engagements with Heidegger (which stretch from his earliest publications to his final seminars) constantly return to the problem of worldlessness. Even if worldlessness remains only a seemingly marginal theme in some of these texts, it nevertheless remains one of the central threads that connects these investigations.

In this context, '*Geschlecht I:* Sexual Difference, Ontological Difference' (1983) is exemplary because it ties the interrogation of the ontological difference to the problem of auto-affection. We could say that we encounter two analogous structures here: the phenomenological difference in Husserl (the difference between the transcendental subject and the empirical self) and the ontological difference in Heidegger (the difference between Being and beings) both encounter an essential limitation in the specific structure of a self-relation. In the case of Heidegger, however, we are no longer concerned with the possibility of the self-relational constitution of the transcendental subject, but with the auto-affective structure of Dasein itself.

Derrida focuses on the problem of Dasein's supposed neutrality. Heidegger makes it clear that in order to access the part of the human being that we can justly call Dasein, we have to suspend all anthropological determinations. Dasein is not simply *anthropos*. Heidegger claims that he chose the name 'Dasein' precisely because of its neutrality. But this originary neutrality

214

of Dasein is not immediately given to us in everyday experience. The being-there of Dasein, therefore, is neutral in the sense that Dasein is accessible to us only through the neutralisation of all of its predicates except for a pure self-relation:

> This is the minimal relation to itself as relation to Being, the relation that the being which we are, as questioning, maintains with itself and with its own proper essence. This relation to self is not a relation to an 'ego' or to an individual, of course. Thus Dasein designates the being that, 'in a definite sense', is not 'indifferent' to its own essence, or to whom its own being is not indifferent. Neutrality, therefore, is first of all the neutralization of everything but the naked trait of this relation to self, of this interest for its own being in the widest sense of the word 'interest'. (Derrida 2008b: 11)

The question of Dasein's originary neutrality introduces two related problems that will be essential for our discussions of worldlessness. First, it makes clear that we have to separate two levels of analysis in Heidegger's discourse. Although Dasein is always already in a specific 'factical' relation to its own being, it is nevertheless possible to isolate in its structure the originary dimension of self-relation as a relation to Being itself. This separation of the factical and neutral dimensions of Dasein, however, takes us to a second problem: In what terms should we describe the process of neutralisation that takes us from the state of factical dispersion to the domain of this originary auto-affection? Is this necessarily a form of negativity? Or should we rather define it in terms of some kind of originary positivity?

This is where the central argument of Derrida's essay concerning sexual difference comes into play. Dasein's neutrality implies that, on this level, it is defined by a certain essential 'sexlessness' (*Geschlechtlosigkeit*). As Derrida points out, in Heidegger's analysis sexual difference is something like a privileged example of what needs to be neutralised in order to access Dasein's authentic neutrality. Derrida, however, tries to show that sexual difference cannot be neutralised in this way and is, in a certain sense, irreducible (Derrida 2008b: 13). The source of this complication in Heidegger's argument is that the neutralisation of sexual difference is not a simple negation or destruction of sexual difference. On the contrary, the issue is that the neutralisation of sexual difference in 'sexlessness' (*Geschlechtlosigkeit*) reveals a different kind of sexuality that is more originary than the dyad of sexual difference: 'the positive and powerful source of every possible "sexuality"' (Derrida 2008b: 14). *Geschlechtlosigkeit* is not simply 'sexless', but an originary condition of sexuality as such that cannot be reduced to sexual difference. This also means that, in spite of the negative lexical formulation, *Geschlechtlosigkeit* does not refer to a negativity but to an originary positivity.

This is where the deconstruction of the supposed purity of the ontological difference becomes possible. Derrida's goal is to show that sexual difference cannot function here as a secondary negativity that must be eliminated in the name of an originary positivity, since sexual difference is itself the very condition of this neutralisation. Sexual difference itself introduces the very negativity into this scheme that, on the one hand, makes neutralisation possible and, on the other hand, that neutralisation aims to erase in order to reveal an originary positivity. As Derrida put it:

> despite appearances, the asexuality and neutrality that must first of all be subtracted from the binary sexual mark, in the analytic of Dasein, are in fact on the same side, on the side of that sexual difference – the binary one – to which one might have thought them simply opposed. (Derrida 2008b: 15)

Dasein's self-relation, therefore, is already marked by a difference. Dasein's ipseity, its selfhood (*Selbstheit*), is certainly defined by a fundamental concern with itself, but in Heidegger's analysis this selfhood itself must be understood in terms of its neutrality: 'Always presupposed, ipseity is therefore also "neutral" with respect to being an "I" and being a "you", "and above all with respect to such things as sexuality" [*und erst recht etwa gegen die 'Geschlechtlichkeit' neutral*]' (Derrida 2008b: 16). How do we understand this irreducible and neutral selfhood of Dasein? It is not a form of egoism, solipsism, isolation or the existential solitude of man (which would all refer us back to Dasein's factical existence) but what we could call the 'metaphysical isolation of the human being' (Derrida 2008b: 17) that refers us to 'the authentic concreteness of the origin, the "not-yet" of factical dissemination, of dissociation, of dissociated-being or of factical dissociality' (Derrida 2008b: 18). As we can see, the issue here is that the hypothesis of this neutrality seems to work against the necessary factical worldliness of Dasein. To put it differently, it is precisely the assumption of neutrality that will show us that we cannot conceive of Dasein's facticity in terms of a simple self-relation that constitutes an immediate self-presence. As Derrida argues, Dasein's dissociated being is not an accident but an originary structure: '*Dasein* is separated in its facticity, subjected to dispersion and division (*zersplittert*), and concomitantly (*ineins damit*) always disunited, disaccorded, split, divided (*zwiespaltig*) by sexuality into a particular sex (*in eine bestimmte Geschlechtlichkeit*)' (Derrida 2008b: 18). To make sure that we do not treat this originary structure in purely negative terms, Heidegger refers to it as a 'multiplication', and he clearly distinguishes multiplication (*Mannigfaltigung*) from a simple multiplicity (*Mannigfaltigkeit*) in order to be able to account for the ontological possibility of this factical dissemination:

> One must also avoid the representation of a large primal being whose simplicity was suddenly dispersed (*zerspaltet*) into many singularities. It is rather a matter of clarifying the intrinsic possibility of multiplication for which *Dasein*'s own embodiment represents an 'organizing factor'. The multiplicity in this case is not a simple formal plurality of determinations or of determinities (*Bestimmtheiten*); it belongs to Being itself. An 'originary dissemination [*ursprüngliche Streuung*]' already belongs to the being of Dasein in general. (Derrida 2008b: 19)

The most important consequence of this analysis of Dasein's factical dispersion is that it leads us to the conclusion that transcendental dispersion belongs to Dasein's essence: 'Dasein affects itself with this movement, and this auto-affection belongs to the ontological structure of its historicality' (Derrida 2008b: 20). This conclusion, then, takes us back to the question concerning the status of the negative in Heidegger's descriptions of the existential structures of Dasein. Commenting on the necessarily 'privative interpretation' of Dasein outlined in *Being and Time*, Derrida asks: 'Why do negative determinations impose themselves so often in this ontological characteristic?' And his answer is the following: 'It is not at all "accidental". It is because one must remove the originality of the phenomena from what has dissembled, disfigured, displaced or covered them over, from the *Verstellungen* and *Verdeckungen*, from all the pre-interpretations whose negative effects must in their turn be annulled by the negative statements, the genuine "sense" of which is in fact "positive"' (Derrida 2008b: 24). In other words, the existential analytic of Dasein must proceed in an apparently negative language that in fact carries positive significations.

The foundation of this strange linguistic necessity (to speak in negative terms about positive conditions) is the fact that the history of Being itself is marked by movements that appear to be negative when in fact they stem from the positive essence of Being itself: '*Uneigentlichkeit*, *Verstellungen*, and *Verdeckungen* are not of the order of negativity (the false or the evil, error or sin)' (Derrida 2008b: 24). The apparently negative movements of Being that are in reality necessary components of its structure need to be addressed in a language that necessarily appears to be negative even if it intends to capture positive possibilities of Being. This split between structural necessity and factical negativity is what defines the language of worldlessness itself as one the most significant negative historical possibilities of Being.

Derrida, however, clearly demonstrates that in spite of this neutralising analysis of structural necessities, Heidegger's discourse remains hierarchical: 'In certain contexts, dispersion marks the most general structure of *Dasein* [. . .] Yet elsewhere dispersion and distraction (*Zerstreuung* in both senses) characterize the inauthentic ipseity of *Dasein*' (Derrida 2008b: 25). The consequence of this tension between the neutral and the hierarchical is that 'Dispersion is thus marked twice: as general structure of *Dasein* and as mode of inauthenticity' (Derrida 2008b: 25). Although in this essay Derrida stays away from an explicit analysis of the structures of worldlessness, his analysis shows that this tension remains one of the central legacies of Heidegger's philosophy today when it comes to an encounter with the problem of worldlessness: worldlessness is a neutral condition that is marked twice in a hierarchy without foundations.

★ ★ ★

The same tension is then treated in more explicit reference to worldlessness in Derrida's *Of Spirit* (1987), where it surfaces as a conflict between Heidegger's structural and historical accounts of worldlessness. Discussing the priority of the question and the function of philosophy in Heidegger's thought, Derrida discusses Heidegger's historical diagnosis of a 'spiritual decadence' that has taken over the West in the context of the 'geopolitical diagnosis' (Derrida 1989: 44) provided in *Introduction to Metaphysics*: 'Thinking the world is determined as thinking the earth or the planet' (Derrida 1989: 44). Heidegger denounces the spiritual decline that characterises the West today. Caught between America and Russia, Europe (or more precisely the German people) face a new decision that will determine the fate of the world:

> But geopolitics conducts us back again from the earth and the planet to the world and to the world as a world of spirit. Geo-politics is none other than a *Weltpolitik* of spirit. The world is not the earth. On the earth arrives an obscuring of the world (*Weltverdüsterung*): the flight of the gods, the destruction of the earth, the massification of man, the preeminence of the mediocre. (Derrida 1989: 46)

The question for us will be: what is the relationship of this *Weltverdüsterung* as a historical figure of worldlessness to the constitutive *Verfall* of Dasein who is by definition world-forming? In order to address this question, Derrida opposes two statements made by Heidegger concerning the animal's relation to the world.[5] On the one hand, in his 1929–30 Freiburg lecture course, Heidegger famously claimed that the animal is poor in world (*weltarm*); on the other hand, in *Introduction to Metaphysics*, we read that the 'animal has no world' (Derrida 1989: 47). Are these two statements contradictory or consistent with each other? What needs to be clarified here, then, is the exact meaning of 'poverty' and 'privation'. What does it mean to be poor in world and to be deprived of the world? As Derrida explains, the word 'poor' includes two possibilities: it can designate a difference in degree or a difference in essence (Derrida 1989: 48). In the first case, the animal and the human being would be essentially the same, but the animal would be granted less of the spirit than the human being. In the second, more complicated case, we run into the problem of alterity and all that it implies for our analysis:

> This poverty is not an indigence, a meagerness of world. It has, without doubt, the sense of a privation (*Entbehrung*), of a lack: the animal does not have enough world, to be sure. But this lack is not to be evaluated as a quantitative relation to the entities of the world. It is not that the animal has a lesser relationship, a more limited access to entities, it has an other relationship. (Derrida 1989: 49)

Derrida claims that, although Heidegger opts for the second option, his argument gets caught up in unintended ambiguities and complications. The problem is that the definition of privation as an essential difference allows Heidegger to avoid a certain philosophical anthropocentrism, but the terms he uses to articulate this difference reintroduce the human measure as the basic standard of comparison. While it is true that there is here a move away from the human, it nevertheless remains a fact that the animal's specific position between the lifeless stone and world-forming Dasein must be defined in relation to something other than itself. Thus, the animal's alterity and the alterity of the animal's relation to the world are still defined on the basis of Dasein's relation to the world. The key to this subtle adjustment concerns the status of the phenomenological 'as such'. This is where the contradiction between not having a world and being world-poor becomes apparent again. The stone has no world, but this worldlessness is not a privation. But what can we say about this animal that supposedly does not have a world and is at the same time poor in world? The solution to the apparent contradiction is that the animal does not have a world, but this not–having–a–world is a way of having a world:

> The animal has no world either, because it is deprived of it, but its privation means that its not-having is a mode of having and even a certain relation to having-a-world. The *without* of the *without-world* does not have the same sense and does not bespeak the same negativity, for animal and for stone: privation in one case, pure and simple absence in the other. The animal has a world in the mode of not-having, or, conversely, it is deprived of world because it can have a world. Heidegger talks of a 'poverty' (or privation) as a form of *not-having* in the *being-able-to-have* (*Armut —Entbehren — als Nichthaben im Habenkönnen*). (Derrida 1989: 50)

The proposition according to which 'The animal has and does not have a world' (Derrida 1989: 59), therefore, is not a logical contradiction that would have a dialectical resolution. What makes the two statements consistent with each other is precisely the 'as such'. Derrida identifies in this move the essence of Heidegger's 'strategy' (Derrida 1989: 54). The absolute limit instituted by Heidegger between the living creature and human Dasein breaks with anthropomorphism, biologism and its political effects. But allowing for 'the subtle but decisive phenomenological structure of the "as such"' (Derrida 1989: 55) introduces 'essential difficulties' into Heidegger's argument that render the three theses (about the stone, the animal and Dasein in their relations to the world) problematic. The 'as such' allows Heidegger to speak (if ever so indirectly) about two forms of privation. First, we have Dasein's privation as it is described in *Being and Time* in terms of a *Privation* which occurs within the structure of understanding 'something as something'. At the same time, we also have to reckon with the animal's privation as an *Entbehrung*: 'The animal can have a world because it has access to entities, but it is deprived of a world because it does not have access to entities as such and in their Being' (Derrida 1989: 51). As Derrida puts it, this reduplication of privations, this 'discrepant analogy between these two "privations" remains troubling' (Derrida 1989: 51).

★ ★ ★

In the context of these Derridean reflections on the worldlessness of the stone and the world-poverty of the animal, how can we address the Heideggerian tension between Dasein's constitutive worldliness and its simultaneous exposure to the dangers of historical worldlessness? In other words, what is the relationship between the darkening of the world (*Weltverdüsterung*) and the destitution of spirit (*Entmachtung der Geist*) renounced by Heidegger? Derrida turns to Heidegger's readings of Trakl to address this problem. It is a single line from Trakl's poem 'Frühling der Seele' that provides the central clue here: '*Es ist die Seele ein Fremdes auf Erden.*/Yes, the soul is a stranger upon the earth' (Derrida 1989: 87). Derrida traces the way Heidegger inverts what could be called a Platonic–Christian interpretation of this line. According to this new interpretation (based on the *althochdeutsch* meaning of the word *fremd* as 'being on the way towards something'), the soul is a stranger on earth but not because it is exiled on earth like a fallen angel: 'The souls is a stranger because it does not yet inhabit the earth' (Derrida 1989: 88). The reversal of this temporality allows Heidegger to distinguish two forms of worldlessness. On the one hand, we have a spiritual darkening (*Geistliche Dämmerung*); on the other hand, we have the corruption of the human being (*Verwesen*). What concerns Derrida here is that the spiritual darkening is an essential or structural component that includes the possibility of this other corruption of the essence: 'Now this becoming-crepuscular, this *Dämmerung*, which does not signify a decline (*Untergang*) nor an occidentalisation, is of an essential nature (*wesentlichen Wesens*)' (Derrida 1989: 89). Once again, the important point is that in spite of the negative language used to describe it, this function is not a form of negativity: 'Crepuscule or night, as *geistlich*, does not signify the negativity of a decline but what shields the year or shelters this course of the sun' (Derrida 1989: 89). In the reversed temporality outlined by Heidegger, the darkening of the spirit refers to a spiritual journey (the movement of the year) that actually moves forward by moving in the direction of what comes earlier (*die Frühe*). It is this spiritual journey that allows for the possibility of corruption (*Verwesen*).

In this movement towards a more originary thinking of time, we reach one of the central arguments of Derrida's critique of Heidegger. For one of the avowed goals of *Of Spirit* was to question the Heideggerian primacy of the question for thinking. For Heidegger, everything beings with the question. Derrida, however, offers another figure for us in place of the question: the promise (*Versprechen*). What is the function of the promise in this reflection on originary darkening and historical corruption? The answer is in Derrida's formula: 'The *Verwesen* is a *Versprechen*' (Derrida 1989: 94). As Derrida consents, Heidegger is most likely right when he declares, in a famous formulation, that *Die Sprache spricht*. But at the origin of this language that speaks we find the possibility of its corruption itself: *Die Sprache verspricht*.

> The *Verwesen* is a *Versprechen*. In saying this, I have perhaps, doubtless even (how could one be sure?) left the order of commentary, if such a thing exists. Would Heidegger subscribe to an interpretation which would make of this *Versprechen* something other than a modality or modification of *Sprache*? He would, rather [*plutôt*], earlier [*plus tôt*], see the very coming, in the promise, for better and for worse, of the *given word*. It remains to find out whether this *Versprechen* is not the promise which, opening every speaking, makes possible the very question and therefore precedes it without belonging to it: the dissymmetry of an affirmation, of a *yes* before all opposition of *yes* and *no*. The call of Being – every question already responds to it, the promise has already taken place wherever language comes. Language always, *before any question*, and in the very question, comes down to [*revient à*] the promise. This would also be a promise of *spirit*. (Derrida 1989: 94)

The originary corruption of language (*Ver-sprechen* as a kind of mis-speaking) is the genuine promise of language that precedes and makes possible the question itself. In this originary position, the promise of the originary corruption is not a negative category but a genuine affirmation that precedes the very difference between a yes and a no. The promise of spirit is then the inherent corruption (*Verwesen*) that belongs to the essence of spiritual darkening. In Derrida's reading, the Heideggerian tension between a positive structural form of worldlessness and its negative historical manifestation is undermined by the re-inscription of the latter in the former as its very condition.

While in Husserl it was the constitutive worldlessness of the transcendental subject that had to be deconstructed, in Heidegger it is the supposed factical worldliness of Dasein that proves to be unsustainable. The secondary, merely ontic corruption of Dasein in its historical worldlessness turns out to be the very condition of the originary positive assertion of its essence in the first place. Worldlessness as *Verwesen* is reinscribed in the very essence (*Wesen*) of Dasein. Thus, we come full circle here in our description of Derrida's strategy: phenomenological worldlessness is contaminated by a constitutive worldliness, and ontological worldliness is contaminated by structural worldlessness.[6] And this is where we reach an inherent limitation of deconstruction itself that is simultaneously an enabling condition and an ultimate horizon for its project: the thought of différance simultaneously affirms the worldlessness of Being and the worldliness of appearing in such a way that the two constantly contaminate each other. Ontology as 'hauntology' shows us that the radical indeterminacy of Being itself functions as the very condition of Being's self-externalisation in appearing. But, according to the logic of the same necessity, this condition is also a condition of impossibility as the field of appearing will never be able to obtain the consistency of a closed order (as both the transcendental ego and the phenomenal form of the world are in essence 'spectral') (Derrida 1994: 135). This generalised state of worldlessness is haunted by the ghostly possibility of the world.

★ ★ ★

226

In a well-known passage of 'Force of Law' (1990/1994), Derrida spoke of the two 'styles' of deconstruction in the following terms:

> Deconstruction is generally practiced in two ways or two styles, and it most often grafts one on to the other. One takes on the demonstrative and apparently ahistorical allure of logico-formal paradoxes. The other, more historical or more anamnesic, seems to proceed through readings of texts, meticulous interpretations and genealogies. (Derrida 2002: 250)

These two styles directly correspond to the Derridean strategy that we have outlined above: when deconstruction encounters metaphysical assertions of the primacy of worldlessness, it responds by a 'genealogical' reinsertion of what appears to be worldless into history and, thus, into the world (phenomenological worldlessness is contaminated by a constitutive worldliness); but when deconstruction comes face to face with metaphysical assertions of worldliness, it retreats into the apparently 'ahistorical' domain of the worldlessness of thought (ontological worldliness is contaminated by structural worldlessness). Yet, the potentially infinite oscillation of these two strategies that are grafted onto each other does have a stable centre: the necessity of appearance. For, the entire problematic of 'spectrality' is organised by the assumption that the ghost must appear. In other words, the necessity of appearance functions here as the undeconstructible condition of the play of worldliness and worldlessness. Without the haunting appearance of the ghost, there would be no world; but once the haunting gets underway, the world cannot be said to exist anymore.

Therefore, all of our discussions so far point in the direction of an unavoidable conclusion: we need to add a third, properly phenomenological 'style' to the inherently 'worldly' genealogical and the fundamentally 'worldless' logical modes of deconstruction. This new style functions simultaneously as the condition and as the ultimate horizon of the other two. It is what renders deconstruction itself into a kind of experience. Before it can become a demonstration of a historical erudition and logical bravado, deconstruction is an ordinary experience. This experience then is what the other styles of deconstruction set out to formalise in their more or less rigorous manners. But the ultimate goal of logical and genealogical deconstructions is to reproduce this experience in a new language and in a new conceptual apparatus. It is not an accident that Derrida refers to all major concepts or 'quasi-concept' of deconstruction (différance, the promise, mourning, freedom, friendship, justice, haunting, the messianic, aporia and even deconstruction) as experiences. In fact, the reason why the very term 'quasi-concept' had to be invented was to mark the impossibility of pure conceptualisation as mere abstraction. These quasi-concepts never cease to be experiences. And we can clearly articulate now what this experience consists of that constitutes the very condition of deconstruction: it is the experience of worldlessness.

We could scour Derrida's text for different illustrations of this abysmal yet fundamental experience, but one of the best-known examples remains Derrida's encounter with his own cat as it was recorded in *The Animal That Therefore I Am*. This scene functions like the primal scene of deconstruction. The story is simple and has the structure of an event: Derrida is seen naked by his cat as he exits his shower. The cat is a real cat, '*this* irreplaceable living being [. . .] that refuses to be conceptualized' (Derrida 2008a: 9). In its singularity, it is wholly other, which in Derrida's language means that, in its very being, it confirms to the principle that 'every other is wholly other' ('tout autre est tout autre'). This famous proposition is precisely the deconstructive ontological and ethical formula for worldlessness: being with the wholly other means that being is radically open to the degree that its internal alterity cannot ever be reduced to the closed economy of sameness. If every instance of alterity is other in a different way, there is no ontological ground for the constitution of a common world other than this radical openness that simultaneously renders ipseity and alterity non-totalisable.

As Derrida tells the story, the surprising feeling of shame in front of the animal leads to a state of disorientation and confusion that, ultimately, consists of the destitution of the self:

> For I no longer know who, therefore, I am (following) or who it is I am chasing, who is following me or hunting me. Who comes before and who is after whom? I no longer know which end my head is. Madness: 'We're all mad here. I'm mad. You're mad'. I no longer know how to respond, or even to respond to the question that compels me or asks me who I am (following) or after whom I am (following), but am so as I am running [*et suis ainsi en train de courir*]. (Derrida 2008a: 10)

Derrida also makes it clear that what is at stake in this experience is precisely the status of the world as a moment of a *Mitsein*: 'what is meant by living, speaking, dying, being and world as in being-in-the-world or being-within-the- world, or being-with, being-before, being-behind, being-after, being and following, being followed or being following, there where *I am*, in one way or another, but unimpeachably, *near* what they call the animal' (Derrida 2008a: 11). In place of the traditional 'with' of a classic being-with the world, we now have a being after, alongside, near and next to, a being-pressed or being-huddled-together (Derrida 2008a: 10). Co-existence with the wholly other implies some kind of a proximity but this closeness cannot be reduced to a simple 'with' (that would imply some kind of a more or less harmonious community).

This is why, when he looks into his cat's eyes, Derrida sees something other than a common world – namely, 'the abyssal limit of the human':

> And in these moments of nakedness, as regards the animal, everything can happen to me, I am like a child ready for the apocalypse, *I am (following) the apocalypse itself*, that is to say, the ultimate and first event of the end, the unveiling and the verdict. I am (following) it, the apocalypse, I identify with it by running behind it, after it, after its whole zoo-logy. When the instant of extreme passion passes, and I find peace again, then I can speak calmly of the beasts of the Apocalypse, visit them in the museum, see them in a painting (but for the Greeks 'zoography' referred to the portraiture of the living in general and not just the painting of animals); I can visit them at the zoo, read about them in the Bible or speak about them as in a book. (Derrida 2008a: 12)

The dynamics of this experience is laid out here with exceptional clarity. The encounter with the other as absolute other brings an end to the world as it ushers in an apocalypse. But this is not an ordinary catastrophe, as it leads to an identification: *je suis l'apocalypse même* – I am the apocalypse/I follow the apocalypse. The semantic ambiguity exploited by Derrida here suggests that this is not a passive experience as it involves an active following, a search, and who knows, maybe even a desire for worldlessness. The experience of worldlessness, after all, is an 'extreme passion' – not a catatonic state of passive isolation. Once the intensity of the experience subsides, once the world is restored, the apocalypse itself comes to an end. At this point, it becomes possible to contain the experience of worldlessness in a conceptual apparatus. It becomes possible to describe it, represent it and analyze it. In short, the discourse on worldlessness is institutionalised.

The moral of the story, then, is best understood as a reflection on the philosophical problem of *Mitsein*. The disturbing conclusion is that 'being-with' in the mode of being with the wholly other is not necessarily a world-constituting experience. No doubt, we need some kind of a relation to the non-self in order to have a world. But the experience of radical alterity is precisely the experience of worldlessness: it reveals a proximity that cannot be contained or totalised. What the encounter with the animal shows here is that *Mitsein* is not only *Mitsein* with another Dasein as being-in-the-world: *Mitsein* is essentially the opening onto worldlessness. The encounter with the other is world-constituting only as long as the alterity of the other is mastered, domesticated or masked. It now appears that the world (in the sense of the world of the same) is always a defense against the other.

★ ★ ★

It is, then, more than a mere coincidence that in his final seminars Derrida once again returned to Heidegger and the question of worldlessness. The thematic of worldlessness, with all of its complications and connotations, appears to frame his entire oeuvre. Derrida opened the seminar with the announcement that the year's topic would reflect on the meaning of a sentence: 'I am alone in the world' (Derrida 2011a: 3). As part of this preparatory work for a set of parallel readings of Daniel Defoe's

Robinson Crusoe and Heidegger's *The Fundamental Concepts of Metaphysics*, during the first session of the seminar Derrida announced a threefold thesis about the world in response to the question: 'What do beasts and man have in common?' (Derrida 2011a: 8). The three propositions concerning the community of the world unfold in a quasi-dialectical fashion. First, it appears to be undeniably true that human beings and animals inhabit the same objective world even if they have radically different experiences of this same world. Second, it appears to be equally unquestionable that they do not inhabit the same the world, since there appears to be an insurmountable difference between the two worlds. At this point, then, we have two contradictory propositions that are both, nevertheless, true. Human beings and animals share and do not share the same world. Once again, the task is not to find a logical resolution to the contradiction but to see that our very definition of the world is inadequate.

This is, then, the function of the third thesis, which amounts to a straightforward assertion of worldlessness. What humans and animals have in common is not the world but the state of worldlessness:

> In spite of this identity and this difference, neither animals of different species, nor humans of different cultures, nor any animal or human individual inhabit the same world as another, however close and similar these living individuals may be (be they humans or animals), and the difference between one world and another will remain always unbridgeable, because the community of the world is always constructed, simulated by a set of stabilizing apparatuses, more or less stable, then, and never natural, language in the broad sense, codes of traces being designed, among all living beings, to construct a unity of the world that is always deconstructible, nowhere and never given in nature. Between my world, the 'my world', what I call 'my

world' – and there is no other for me, as any other world is part
of it – between my world and any other world there is first the
space and the time of an infinite difference, an interruption
that is incommensurable with all attempts to make a passage, a
bridge, an isthmus, all attempts at communication, translation,
trope and transfer that the desire for a world or the want of
a world, the being wanting a world will try to pose, impose,
propose, stabilize. There is no world, there are only islands.
(Derrida 2011a: 8–9)

As the passage indicates, Derrida's argument is pulled in two
directions. On the one hand, Derrida clearly asserts that there
is no such thing as a common world because there is an infinity
of private worlds ('my world'). As a result of this uncontrollable
multiplication of worlds, it might be improper to speak of a
'world' that is, in the end, nothing but the relation of the self to
itself. The more appropriate term offered by Derrida is 'island'.
On the other hand, there also appears to be an inherent 'desire
for a world' at work in this ontology of worldlessness. Even if
the ontological absence of the world is an undeniable fact, so is
this desire that will always be at work (presumably at least in the
human being) on constructing a world. The impossibility and the
necessity of the world are tied together in this basic insight: the
world is always deconstructible. A stronger formulation of this
insight would hold that it is always a world that is deconstructible.
If it is a world, by definition, it is deconstructible; but if it is
deconstructible, it bears the mark of a certain kind of worldliness.
But the undeconstructible condition of deconstruction will be
impossible to reduce to a world. Deconstruction is, therefore,
worldless in this basic sense: the worldlessness that is its fundamental ontological presupposition remains undeconstructible
and functions as the very condition of deconstruction itself.

★ ★ ★

These final seminars, therefore, point in the direction of what we could call the ultimate horizon of Derrida's thought. They articulate an internal limit to deconstruction itself that simultaneously accounts for the very possibility of deconstruction and, at the same time, gestures in the direction of the necessary suspension of its operation. It is here that we can identify in its most explicit form Derrida's decision concerning worldlessness. The argument is clearly animated by a simultaneous harmony and tension between the ontology of worldlessness and the ethics of worldliness. On the one hand, it appears to be undeniable that the world does not exist. This ontological fact is the very condition of any ethical behaviour as well: ethics exists because there is no world. On the other hand, our ethical duty appears to be to live life *as if* the world existed. For some reason, the possibilities of inhabiting and, more importantly, co-inhabiting worldlessness are simply discarded by Derrida in favour a different kind of ethics.

The focus of this inquiry is a line from Paul Celan's poetry: '*Die Welt is fort, ich muss dich tragen*'. Here is Derrida's translation:

> That is one of the thousand directions in which I would be <tempted> to interpret the last line of a short and great poem by Celan: 'Die Welt ist fort, ich muss dich tragen', a poem of mourning or birth that I do not have time to read with you: the world has gone, the world has gone away, the world is far off, the world is lost, there is no world any more (to sustain us or ground [*fonder*] the two of us like a ground [*sol*]), I must carry you (either in me as in mourning, or else in me as in birth (for *tragen* is also said of the mother carrying a child, in her arms or in her womb). We are *weltlos*, I can only carry you, I am the only one who can and must carry you, etc.; but are we *weltlos*,

without world, as Heidegger says of the stone and the material thing that they are *weltlos?* – clearly not. So how are we to think the absence of world, the non-world? A non-world that is not *immonde* [filthy, revolting]? (Derrida 2011a: 9)

This final question indicates that what is at stake here is a positive (or at least not 'revolting') definition of worldlessness. The task is to imagine the absence of the world in terms that are not immediately negative – even if Derrida's 'clearly not' indicates an unmistakable desire to define the specificity of the human relation to worldlessness in distinction to other non-human forms of worldlessness. This is how worldlessness becomes the condition of ethics. The two parts of Celan's statement clearly align with the ontological and the ethical. The first part (which states that the world is gone) is a direct ontological axiom from which the ethical imperative of the second part must be derived (I am responsible for the other). The ethical duty in relation to the other is born precisely at the moment when the world ceases to exist.

In the concluding tenth session of the seminar, the same line from Celan becomes the occasion for the decision concerning worldlessness. Here Derrida is now speaking about the absolute necessity of thinking worldlessness and cautions us of the risks of this dangerous task. Once again, the same tension between the impossibility and the necessity of the world returns to structure his argument. First, as Derrida puts it, no one can demonstrate the unity of the world:

Of course, one can always question the supposed unity or identity of the world, not only between animal and human, but already from one living being to another. No one will ever be able to demonstrate, what is called *demonstrate* in all rigor, that two human beings, you and I for example, inhabit the same world, that the world is one and the same thing for both of us. Of course, and this argument, which I hope to be a serious one, could and should be taken very far, in more than dangerous fashion. (Derrida 2011a: 265; emphasis in original)

But what appears to tame the edge of this dangerous task is the second step of his argument, which insists on the necessity of the anticipated unity of this world: 'But in a more current sense, and one that does not contradict this one, there really must be a certain *presumed, anticipated* unity of the world even in order discursively to sustain within it multiplicity, untranslatable and un-gatherable, the dissemination of possible worlds' (Derrida 2011a: 265; emphasis in original). Even if we cannot demonstrate the unity of the world, we 'really must' anticipate this non-existent unity that nevertheless includes the multiplicity of possible worlds. The ethical task is contained in this 'must', whose possibility is not in contradiction with the ontological thesis (and, therefore, presumably can be derived from it).

What is interesting, then, in this argument is that Derrida explicitly formulates the problem in terms of a defense mechanism. It appears that we need to be protected from the ontological fact of worldlessness. In order to demonstrate this necessity, he separates the fact from the word. It is the ontological fact of worldlessness that guarantees and necessitates the radical semantic dissemination of the word. But this radical dissemination threatens the very possibility of meaning. Therefore, the constructed semantic unity of the meaning of the word 'world' is a defense against this fundamental worldlessness:

Not only a multiplicity and an equivocality of the world, of the word 'world' (*cosmos, mundus, Welt, world, Mundo*) which would retain a common horizon of univocity, but a dissemination without a common semantic horizon, the noun 'world', as a word void of meaning or the meaning without use of the word 'world' being merely an artificial effect, a cobbled-together verbal and terminological construction, destined to mask our panic (that of a baby who would be born without coming into the world), destined then to protect us against the infantile but infinite anxiety of the fact that *there is not the world*, that nothing is less certain than the world itself, that there is perhaps no longer a world and no doubt there never was one as totality of anything at all, habitable and co-habitable world, and that radical dissemination, i.e. the absence of a common world, the irremediable solitude without salvation of the living being, depends first on the absence without recourse of any world, i.e. of any common meaning of the word 'world', in sum of any common meaning at all. (Derrida 2011a: 265–6)

Hence the absolute necessity of thinking worldlessness. As Derrida insists, this confrontation with the undeniable fact of worldlessness is not a form of apocalypticism but a common experience ('our most constant and quotidian experience') and a logical necessity ('what I must think and say according to the most implacable necessity') (Derrida 2011a: 266). And yet, this experience – which induces panic and anxiety in us – is constantly denied. Derrida again highlights here the structure of a defense mechanism when he speaks about the 'permanently denied' knowledge of the 'abysmal unshareable' (Derrida 2011a: 266). Our relation to worldlessness, therefore, is determined by a permanent denial of the undeniable: 'the undeniable fact that there is no world, not even a world, not even one and the same world, no world that is one: *the* world, *a* world, a world that is *one*, is what there is not' (Derrida 2011a: 266). This is where the function of language can be thematised. Against the background of the undeniable fact of worldlessness, among other things, language offers us an escape from this reality:

> the presumed community of the world is a word, a vocable, a convenient and reassuring bit of chatter, the name of a life insurance policy for living beings losing their world, a life belt on the high seas that we pretend to be leaving, long enough to spend a moment during which we pretend to say 'we' and to be together together. (Derrida 2011a: 267)

In other words, language accomplishes the impossible when it crosses the uncrossable by providing us with the 'vague comforting feeling of understanding each other' (Derrida 2011a: 267). This is an agreement in the name of survival which, however, essentially has the structure of a fiction. We pretend that the world exists.

To put it in Derrida's (and Kant's) language, we decide to act *as if* the world existed (Derrida 2011a: 268). And this is the crucial moment of decision concerning worldlessness, a decision whose structure carries the entire weight of the argument. Derrida insists that, given the undeniable fact of worldlessness, there are two and only two mutually exclusive possibilities available for us: one is the unconditional affirmation of this worldlessness with all of its consequences; the other is the unconditional affirmation of the fiction of the world in the form of the 'as if'. The first one provides us with the minimal community of the negative knowledge of the non-existence of the world, but leaves no room for anything else. It amounts to a co-existence in the void where 'nothing will happen to us nor welcome us ever on any island or any shore' (Derrida 2011a: 268). In this case, the ethical duty in relation to the other is partially to carry the other over into worldlessness, to bring this negative knowledge to the other and to sustain the other as much as possible in the void.

The second option is described in significantly more detail by Derrida and, therefore, presents a more complex set of possibilities. The ethical duty here is the opposite of what we have seen in the first one: 'where there is no world, [. . .] what I must do, with you and carrying you, is make it that there be precisely a world, just a world, if not a just world, or to do things so as to make *as if* there were just a world' (Derrida 2011a: 268). But the structure of this ethical imperative is now different from the previous one: even if I know very well that the world does not exist, I still have the potential of creating the fiction of the world for the other. This is the poetical gift of the world to the other that I can make. And, in turn, this gift to the other is what supposedly makes my own life possible and bearable. I bear my life as I bear the other. But the movement of this gift, then, is inscribed in the logic of the trace: I leave a disappearing trace in the world that is itself in the process of disappearing since it is itself nothing but a trace. The world as fiction is structured like a trace: 'a world that has forever been going to leave and has just left, going away with no trace, the trace becoming trace only by being able to erase itself' (Derrida 2011a: 268). Neither absolutely worldly, nor absolutely worldless, the world is a permanently disappearing trace.

Which one of the two options does Derrida choose in the end? While there is no direct answer to this question in the text of the seminar, a common interpretation holds that it is clearly the second option that he would have preferred.[7] This interpretation is supported by the context in which the two options are outlined for us, for the remainder of the final session of the seminar is mostly concerned with staging a confrontation between the Heideggerian 'as such' (the *als-Struktrur*) and the Kantian 'as if' (what Derrida will now refer to as the

Alsobstruktur).[8] In this reading, the very possibility of the phenomenological 'as such' that guarantees Dasein's special access to the world in contrast to the stone and the animal undergoes a process of fictionalisation. Following this logic, we could say that what Heidegger did not see in his analyses of the ontological difference as *Unter-Schied* and *Austrag* is that the violence of the excessive sovereignty of *Walten* that holds sway over everything in Being and opens up the very possibility of the 'as such' is contaminated by the mere phantasm of the world. It is this conclusion, sustained by Derrida's temptation to act *as if* he had no objection to the Kantian *as if* (Derrida 2011a: 271), that shows his preference for the second option. To put it differently, Derrida discovers in the Heideggerian thematics of *Walten* a powerful figure of worldlessness (in effect arguing that according to Heidegger himself Being is inherently worldless since *physis* is nothing but the originary force of emergence that precedes any world), but then he immediately ties this discovery to the thesis of the absolute necessity of the fiction of the world.

★ ★ ★

The interrogation of this theoretical decision, however, also functions as a potential site for the contemporary radicalisation of the programme of deconstruction. If both options are equally valid consequences of the deconstructive ontology of worldlessness, the reason for choosing one over the other remains forever a strategic decision. We do not have a solid ground to stand on when we choose the second option. Therefore, it could be consistent with the logic of deconstruction to say that under certain historical circumstances it is the first option that remains 'more promising'. This choice would remain compatible with everything that Derrida has said – except for the decision to choose the second option. In a less generous reading, one could insist that Derrida's choice will always remain dangerously close to the structure of a perversion and announces a perverted ethics that, nevertheless, remains the only possible ethics that is available to us. This is the logic of the fetishisation of the world: 'I know very well that the world does not exist, yet I decide to act as if it did exist.' Even the Kafkaesque displacement ('there is hope but not for us') of this Kantian principle in the 'there is a world but not for us, only for the other' does not go far enough, since it remains sacrificial in nature. The self carries the other by sacrificing his or her own relation to the possibilities of world-lessness. The ethical pathos of this solution consists in assuming the burden of worldlessness in place of the other.

Deconstruction tries to protect itself from the consequences of this fetishisation by simultaneously asserting the impossibility and the necessity of the world. The necessary world is only a fiction whose impossibility can always be demonstrated and, therefore, the process of fetishisation can always be interrupted. But as a fiction, the world is, nevertheless, real and necessary. There is no 'as such' of the world, but its 'as if' imposes itself on us with the force of an unavoidable fate. In the end, it is precisely this necessity that provides for deconstruction a way out of the aporia of the world. This undeconstructible necessity of the fiction of the world (which, in the end, is the necessity of appearing) provides us with a foothold in the worldlessness of différance: it is now possible to evoke an ethics whose foundation is the tragic necessity of the world. At best, it will be a two-sided ethics that simultaneously asks us to save and sacrifice the world whenever the need arises. The infinite labour of creating and destroying the world will become a dialectics without an end.

The question for us, however, is whether choosing the first option discarded by Derrida could offer us something other than this fetishism? After all, this is the choice that arguably amounts to the unconditional affirmation of worldlessness as the undeconstructible condition of both this fetishism and of its deconstruction as well. If the impossibility of the world is the necessity of worldlessness, could the affirmation of worldlessness avoid the risks of fetishisation? What if the only genuine necessity is not that of the world but of worldlessness itself?

Notes

1   This chapter will exclusively focus on Derrida's engagement of the phenomenological tradition. In the context of our previous arguments, however, it is evident that Derrida's readings of psychoanalysis are equally relevant for this discussion. From his early engagements of Freudian metaphysics to his reflections on 'geo-psychoanalysis', Derrida's relevant texts offer a wide range of possible reflections on worldlessness. For example, it is quite significant that in one of his early writings Derrida inscribes the logic of différance into that of the death drive with the following words: 'No doubt life protects itself by repetition, trace, *différance* (deferral). But we must be wary of this formulation: there is no life present *at first* which would *then* come to protect, postpone, or reserve itself in *différance*. The latter constitutes the essence of life. Or rather: as *différance* is not an essence, as it is not anything, it *is not* life, if Being is determined as *ousia*, presence, essence/existence, substance or subject. Life must be thought of as trace before Being may be determined as presence. This is the only condition on which we can say that life *is* death, that repetition and the beyond of the pleasure principle are native and congenital to that which they transgress' (Derrida 1978: 203). The psychoanalytic conception of the worldlessness of life is reinterpreted here in terms of the formula: life is différance.

2   As Jeffrey Nealon observed, for Derrida '[i]f it's alive, it has a world, and vice versa. This is axiomatic [. . .] in Derrida. But of course "life" [. . .] isn't all there is in Derrida' (Nealon 2016: 80). I do not pursue any further this line of reasoning in this chapter, but recent critical discussion of the concept of 'life' in Derrida's works is quite relevant for our understanding

of worldlessness. For example, Nealon has also argued that this proximity of the world to life is precisely the point where we can demonstrate a certain latent Heideggerianism in Derrida's works: 'Derrida wants first and foremost to question Heidegger's confidence concerning humans' privileged and exclusive access to this thing called world (and to wonder whether there's ever any access to anything "as such"). But throughout Derrida's late work he continues to follow Heidegger in defining life (and death) through this overarching thematic of world' (Nealon 2016: 54). In addition, Martin Hägglund's argument that for Derrida 'everything in time is surviving, but not everything is alive' remains significant in this context, because it allows us to identify a larger domain of worldlessness (that of the generalised field of survival) in excess of life (which is constituted by the unconditional affirmation of survival) (Hägglund 2008: 96). Nevertheless, these discussions clearly show that the thesis of the worldlessness of life that we have been pursuing in our previous chapters is at odds with Derrida's definition of life.

3   It might be worth noting here that recent attempts to reconcile Derrida's thought with various forms of philosophical realism and materialism all have to pass through the ordeal of worldlessness. In this sense, these readings often try to save Derrida from charges of linguistic idealism by asserting that, according to the very logic of Derrida's thinking, what is truly real is located in a domain where the world no longer holds sway in an absolute manner. For an attempt to identify a 'post-deconstructive realism' at work in Derrida's works by locating the logic différance in the event of the thing, see Marder (2009); for a discussion of Derrida (and the worldlessness of the stone) in the context of 'new materialism', see Crockett (2017: 74–92).

4   Here we should follow the lead of Leonard Lawlor, who argued that it was the problem of the 'origin of the world' that constituted the starting point for Derridean deconstruction. Commenting on Eugen Fink's essay 'The Phenomenological Philosophy of Edmund Husserl and Contemporary Criticism', Lawlor writes: 'Fink's 1933 "The Phenomenological Philosophy of Edmund Husserl" shows us that the basic problem of phenomenology is the basic problem with which Derrida starts: the origin of the world' (Lawlor 2002: 21). For the argument that deconstruction constitutes a 'phenomenology of the "extra-mundane"', see O'Connor (2010: 13). As O'Connor argues, 'it is perhaps the loss of world more than anything that permeates Derrida's thought from beginning to end' (O'Connor 2010: 13).

5   The question of the animal has been at the forefront of a large number of critical debates about Derrida that cut across various disciplines. For useful interventions and overviews of these debates, see Lawlor (2007); Calarco (2008); Krell (2013); Nealon (2015).

6   In a different context, Paola Marrati has already made a similar argument when she claimed that 'it is not by chance that Derrida plays the question of ontology off against Husserl and, at the same time, holds onto the question of the transcendental and the empirical in order to demonstrate their irreducible contamination instead of following Heidegger and simply allowing this question to drop' (Marrati 2005: 17).

7   This is, at least, Michael Naas's interpretation of this problem. See *The End of the World and Other Teachable Moments: Jacques Derrida's Final Seminar* (Naas 2015: 59–60). In addition, Timothy Clark raised a similar point when he argued that for Derrida the world is 'something delusory in which one cannot not believe, simply by being alive, just as one cannot imagine being dead without, impossibly, also projecting oneself as the imagined witness to that condition' (Clark 2013: 18).

8   For useful discussions of the 'as such' and the 'as if' in Derrida, see Lawlor (2007: 46–70); Naas (2008: 37–66); Dickinson (2011).

5

The Logics of Worldlessness

The event is worldless. The postwar radicalisation of the theory of the event undoubtedly points in this direction.[1] A common element of this line of thinking is that the very possibility of the event shows that there is something other than the world that we take for granted. Without the event, in effect, nothing new would ever happen in a world. Inside the limits of a given world, there are only worldly occurrences, whose dynamics remain subjugated to the laws of that world. When an event takes place, it happens as a breach in the texture of the world. The alterity of the event, thus, also implies that within the confines of a specific world, we cannot really speak of an ontology of the event, only a phenomenology of its worldlessness. But it is an equally important part of the theorisation of the event that this alterity comes to us from a location that cannot be described in worldly terms. When an event finally irrupts into the world, it cannot be construed as a message from another fully constituted world. The location from which the event arrives cannot be a world. If it came from another world, its event-ness would only be 'relative'. It would not be an absolute event 'in itself' but only an event 'for us' (that is, for our world). The radicalisation of the thought of the event, however, points in the direction of the absolute event. The event, if it is worthy of the name, does not stop being an event: it cannot be normalised as a regular element of any world. In this sense, being and event cannot be fully reconciled. But if the source of the event cannot simply be another world in which the event would cease to be an exceptional occurrence and would be merely another normal element of the world, the thinking of the event must also be a thought of worldlessness even if we assume that its worldly manifestation is a necessary part of its destiny. Even if it manifests itself in a world, even if the event must assume a worldly presence, something of the event remains forever worldless.

No doubt, this theorisation of the event reached one if its highest points in Alain Badiou's philosophy. We could say without exaggeration that *Being and Event* (1988) was one of the most consistent efforts of our times to elaborate a systematic ontology of worldlessness. As is well known, this explicitly anti-Heideggerian book offers us an ontology that grasps being as a pure multiplicity that has no other limit to its infinity than the void from which it is woven.[2] In other words, there is no external totality of being in the form of a closed world, only an internal limit to its infinite dissemination that can be mathematically grasped as an empty set. The worldlessness of being means here that 'the one *is not*' (Badiou 2005: 23). But this proposition does not mean that being is mere chaos, since the one is retained by Badiou in the form of an operation: the count-as-one (Badiou 2005: 24). This is why ontology can grasp the structures of being in the form of 'situations'. *Being and Event*, then, proposes a rigorous way of moving from the empty set through the inconsistent multiplicity (being as the multiplicity of multiplicities) to the structure of the situation (presentation as the counting for one) and, finally, to the state of the situation (representation as the metastructure of the situation that counts the counting itself). The chain of these arguments suggests that we can move from the empty set (the ontological name of worldlessness) to the situation (which is Badiou's early term for what later will be called a 'world') in such a way that worldlessness remains the truth of this sequence. Yet, the worldlessness of being does not mean that being is without a structuring principle. In fact, for Badiou, it is precisely the worldlessness of being that accounts for the possibility of the ontological structuration of being.

In this context, the function of the event is to reveal the truth of the situation: namely, that the very being of the situation is pure inconsistency. Thus, the event reveals the void of the situation itself: in its being, the situation (the world) is worldless. If being is pure multiplicity, the event has no other ontological status apart from the interruption of the structure of the situation. We could then say that the event is worldless: 'It is not from the world, even ideally, that the event gets its inexhaustible reserve, its silent (or indiscernible) excess, but *from its not being attached to it*, from its being separated, interrupted or [. . .] "pure"' (Badiou 1994: 65; emphasis in original).[3] This means that the event is of course a multiple (like everything else for Badiou), but it counts for nothing in the given situation: 'The event is not actually internal to the analytic of the multiple. Even though it can always be localized within presentation, it is not, as such, presented, nor is it presentable. It is – not being – supernumerary' (Badiou 2005: 178). Thus, the event always manifests itself as the potential ruin of a world. Similarly, the subject who declares fidelity to an undecidable event intensifies its existence precisely by stepping outside of the ordinary world. The subject is not a mere individual for Badiou precisely to the degree that it no longer belongs to the world that was constituted by the state of a given situation. It is the subject of a worldless event.

What this means, however, is that both being and the event are worldless for Badiou. In other words, mathematics as ontology cannot give us a world. The theoretical impasse of *Being and Event* is precisely this generalised ontological worldlessness that includes both being (which can be described in formal terms by ontology) and the event (which, in a sense, escapes ontology). Badiou, therefore, still needs to account for the world: he needs the category of the 'world' to be able to articulate the relation between these two different forms of worldlessness. The worldlessness of the event needs a place in which it manifests itself as different from the worldlessness of being. That is to say, between worldless being and the worldless event, another space had to be opened up where truth can take place. Truth needs the world in order to be able to unfold in the form of a subjectivised body.

This is why the sequel to *Being and Event* shifts the focus from the ontology of worldlessness to the logics of worldliness. Against the background of the pure multiplicity of being, Badiou's *Logics of Worlds* (2006) is concerned with the necessary appearance of worlds. As Badiou explains, in this second book we shift from the analysis of the *onto*-logy of pure being (being-qua-being, the multiple without One), which is in essence a mathematics of being, to the onto-*logy* of being-there, that is to a 'phenomenology' of appearing (Badiou 2009a: 39). The recourse to the term phenomenology, however, remains somewhat misleading, since the core of Badiou's project is to rethink the relationship between ontology and phenomenology. Nevertheless, we could still say, in a language that is not Badiou's, that the fundamental goal of this project is to reconcile a consistent ontology of worldlessness with a necessary phenomenology of worldliness. How can we maintain simultaneously that being is worldless yet it belongs to its essence to manifest itself in the infinity of worlds?

In the course of this realignment, new possibilities are opened up for the phenomenology of worldlessness. We could in fact argue that this move from the ontology of worldlessness to the logics of worlds makes Badiou into something like the last phenomenologist: he announces to us a radical break with the phenomenological tradition all the while retaining a central category of this tradition, the world as the function of appearing. In this sense, he produces for us not so much a phenomenology without the world, but a world without a proper phenomenology. Badiou accepts one of the basic tenets of phenomenology (the necessity of appearing) but, as far as classic phenomenology is concerned, he draws a few monstrous conclusions from this premise. In this sense, what he proposes under the title of a 'Greater Logic' would be simply unrecognisable by our phenomenologists. And yet, what Badiou outlines is, nevertheless, a phenomenology but only in the minimal sense that its goal is to account for the logic of appearing. The necessity of appearing (and this necessity's relation to being remains a crucial question to be explored here) naturally leads us to the necessity of worlds. Since being is neither Whole nor One for Badiou, the necessity of this worldlessness already prescribes the plurality and even infinity of worlds.

* * *

Badiou's intervention could be described as the invention of an altogether new kind of phenomenological reduction, a new kind of transcendental epoché. While the classic phenomenological epoché aims to suspend human immanence in the world to thematise the transcendental ego, Badiou's method offers us the exact reverse of this process. Badiou, in effect, asks us to start by suspending the ego in order to thematise the asubjective transcendental structures of the world.[4] The term Badiou introduces for this new method is 'objective phenomenology':

> What we are attempting here is a *calculated phenomenology*. The method employed in these examples can in fact be related to a phenomenology, but only to an objective phenomenology. This means that the consistency of what one speaks about [. . .] must be allowed to emerge by neutralising, not its real existence as in Husserl, but on the contrary its intentional or lived dimension. (Badiou 2009a: 38–9)

This new phenomenological epoché is, therefore, still 'transcendental' in nature, but in a sense that is fully at odds with the traditional phenomenological definition of the term. It suspends everything but the world in order to bring to light the logical composition of a localised region of being independently of any subjective intervention:

> The transcendental that is at stake in this book is altogether anterior to every subjective constitution, for it is an immanent given of any situation whatever. As we shall see, it is what imposes upon every situated multiplicity the constraint of a logic, which is also the law of its appearing, or the rule in accordance with which the 'there' of being-there allows the multiple to come forth as essentially bound. That every world possesses a singular transcendental organization means that, since the thinking of being cannot on its own account for the world's manifestation, the intelligibility of this manifestation must be made possible by immanent operations. 'Transcendental' is the name for these operations. The final maxim can be stated as follows: with

regard to the inconsistency of being, 'logic' and 'appearing' are one and the same thing. (Badiou 2009a: 101)

As we can see, Badiou changes the meaning of the 'transcendental' by completely separating the problem of appearing from the subjective field. The transcendental is no longer tied to intentional consciousness as it now refers to the asubjective structures of appearing. What follows from this proposition is that the 'transcendental' actually names the 'immanent' composition of any situation whatever. This shift of focus means that the problem of appearing must be construed as an immanent operation of the given situation. Being appears according to a set of rules that are immanent to localised situations of being. The conclusion to be drawn from these theses is that 'appearing' is an asubjective immanent operation of being that can be formalised as a logic. Being possesses a 'transcendental' logic in the sense that this logic both precedes the constitution of consciousness and it escapes the discourse of ontology (since the system of indexation that constitutes a world cannot be grasped as a positive entity of the given world itself). It is neither consciousness, nor pure being qua being.

This new epoché, therefore, allows us to perceive the equivalence between appearance and logic (phenomenon and logos) and completely changes the meaning of 'phenomenology'. Taken in the sense of the 'logic of appearance', phenomenology is on the side or even on the inside of ontology as it is now best described as 'onto-*logy*'. The task this redefinition poses for Badiou, then, is to account for the fact that the pure multiplicity of being is not without some kind of inherent process of structuration or, to put it differently, being is not without its logic. The logic of being, then, is its appearance, which is not an appearance for an intentional consciousness but an objective quality of localised being itself.

Yet, in spite of the fact that the possibility of the logic of appearance is inherent in being itself, being and appearing are not the same for Badiou. Their relationship is best described as a specific kind of mutual determination: while being contains the possibility of appearing, appearing retroactively changes being. Badiou lays out the complications of this situation in explicit terms:

> Appearing, though irreducible to pure being (which is accessible to thinking only through mathematics), is nonetheless what beings must endure, once the Whole is impossible, in order for their being to be guaranteed: beings must always manifest themselves locally, without any possible recollection of the innumerable worlds of this manifestation. The logic of a world is what regulates this necessity, by affecting a being with a variable degree of identity (and consequently of difference) to the other beings of the same world. (Badiou 2009a: 119)

We could paraphrase this passage by saying that the worldlessness of being (the fact that the Whole does not exist) is the ontological condition of appearance. Beings appear because being is not a whole. Or to put it in seemingly paradoxical terms: there are worlds because being is worldless. If there is no Whole, being must appear. But if there were a Whole – if being were constituted as a unified world – it is not entirely clear if appearing would be possible at all. At the same time, this ontological fact also establishes not only the possibility but also the necessity of this appearance. If being is worldless, the being of beings lacks a guarantee. The only possible guarantee that we can account for in the state of worldlessness is appearing itself: the being of these beings is not guaranteed by reference to the whole of beings as such but in relation to each other (and to themselves) as worldless beings. If being is worldless, only this relation among beings (which is the essence of appearance) can guarantee the being of beings. Appearing, therefore, names the system of immanent relations among worldless beings.[5] And the necessity of appearance is regulated by a specific logic that determines the identities of the beings that appear in a world. The wager of Badiou's project is that this logic can in fact be formalised in the form of a 'minimal phenomenology' (Badiou 2009a: 103).

Badiou repeats the same argument in another passage where he addresses the Heideggerian problem of the 'ontological difference':

> The stages which develop this parameter have as their point of departure the impossibility of determining a being of the Whole, and finally the thesis according to which there is no Whole. Contrary to a Heideggerian proposition, it is irrational to evoke 'beings-as-a-whole'. It follows that every singular being [*étant*] is only manifested in its being [*être*] locally: the appearing of the being of beings [*l'être de l'étant*] is being-there. It is this necessity of the 'there' which, for a being thought in its multiple-being, entails a transcendental constitution (without subject). (Badiou 2009a: 102)

If there is no such thing as 'beings-as-a-whole', the state of worldlessness is not a negative limit to being but a productive condition. It is this worldlessness of being that allows Badiou to hypothesise the coincidence of opposites here: the 'there' of being must be now included in the being of beings. To put it differently, the ontological difference is turned inside out here, since it is now the singular being that guarantees the intelligibility of pure being. As soon as we evoke the 'necessity' of the 'there', however, we are really equating these two categories:

there is necessity in contingent being because there is the 'there'; and the content of this necessity is that being must be manifested in singular beings locally. It is then this necessity (the only one that we can clearly articulate in this system) that introduces its constraints on being. But mathematics fails in the face of this necessity, as it can give us only the pure being of the being in its contingency. As a result, the constraint of this necessity must be formalised in the register of a different system of formalisation: the logic of appearing (since now logic and appearing designate the same thing).

* * *

So, what is the world according to Badiou? The short answer is that the world is the 'transcendental indexing' of a given situation of being that determines the degree of identity of a specific element to itself as well as to other elements in the same situation. In other words, every situation of being consists of the pure multiple and the transcendental organisation of this multiple. As we have seen, this transcendental organisation (the asubjective immanent operation in the local constitution of a given situation) is the direct result of the necessity of appearing. The central aim of Badiou's 'Greater Logic' is to show that this necessary appearance has a differential composition and must present itself in terms of a scale of degrees. The fact that the transcendental possesses an 'order-structure' implies for Badiou that it must make possible a 'more' and a 'less'. To articulate the various degrees of this order, Badiou calls for a 'minimal phenomenology of abstract appearing' that he describes as an 'operational phenomenology' that 'identifies the conditions of possibility for the worldliness of the world, or the logic of the localization of the being-there of any being whatever' (Badiou 2009a: 103).

At the same time, it is now also clear that in Badiou's system we must always speak about the world in plural terms. The necessary plurality of worlds follows directly from the thesis of worldlessness:

> we will call universe the (empty) concept of a being of the Whole. We will call world a 'complete' situation of being [. . .] Obviously, since we show that there is no universe, it belongs to the essence of the world that there are several worlds, since if there were only one it would be the universe. (Badiou 2009a: 102)

The necessary worldlessness of being (the fact that there is no 'universe') is not the simple negation of the world but precisely the ontological condition of the infinite multiplication of worlds. The thesis according to which there is no such thing as '*the* world' means that there is an infinite number of worlds. But this emphasis on plurality is not where the originality of Badiou's definition of the world lies. The mere emphasis on the infinity of the worlds could still be misconstrued as a subjectivist argument. As we have already seen, however, the whole point is that we are now talking about the objective plurality of worlds. Thus, the originality of this definition of the world lies in the formalising tendency of Badiou's thought. To put it differently, for Badiou the idea of the world concerns the localisation of being, but this does not mean that the world is the place 'in' which beings appear. Speaking of 'the logical operators capable of lending coherence to appearing "in" one of the worlds in which multiples come to be' (Badiou 2009a: 102), Badiou writes the following:

I write 'in' a world (in quotation marks) to indicate that we are dealing with a metaphor for the localization of multiples. As a situation of being, a world is not an empty place – akin to Newton's space – which multiple beings would come to inhabit. For a world is nothing but a logic of being-there, and it is identified with the singularity of this logic. A world articulates the cohesion of multiples around a structured operator (the transcendental). (Badiou 2009a: 102)

Thus, we must emphasise that the 'world' is a purely formal concept here. The world is the singular formal operation of the localisation of an inconsistent multiplicity. It is 'nothing but a logic of being-there', which means that it is an immanent operation in a situation of being that establishes a network of comparative relations that crystallise into a system of consistency. In this sense, as Badiou insists, the world is nothing but a logic. The difficulty that this definition poses is that the world that it offers us for contemplation is neither a place, nor a substance, nor a subject. As Badiou puts it, it is a 'transcendental fiction' (Badiou 2009a: 221) that is nevertheless real.

★ ★ ★

Given this definition of the world, the question that organises Badiou's arguments concerns the relationship between being and appearing, the pure multiple and being-there – or in our language, between ontological worldlessness and the transcendental indexing of a world. As we have already seen, Badiou provides us with two different answers to this question: being and appearing are irreducible to each other, yet they are tied to each other by a relation of necessity. Let us examine this

256

argument in two steps. First, Badiou insists that appearing is not ontologically deducible. This first answer suggests an insuperable gap between being and appearing. This way of formulating the problem indicates that we need to clarify the status of the concept of 'relation' in this argument.

What is quite striking about Badiou's definition is that he treats the world like a 'differential network' (Badiou 2009a: 118). In other words, the very possibility of a 'relation' emerges only on this level of analysis, only in relation to a world. The problem is that this line of reasoning suggests that the worldlessness of being is an undifferentiated lack of relations. This thesis is quite clearly articulated in those passages where Badiou tries to clarify the difference between *Being and Event* and *Logics of Worlds*. Here Badiou writes: 'In *Being and Event*, I assumed the dissemination of the indifferent multiple as the ground of all that there is, and consequently affirmed the ontological non-being of relation' (Badiou 2009a: 99). He then adds that in the new book he will show 'that being-there as appearing-in-a-world has a relational consistency' (Badiou 2009a: 99). For example, when Badiou speaks of the problem of 'ontological identity', he makes it clear that the determination of this identity does not involve a differential network:

> For its part, ontological identity does not entail any difference with itself, nor any degree of difference with regard to another. A pure multiple is entirely identified by its immanent composition, so that it is meaningless to say that it is 'more or less' identical to itself. If it differs from an other, be it by a single element in an infinity thereof, it differs absolutely. (Badiou 2009a: 118)

A pure multiple is simply absolutely identical with itself, just as it is absolutely different from all other multiples. This is why we cannot speak of a system of relations here since all we get on the level of being is absolute identity and absolute difference. Once again, we find that mathematics as ontology cannot give us a world.

What follows from this understanding of ontological identity is that appearing is not logically deducible from the mere fact of being:

> the mathematical theory of the pure multiple doubtlessly exhausts the question of the being of a being, except for the fact that its appearing – logically localized by its relations to other beings – is not ontologically deducible. We therefore need a special logical machinery to account for the intra-worldly cohesion of appearing. (Badiou 2009a: 121–2)

Badiou seems to suggest two things here: first, differential relations do not exist in the domain of being as pure multiplicity; and second, that the very relation between ontology and phenomenology (as the logic of appearing) must be rethought, since ontology cannot account for the logic of appearing.

If there were an insuperable gap between the pure multiple (being) and being-there (appearing) as well as between ontology (mathematics) and phenomenology (logic), we would find ourselves in a desperate situation. We would have to conclude that being is the domain of ontological worldlessness, which implies an absolute lack of relations (since pure multiples are absolutely identical to themselves and absolutely different from each other). Appearing, on the other hand, is nothing other than the logical constitution of a differential network of relations. The question, therefore, concerns the exact nature of the relations between these two domains that represent two different conceptions of relationality: the minimal relationality of being (since on this level mathematics recognises only the relation of belonging), and the differential relationality of appearing (logic establishes degrees of identities and differences internal to a world).

★ ★ ★

But, in a second step, Badiou provides a more refined model to account for the retroactive structuring effect of appearing on being itself. In order to make sense of this point, we need to take up Badiou's argument about what he calls the atomic logic of appearing, a basic postulate of his philosophical materialism. Incidentally, this part of Badiou's argument is also the explicit site of a pure theoretical decision concerning worldlessness. This decision, then, occurs in the context of a new theory of the object. Badiou distinguishes three levels of analysis: the 'phenomenon' refers us to the transcendental evaluation of differences; within the field of phenomenality, it becomes possible to raise the question of 'existence' (as clearly distinct from the question of being) in the form of a pure logic; and, finally, in order to move to the level of 'objectivity', we have to be able to locate the real of the One within the field of phenomenal existence (Badiou 2009a: 194). The goal is to be able to pursue the analysis of the object down into its smallest components until we reach the point where it is sutured to the smallest components of the pure multiple itself. This phenomenological method, therefore, proceeds by moving from appearing towards being: it looks for 'an intelligible intersection between an "atom of appearing" and "an atom of being", that is between a minimal component of what is given as localized in a world, and the elementary composition of the multiple-being which underlies this givenness' (Badiou 2009a: 195–6). The task is, then, to identify the minimal unit of being and the minimal unit of appearing, and to establish some kind of a relation between the two.

The fact that being can be broken down to its components clearly follows from Badiou's earlier work, where it has already been established that, ontologically speaking, every set has subsets (or parts). The analytic of these parts reaches an evident halting point with the 'empty set' (which is a part of every multiple but itself does not contain any parts) and the so-called 'minimal part' (the one-member subset of a set). But the question for Badiou is whether 'appearing admits of the One' (Badiou 2009a: 212), which would function as 'a minimal threshold of appearing' (Badiou 2009a: 212) and would provide us with 'the analytical edge of appearing' (Badiou 2009a: 213).

The crux of the argument, of course, is that this atom of appearing can in fact be identified. There is a non-decomposable component of appearing itself: a minimal component. Following the logic of Badiou's argument, we see that this minimality must be a specific type of correspondence between the elements of a world and the transcendental indexing that constitutes this world. To put it simply, the elements that make up a being-there can be said to belong to this being-there in different degrees. So, we can conceive of a function that associates a transcendental degree of belonging to every such element. Those elements that are assigned the maximal value can be said to absolutely belong to this being-there; while those elements that are assigned the minimal value can be said to belong to it in a minimal degree. Between these two extreme positions, we have a scale of inter-mediary degrees of belonging that defines the diversity of a given world.

Badiou argues that an atomic phenomenal component can 'absolutely' contain at most one element (Badiou 2009a: 214). The reason for this unicity is simple: if an element belongs absolutely to the component, any other element that would also belong to it absolutely would have to have the exact same transcendental value and, therefore, would have to be absolutely identical to the first element. As Badiou puts it:

> That is why an atom of appearing is a phenomenal component such that, if an apparent absolutely establishes itself within it in the world, then every other apparent which comes under this case will be identical to the first ('identical' in the sense of appearing, that is of transcendental indexing)..The atom in appearing, or in the logical (rather than ontological) sense, is not 'one and only one, which is indivisible' but 'if one, not more than one and if not none'. (Badiou 2009a: 214)

This definition, of course, also implies that we are speaking of 'uniqueness' only in the domain of appearing here, and it is possible for two ontologically distinct multiple-beings to belong to the same atomic component. As a result, 'an atom of appearing can be an ontologically multiple phenomenal component. It is enough for the logic of appearing to prescribe the identity-in-the-world of its elements for its atomicity to be acknowledged' (Badiou 2009a: 216).

After establishing the existence of atoms of being as well as atoms of appearing, Badiou can raise the crucial question of his atomic logic: the question concerning the nature of their relations. The problem of the possible (and even necessary) correspondence between minimal units of being and minimal units of appearing is important since the meeting point of these two domains (where they are sutured to one another) is precisely the site of the theoretical decision concerning worldlessness in Badiou. The essence of this decision (a genuine decision without a logical foundation) is that being and appearing must be somehow tied together at a specific point. Even if ontology cannot logically found phenomenology, we can say that being and appearing are not freely floating domains that have nothing to do with each other. In the end, appearing is anchored in being. In Badiou's analysis, this is the fundamental worldlessness of materialism: every genuine materialism is a philosophy of worldlessness.

Being and appearing meet in what Badiou calls 'real atoms'. A real atom is a minimal unit of appearing that can be assigned to a unit of being. In other words, the existence of real atoms proves that appearing is not mere appearance:

> Let us gauge the importance of the existence of real atoms; it attests to the appearance, in appearing, of the being of appearing. For every pure multiplicity A led to be there in a world, we are certain that to the ontological composition of A (the elementary belonging of the multiple a to the multiple A) there corresponds its logical composition (an atomic component of its being-there-in-this-world). We encounter in this point another ontological connection which, unlike the Kantian dualism of the phenomenon and the noumenon, anchors the logic of appearing – at the fine point of the One – in the ontology of formal multiplicities. (Badiou 2009a: 218)

Needless to say, Badiou's language is quite dense here, but the basic point is clear: a real atom attests to the appearance of the being of appearing. In other words, the being of appearing itself must appear. This is precisely the proposition that undoes Kantian metaphysics, since for Badiou the dualism of the thing-in-itself and mere appearance is a false hypothesis. At the point of its own being, appearance is directly tied to the being of the thing. But this ontological monism also clearly anchors phenomenology in ontology (appearing in the pure multiple).

Badiou's point, however, is not that, if we are lucky, we can identify real atoms where being and appearing are essentially tied together. On the contrary, Badiou is trying to formulate here a general principle that applies to the whole field of appearing. The point is not that there are some real atoms, but that every atom is real (otherwise it would not be an atom). This is how Badiou raises the question of the reciprocity of this relation between being and appearing:

> It turns out that every constitutive element of a worldly being prescribes an atom of appearing. Is it true, reciprocally, that every atom of appearing is prescribed by an element of a multiple that appears? In other words, at the point of the One or of uniqueness is there identity, or total suture, between the logic of appearing and the ontology of the multiple? (Badiou 2009a: 168)

To paraphrase this question: if it is true that being must appear, does this ontological fact also mean that appearing is always the appearance of something in being? The stakes of this question are clear. If the answer is yes, then at the level of the real atom (at the level of the One) ontology and phenomenology are one and indistinguishable, since appearing and being are totally sutured to one another.

Needless to say, Badiou's answer is an emphatic yes. Invoking Lacan's vocabulary, Badiou writes: 'the One (the atom) is the quilting point of appearing within being' (Badiou 2009a: 218). This is in fact what Badiou calls the 'postulate of materialism' (Badiou 2009a: 218): '*every atom of appearing is real*' (Badiou

2009a: 218). Simplifying things, we could say that this defini-tion merely states that a minimal unit of appearing will always correspond to something in being. At the point of the One (the place of the atomic function), where appearing corresponds to something in being, logic is anchored in a mathematical element. Or as Badiou puts it, the materialist postulate 'demands that what is atomically counted as one in appearing already have been counted as one in being' (Badiou 2009a: 219).

But as Badiou makes clear, at this point in his argument 'logic' (understood as the logic of appearing) reaches one of its inherent limits, for the materialist postulate in itself is not something that we can derive from Badiou's formal analysis of the logic of appearing as a system of transcendental indexation. Logic in itself cannot prescribe in a logical manner the necessity of the materialist postulate:

> We have reached the point of a speculative decision, for which there is no transcendental deduction. This decision excludes that appearing may be rooted in something virtual. In effect it requires that an actual dimension of the multiple (of ontologi-cal composition) be involved in the identification of every unit of appearing. There where the one appears, the One is. This explains why appearing, there where it is One, cannot be other than it is. In an elementary sense, there is an 'it's like that' of what appears where the 'it's' is an 'it's one'. For the postulate of materialism ('every atom is real') requires that the 'it's one' be sustained by some one-that-is [*un-qui-est*]. It will not be in vain to refer to it as the *unease* [*l'inquiet*], to the extent that it is indeed there where logic draws its consistency from the onto-logical that thought can enter into its most fecund unease [*in-quiétude*] (the one-who-studies [*l'un-qui-étudie*]). (Badiou 2009a: 219)

The essence of the speculative decision is clear: the materialist postulate demands that we anchor every world in worldlessness for the simple reason that worldlessness is what is real. This necessity, however, cannot be deduced either mathematically or logically. Mathematics as ontology cannot give us a world; but the logic of appearing on its own cannot give us anything real. In a certain sense, we encounter here what we could call the parallax of being: neither of the two available perspectives provides us with a complete picture. Hence the 'unease' that Badiou is talking about. If every world draws its consistency from worldlessness, at the anchoring point of being and appearing, of mathematics and logics, the world and worldlessness are One. The task of thinking, then, is precisely to study the unease of this relation.

★ ★ ★

In light of this purely formal definition of the world (as an immanent system of transcendental indexation that is always anchored in the real of worldlessness), it is not surprising that Badiou's definitions of the 'object' and the 'subject' take similar routes. In fact, Badiou makes it clear that he considers one of the main achievements of *Logics of Worlds* to be a new theory of the object. As he puts it, the book proposes 'an entirely new concept of what an object is', since it offers a definition of the object that is finally completely independent of the subject (Badiou 2009a: 193). This 'subject-less object' (Badiou 2009a: 193) occupies a special position within his completed system between metaphysics (understood here as the purely formal theory of the subject) and physics (which Badiou defines here as the theory of subjectivisable bodies). The function of the object (as the moment of the One within appearing) is to provide an objective support for the appearing of the subject.

Badiou's definition of the object once again takes us back to the materialist postulate (Badiou 2009a: 220). In effect, this definition holds that an object is the operational couple formed by a multiple and the transcendental indexation of this multiple in such a way that the materialist prescription holds true for all the atoms of appearing of the object. What follows from this definition is that for Badiou the object is neither a subjective 'representation' nor an objective 'substance', but a purely formal function of the subjectless suturing of a world of appearing to the worldlessness of being. This is why Badiou insists here that the object is an 'ontological category par excellence':

> It is fully logical, in that it designates being as being-there. 'Appearing' is nothing else, for a being – initially conceived in its being as pure multiple – than a becoming-object. But 'object' is also a fully ontological category, in that it only composes its atoms of appearing – or stopping-points-according-to-the-One of the there-multiple – in accordance with the mathematical law of belonging, or of pure presentation. (Badiou 2009a: 220–1)

In other words, this subjectless object is the becoming-object of being in the sense that it designates the formal meeting point of the worldlessness of being and the being-there of a world. The necessity of appearing means that being is necessarily becoming-object, but this becoming is still determined by the purely ontological (mathematical) law of worldless belonging.

It is in this context, then, that Badiou refers to the 'transcendental fiction' of the world: 'The only inflexible truth regarding the intimate decomposition of the worldly fiction of being-there is that of being-qua-being. The object objects to the transcendental fiction, which it nevertheless is, the "fixion" of the One in being' (Badiou 2009a: 221). The reference to the Lacanian concept of 'fixion' (which combines 'fixation' with 'fiction') also makes it clear that we are now directly talking about the real of worldlessness. If there is no world in an ontological sense, any world is an objective transcendental fiction (or, to put it differently, the localisation of being as being-there is a 'worldly fiction'). If the operation of the object takes place at the point where the fiction of the world is sutured to being-qua-being, the object becomes a site of a specific type of tension between worldliness and the world. As a purely formal operation, the object itself must be understood as a transcendental fiction. But, as the site of 'the "fixion" of the One in being', the object objects to this fiction in the sense that it provides access to the only inflexible truth that brings to ruin the fiction of the world. Therefore, the object is the polemical site of the anchoring of the world in the real of worldlessness.

Badiou gives a concrete name to this objective dynamic: 'localization' (Badiou 2009a: 221). The interesting point here is that localisation (the function that assigns to every being of a world a transcendental degree of belonging to this world) becomes the operation whereby appearing (the transcendental fiction) itself has a structuring effect on being (the real):

> What we are moving towards is the retroaction of appearing on being. The concept of the object is pivotal to this retroaction. What is at stake is knowing what becomes of a pure multiple once it will be there, in the world. This means asking what happens to a being in its being, insofar as it becomes an object, the material form of localization in the world. (Badiou 2009a: 221)

Badiou wants to show that, under the constraints of the materialist postulate, the very process of transcendental indexation is inscribed into multiple-being itself. As he puts it, an atom is a 'rule-governed relationship' between an element of a multiple and the transcendental of a world (Badiou 2009a: 222). A 'real atom', then, is a specific 'function' that carries 'values' (which are, in this case, transcendental degrees) in such a way that the function is prescribed by an element of the multiple. Thus, the logic of atoms is ultimately concerned with the 'correlation' between elements of a specific multiple and the transcendental degrees of a world (Badiou 2009a: 222). This correlation defines the essence of localisation.

Based on this definition of atomic logic (as the logical capture of the being of a multiple), Badiou identifies an internal recursion in the very structure of localisation. As he argues, every localisation of an atom gives us a new atom: 'every assignation of an atom to a degree – every localization – is itself an atom' (Badiou 2009a: 224). Badiou needs to make this point (that he himself calls 'rather difficult' [Badiou 2009a: 224]) in order to be able to anchor the very process of indexation in being itself. According to this logic, an atom of being prescribes an atom of appearing by way of localisation (by the assignation of a transcendental value to the atom of appearing). But the nature of this localisation is such that the very act of localisation must be prescribed by another element of the multiple. This way, the process of localisation can be mapped as a triangular relationship between two elements of a multiple (being) that is mediated through a rule-governed relationship in the field of appearing (world). Here is Badiou's more technical explanation:

Consequently, every localization of an atom on a transcendental degree is an atom. But, by the postulate of materialism, every atom is real. [. . .] Thus, through the mediation of the transcendental, we define a relation that is immanent to the multiple. We thus have the sketch of a retroaction of appearing onto being. Since A appears in a world where the transcendental is established, it follows that some elements of A are localizations of other elements of the same multiple. (Badiou 2009a: 225)

As Badiou's language makes clear here, the crucial point is that localisation itself becomes a relation immanent to the multiple itself. The transcendental indexation that constitutes a world does not simply emerge out of nowhere. It is not an inexplicable supplement to pure being. Badiou's points now can be paraphrased by saying that the transcendental fiction of the world is a specific kind of relationship between two elements of being. The world is the way the worldlessness of being relates to itself in an immanent fashion.

This redefinition of localisation as an immanent relation of being implies that it has a direct effect on the structures of the multiple (Badiou 2009a: 225). This is the retroactive effect of the logic of appearance on being: as an immanent relation, localisation oversees the immanent self-organisation of being itself. In this context, Badiou speaks of the 'solidarity' between the immanent structures of being and appearing:

On the basis of this primitive relation between two elements of a multiple-being such as it appears in a world, we will try to set out a *relational form of being-there* capable of lending consistency to the multiple in the space of its appearing, so that ultimately there is a solidarity between the ontological count as one of a given region of multiplicity and the logical synthesis of the same region. (Badiou 2009a: 226; emphasis in original)

As Badiou argues, no matter how wide the gap between being and appearing, between mathematics and logic might appear, in reality we are dealing with a twofold connection. On the one hand, as we have already seen, the One provides a quilting point for the anchoring of appearing in being itself. On the other hand, 'there exist relations immanent to any being which is inscribed in a world' (Badiou 2009a: 226). These immanent relations allow us to conceptualise the 'synthetic unity of a multiple that appears': 'This unity is at one and the same time dependent on the multiple-composition of the being, that is on its being, and on the transcendental, that is on the laws of appearing' (Badiou 2009a: 226).

The consequences of this argument for a theory of world-lessness are far-reaching. Effectively, Badiou shows that the worldlessness of being is organised by immanent relations that are different from worldly relations but are not entirely independent from them. Abandoning the confines of Badiou's argument, we could say that this is the point where the logics of worlds could be grasped as the 'logics' of worldlessness. If being always already organises itself, this immanent organisation is the ontological condition of the emergence of a world (of the logic of appearance). Thus, the world is the way an immanent relationality of pure being produces transcendental effects that, in turn, affect the organisational structure of being itself. The logic of worlds can be grasped as a moment in the immanent logic of world-lessness, alienating itself in a transcendental indexing, which creates a world in the image of its ontological worldlessness. As Badiou claims, after all, the world does have a retroactive effect on worldlessness. But worldlessness is what is real, and it is the fiction of the world that reveals the real immanent organisational structures of worldlessness.

★ ★ ★

The formal theory of the subject offered by Badiou represents another decisive step in the separation of the object and the subject from each other. Similarly to the object, the subject also needs to be anchored in a theory of worldlessness. As Badiou clearly explains, the condition for the emergence of a subject is the irruption of an event that produces 'a local rearrangement of the transcendental of this world' (Badiou 2009a: 222). The world itself must first change before a subject is born: in this sense, the subject is the ruin of the object. The subject begins where a specific regime of objectivity threatens to come to an end: 'This modification of the conditions of appearing may be seen as an alteration of objectivity, or of what an object in the world is [. . .] The precondition for becoming a subject in a determinate world is that the logic of the object be unsettled' (Badiou 2009a: 222). As a first approximation, then, we could say that the subject is even less substantial an entity than the object. If the object is nothing but a purely formal operation that tries to anchor the transcendental fiction of the world to something in being, the subject is actually merely the effect of an interruption of this formal procedure. The subject is the formal capture of the displacement of the formalism of the object.

All this, of course, does not mean that the subject dissolves into nothingness right in front of our eyes. The same way that the object is something like a mediating function between a world and the worldlessness of being, the subject itself assumes a double role. On the one hand, the subject is the effect of the impending ruin of a world. On the other hand, the subject never properly speaking leaves the world: 'Subjective formalism is always invested in a world, in the sense that, borne by a real

271

body, it proceeds according to the inaugural determinations of a truth' (Badiou 2009a: 69). This why Badiou speaks of it in terms of a 'compromise':

> We begin directly with the underlying ontological components: world and event – the latter breaking with the presentational logic of the former. The subjective form is then assigned to a localization in being which is ambiguous. On the one hand, the subject is only a set of the world's elements, and therefore an object in the scene on which the world presents multiplicities; on the other, the subject orients this object – in terms of the effects it is capable of producing – in a direction that stems from an event. The subject can therefore be said to be the only known form of a conceivable 'compromise' between the phenomenal persistence of a world and its evental rearrangement. (Badiou 2009a: 79)

According to this dual ontology that distinguishes the world from the event, the subject is the exceptional object that orients itself around the trace of an event. It is the part of the objective world that takes upon itself the task of reorganising the world according to something that remains alien to the world. But, in the end, this means that the subject is precisely not an object but a 'pure act' (Badiou 2009a: 49). The paradox of the subject is that although it is irreducible to being a mere object of the world, it is still endowed with being and appearing. The task of metaphysics is to provide a theory of the subject as a pure act that endows 'an efficacious body with an appropriate formalism' (Badiou 2009a: 49). The task of physics, then, is to account for the way this body emerges as a worldly being in the wake of an event.

Hence Badiou's thesis: 'A subject is an indirect creative relation between an event and a world' (Badiou 2009a: 79). This definition positions the subject between a specific figure of worldlessness (the event) and the world. To be more precise, according to Badiou, the subject exists in the form of a relation between the worldly manifestation of the event and a set of local objects internal to the world. In this relation, therefore, the event is represented by what Badiou calls its innerworldly 'trace', while the world itself is represented by a composite element of this world that Badiou designates as the 'body'. The subject, then, is an innerworldly relation oriented by the worldlessness of the event: 'The real of a subject resides in the consequences (consequences in a world) of the relation, which constitutes this subject, between a trace and body' (Badiou 2009a: 81). Tracing the consequences of this relation means that the subject encounters 'points' in the world, where the multiplicity of the world is reduced to an either/or decision (a yes or a no, an affirmation or a negation). This way the subject becomes the formal site of the constitution of a new world: 'A new world is subjectively created, point by point' (Badiou 2009a: 84).

This definition, however, also implies that the subject comes into being when the world is no longer properly sutured to the worldlessness of being. When the logic of the object is unsettled in a world, what becomes visible is that what we thought to be objective reality is not in fact prescribed by anything real in being. When the event discloses the truth of the situation, the real of worldlessness establishes the hazardous conditions of a difficult reorganisation of the world. The very existence of the subject, therefore, testifies to the truth that there is something other than our world: a different relation to the worldlessness of being is possible. But, if the construction of a new regime of objectivity does in fact have retroactive effects on being, we must assume that the constitution of a new world will produce effects on this level as well. In other words, the most radical implication of Badiou's theory of the subject is that, even if the world is only a transcendental fiction, changing the world can have effects on the immanent organisation of being. Constructing a new world does not simply provide a more accurate 'representation' of the worldlessness of being. The task of the subject is not to 'fix' the mistake of the old world by tightening the solidarity between the count-as-one of being and the transcendental indexation of the world. By changing the world, the subject might effect a change in being itself.

★ ★ ★

It is a striking fact that the conclusion of *Logics of Worlds* frames the entire argument in terms of the themes that we have been tracing: the worldlessness of life and the worldlessness of thought.[6] For, as Badiou claims, the ultimate question of philosophy is 'What is it to live?' And he immediately adds an Aristotelian correction: the true question concerns what it means to live as an immortal. Not surprisingly, for Badiou, life in the true sense of the term is the history of the faithful subject who is contemporaneous with the true present. The possibility of this life is not provided by the world but by the trace of event:

> It is not a world, as given in the logic of its appearing (the infinite of its objects and relations), which induces the possibility of living − at least not if life is something other than existence. The induction of such a possibility depends on that which acts in the world as the trace of the fulgurating disposition that has befallen that world. That is, the trace of a vanished event. (Badiou 2009a: 507)

274

Strictly speaking, life is not possible within the world, if we understand the latter to mean the logic of its appearing. The ontological support of true life will always be an 'inexistent' element of the world: something that prior to the flash of the event did not possess a positive value of existence for the given world.

The task of true life, then, is a genuine 'incorporation' into the consequences of the event through a sequential creation of a present. It is not enough to be a mere witness to the event to be its contemporary. To live is to become an active part of the body organised by the worldly consequences of the event. Thus, life always takes place within a world since it requires a body as a support. But its defining characteristic is its subjective formalism: 'Life is a subjective category. A body is the materiality that life requires, but the becoming of the present depends on the disposition of this body in a subjective formalism' (Badiou 2009a: 508). And this subjective formalism must assume a specific form: 'To live is thus an incorporation into the present under the faithful form of a subject' (Badiou 2009a: 508). It is the faithful subject's disposition towards the event that exposes it to the eternity of truth.

As we can see, the temporal dimension that this life inhabits is the present, but this present is not the simple continuation of a past that could be fetishised in the form of a History (as Badiou puts it: 'History does not exist' [Badiou 2009a: 509]). In order for life to be possible, the present must be experienced in terms of eternity. In light of such a present, the past ceases to be the monumentalised guarantor of cultural depth, and it is reconstituted as a 'legible succession of fragments of eternity' (Badiou 2009a: 509). In order to give a proper name to this experience, Badiou turns to the Platonic Idea: 'If we agree to call "Idea" what both manifests itself in the world — what sets forth the being-there of a body – and is an exception to its transcendental logic, we will say, in line with Platonism, that to experience in the present the eternity that authorizes the creation of this present is to experience an Idea' (Badiou 2009a: 510). The eternal Idea functions here as the worldly manifestation of the worldless exception.

However, under the contemporary hegemony of what Badiou calls 'democratic materialism', we are forced to live according to the inconsistent injunction: 'Live without Idea' (Badiou 2009a: 511). To live without the Idea (a contradiction in terms as far as Badiou is concerned) amounts to the total abandonment of any genuine thought today under the guise of a sceptical relativism. This weak form of scepticism, the contemporary regime of thoughtlessness, is the exact opposite of the genuine scepticism of the ancient Greeks, which was an 'absolute theory of exception' (Badiou 2009a: 511). As Badiou claims, the Greeks did in fact believe that truth is inaccessible for the feeble human intellect. But they also claimed that the true is attainable by the immortal part of the human soul, 'the inhuman excess that lies in man' (Badiou 2009a: 511). In fact, for Badiou, this excess is what defines humanity as such. The human being approximates its concept only by way of orienting its existence by what exceeds it in itself: 'But it is impossible to possess a concept of what is 'human' without dealing with the (eternal, ideal) inhumanity which authorizes man to incorporate himself into the present under the sign of the trace of what changes' (Badiou 2009a: 511).

We could also say here that this excess represents the way something worldless is lodged in the very essence of the human being, since 'the inhuman commands humanity to exceed its being-there' (Badiou 2009a: 511). There is something in the human being that forces it to step outside whatever world it happens to inhabit through happenstance. This essential world-lessness, however, is not a simple withdrawal from the world but manifests itself as the human being's exposure to the infinity of worlds:

> Man is this animal to whom it belongs to participate in numerous worlds, to appear in innumerable places. This kind of objectal ubiquity, which makes him shift almost constantly from one world to another, on the background of the infinity of these worlds and their transcendental organization, is in its own right, without any need for a miracle, a grace: the purely logical grace of innumerable appearing. (Badiou 2009a: 513)

This infinity of human worlds is, then, the ultimate foundation of Badiou's rejection of any reference to finitude: 'The infinite of worlds is what saves us from every finite dis-grace' (Badiou 2009a: 514).

We are saved from the banalities of the contemporary world (its thoughtlessness and, ultimately, its worldlessness) precisely when we accept the fact that life cannot be oriented by only what is possible within the world. Life must be lived in accord-ance with an eternal truth that in itself has no worldly existence and yet functions as the guarantor of the infinity of worlds. Truth is 'transworldly' in the sense that, in spite of the fact that it is created in a specific world, it remains valid for all worlds.[7] As such, it is simultaneously worldly and worldless since it cuts across a plurality (and potentially the totality) of worlds. Life lived according to the Idea, therefore, is a life organised around the possibility and necessity of a specific form of worldlessness: it is the kind of worldlessness that was produced in a concrete world but remains irreducible to any world whatsoever.

★ ★ ★

Given the purely formal definitions that have determined Badiou's arguments, one basic question remains. If the world is defined as the transcendental indexing of the parts of a given multiple, what do we gain by calling this procedure a 'world'? After establishing the essential worldlessness of being with such care, why reintroduce this term for the constitution of an immanent 'differential network' (Badiou 2009a: 118) in the midst of this worldlessness? Why rely on this loaded category? As Badiou makes clear, by redefining the world as a purely formal principle, he intends to break with some of the most salient aspects of the Heideggerian tradition. Neither a unity nor a whole, the world is simply the immanent induction of a logic of identities and differences in the midst of being. In itself, the world is neither subject nor substance but a network of relations. Seen from the perspective of earlier theological and philosophical definitions of the world, we might even say that Badiou's conception of the world is already 'worldless' in the sense that it lacks any substantial essence.

At the same time, it would be hard to deny that there is nothing in Badiou's arguments that truly necessitates the use of the signifier 'world' in this specific context. There is no reason to designate transcendental indexing as a world other than a more or less deferential reference to a tradition that Badiou himself immediately rejects. Of course, it is clear that Badiou wants to distinguish 'ontological situations' from what constitutes the field of appearing. This distinction, however, does not explain why the separation of the two levels of analysis (ontological and logical) must be presented in the language of the conflict between ontological worldlessness and phenomenological worldliness. The decision to follow this path might be strategic, but it is purely rhetorical and not 'logical' (in the traditional sense of the word).

Could we not break with this rhetorical decision and argue that Badiou, in fact, provides us with one of the strongest arguments in favour of a general theory of worldlessness? What Badiou describes as the logical necessity of appearance as a system of transcendental indexing could be treated as an effective description of worldlessness itself. Some forms of transcendental indexing might appear to be worlds to us but, in reality, what Badiou describes as appearance is merely a direct consequence of his ontology of worldlessness which simply continues this ontological argument into the domain of phenomenology. In other words, in Badiou, we could also discover the outlines of a strong phenomenology of worldlessness: appearance is necessary within the worldlessness of being, and this appearance proves to us that worldlessness is not a disorganised chaos but a self-inducing system of differential relations. This is why the crucial part of this argument concerns its 'atomism': the link it wishes to establish between ontology and phenomenology. This link is the key to a common worldlessness: there are only atoms without a cosmos both in being and appearance. The same way that there is no totality of beings on the ontological level (in Badiou's language, there is no 'universe'), logic itself cannot give us the total unity of transcendental indexing. As a network of differential relations, appearing itself cannot make the totality of the network appear. To put it differently, within a concrete system of transcendental indexing the totality of this indexation remains without an index.

Badiou is aware of this fact and defines his methodology as a 'minimal phenomenology' that needs only three operations:

it needs to be able to account for a 'minimum' of appearance; it needs to be able to establish 'conjunctions' by connecting the values of appearance of two multiples; and it needs to identify 'envelopes' that function as globally synthesising values of appearance of any number of multiples (Badiou 2009a: 103). The fundamental method of this phenomenology can be paraphrased in the following terms: degrees of appearing are always determined in relation to a non-appearance (the minimum) in such a way that these values of appearing must be able to enter into relations with each other (conjunction) and, therefore, constitute globally identifiable regions of appearance (envelope). The field of appearing is, therefore, marked by two 'limits': on the one hand, appearing is always structured in reference to something that does not appear; on the other hand, the field of appearing does not constitute an absolute totality, only a series of regions. In other words, Badiou himself provides us with a category for the worldlessness of appearance: in place of unified worlds, appearing itself can be described in terms of 'envelopes'. And there is no envelope of all possible envelopes.

★ ★ ★

The affirmation of the worldlessness of appearing is important since the rhetorical choice of the 'world' contains the risks of an equivocation whose effects show themselves most clearly in Badiou's political arguments. The decision to call transcendental indexing a 'world' justifies a concrete political programme which now appears to have an ontological foundation and a phenomenological justification. On the one hand, this choice allows Badiou to articulate a systematic transition between the ontology of worldlessness and the phenomenology of worlds. Even if being is worldless, there are necessarily an infinite number of worlds. On the other hand, the same move allows him to argue in favour of a politics whose ultimate goal is to save the world. In spite of the fact that the infinity of worlds is ontologically guaranteed, today we are at risk of losing the very possibility of inhabiting meaningful worlds. Two possible uses of the 'world' emerge here. The more or less neutral philosophical definition is supplemented by a political meaning, whose pathos is fully dependent on Badiou's definition of the faithful subject.

In *Logics of Worlds*, this political argument becomes legible in Badiou's critique of what we could call the worldlessness of democratic materialism. The philosophical core of this criticism is Badiou's theory of 'atonic worlds':

> A world is said to be *atonic* when its transcendental is devoid of points. The existence of atonic worlds is both formally demonstrable and empirically corroborated. We have said enough to make it clear that in such worlds no faithful subjective formalism can serve as the agent of a truth, in the absence of the points that would make it possible for the efficacy of a body to confront such a truth. This explains why democratic materialism is particularly well-suited to atonic worlds. Without a point there's no truth, nothing but objects, nothing but bodies and languages. That's the kind of happiness that the advocates of democratic materialism dream of: nothing happens, but for the death that we do our best to put out of sight. (Badiou 2009a: 420)

A world without 'points' is a world without truth. A point is a specific part of a world that condenses the infinite possibilities of the given world into a single decision. As Badiou puts it, a point forces a decision in which 'the totality of the world is at stake in a game of heads or tails' (Badiou 2009a: 400). In a world without points, therefore, there are only objects (bodies and languages), and the powers that be define their task as the seamless management of this subjectless world.

Paraphrasing Badiou, however, we could also argue that a world without points is in reality a 'pure' world. It is the world reduced to its absolute degree zero of worldliness: it is nothing but a world. A world that is wholly worldly lacks the worldlessness of truth. This suggests that one of the most dangerous historical threats humanity can face is being forced to inhabit a world that is nothing but a world and lacks any reference to worldlessness. And, yet, Badiou wants to save the world and not worldlessness. An atonic world is pure transcendental indexing. And what Badiou suggests is that transcendental indexing is not really a world until it receives the test of the Two and the decision. The moment a world truly becomes a world is the moment of decision: when a faithful subject sets out to bring this world into being. Although Badiou does not say this, his arguments suggest that in the emphatic sense of the word 'world', there are worlds only for faithful subjects.

And yet, in another turn of events, Badiou argues that atonic worlds are, strictly speaking, impossible. No world can fully eliminate the necessity of the decision:

> Let us call 'isolate' a non-minimal degree of positive intensity such that nothing is subordinated to it, except for the minimum. In other words, there is nothing between it and the nothing. Where everything communicates infinitely, there exists no point. Empirically, an isolate is an object whose intensity of appearance is non-decomposable. To evaluate its pertinence in a construction of truth we do not need to analyse it, to decompose it and to reduce it. It is a halting point in the world.

> Such a halting point attests that at least in one place the atony of the world is undermined and that one is required to decide to say 'yes' or 'no' to a truth-procedure. (Badiou 2009a: 421)

The theory of the isolate provides formal proof that no world can be fully reduced to its worldliness. The isolate is a minimal element of a world (a non-decomposable object) that functions as a limit-case of worldliness within the given world. There is nothing between the isolate and nothing. In other words, formally speaking, in every single world it is possible to produce at least one situation that has the structure of a binary choice. This is the choice between something and nothing. This means, however, that structurally speaking the possibility of points is by definition part of the constitution of every world. As a result, there is no such thing as a fully atonic world. The isolate, therefore, functions as the barely perceptible and often deliberately hidden little gate through which the traces of worldlessness can enter any possible world.

What follows from the structural presence of the Two even in an atonic world is that declarations of atony might in fact be merely ideological mystifications: 'This lesson is worth reflecting upon today, since the declaration of the atony of a world may be simply ideological' (Badiou 2009a: 422). Democratic materialism produces an atonic world, but the project of the total elimination of the very possibility of a truth-event is necessarily doomed to failure:

> To the violent promise of atony made by an armed democratic materialism, we can therefore oppose the search, in the nooks and crannies of the world, for some isolate on the basis of which it is possible to maintain that a 'yes' authorizes us to become the anonymous heroes of at least one point. To incorporate oneself

into the True, it is always necessary to interrupt the banality of exchanges. (Badiou 2009a: 422)

In light of this description, it appears that the most important problem with democratic materialism is that, under false pretenses, it tries to reduce the world to its empty worldliness. Its ultimate promise is a perfectly managed world of objects – a world without worldlessness. The way to fight this historical tendency whose global onslaught seems to be all but unstoppable, the way to save the world from becoming nothing but a world, is to keep a vigilant eye on the hidden possibilities of worldlessness.

★ ★ ★

In Badiou's polemical writings, the historical catastrophe of worldlessness is explicitly presented in the framework of a critique of capitalism. In one of his essays, Badiou speaks about our historical present in terms of a 'disjunctive synthesis of two nihilisms' (Badiou 2006a: 31). The two nihilisms facing each other are the two opposing sides in our global 'war against terrorism'. On the one side, we have the nihilism of so-called 'Islamic terrorism'. On the other side, we have what Badiou calls 'capitalist nihilism'. This relation is a synthesis because, according to Badiou, Osama Bin Laden and American super-power 'belong to the same world – nihilistic – of money, blind power and cynical rivalry' (Badiou 2006a: 31). Yet, this synthesis remains disjunctive since it institutes a relation that is a specific kind of war. Badiou is certainly sensitive to the drastic historical changes in the infrastructures of warfare that have taken place over the last couple of decades, and points out that this relation is best described in terms of two symmetrical crimes. America's imperial violence is met with acts of terroristic mass murder:

> In the same way as the crime of New York, America's war is unconnected to any law and indifferent to any project. On both sides, it is a matter of striking blindly to demonstrate the strike capacity. It is a matter of bloody and nihilistic games of power without purpose and without truth. (Badiou 2006a: 32)

The core of Badiou's criticism of capitalist nihilism is precisely that it is worldless.[8] He argues that the most significant structural aspect of this kind of nihilism is that it is predicated upon the fantasy of the 'virtual equality' of the commodity: 'The same products are on sale everywhere [. . .] In principle, anybody and everybody is posited as being equal to everybody else, as being able to buy whatever is being sold as a matter of right' (Badiou 2006a: 34). This specious equality is the foundation of the capitalistic elimination of the world: 'In its circumstantial aspect, capitalist nihilism has reached the stage of the non-existence of any world. Yes, today there is no world as such, only some singular and disjointed situations' (Badiou 2006a: 34). Badiou, then, explains the absence of any world today in terms of the historical deterioration of clearly defined symbolic positions:

> No world exists simply because the majority of the planet's inhabitants today do not even have a label, a simple label. When there was class society, (supposedly) proletarian parties, the USSR, the national wars of liberation, etc., any farmer of any region, or any worker of any town, could receive a political denomination. That is not to say that their material situation was better (it certainly was not), nor that that world was excellent. But the symbolic positions existed and that world

was a world. Today, outside of the grand and petty bourgeoisie of imperial cities who proclaim to be 'civilization', there is only the anonymous excluded. 'Excluded' is the name for those who have no name, just as 'market' is the name for a world that is not a world. In fact, apart from certain singular situations – that is, apart from the unremitting undertaking of those who make thought, including political thinking, live – there is nothing apart from the American Army. (Badiou 2006a: 34)

Worldlessness is described here in terms of the elimination of symbolic positions (in the form of strong political names and labels) that would allow the exploited masses to construct genuine emancipatory political projects. Capitalism is worldless because it produces a minimal symbolic organisation by marking within the symbolic order the absence of a stable symbolic order. This strategy of reducing symbolisation to its zero degree produces universal empty categories that simultaneously mark the limits of the symbolic order and try to maintain this order perpetually suspended by these limits: it produces a world that is not a world (the market) and gives an empty name to those who have no name (the excluded). But if those who have no name still have a name (still have a minimal mark within the symbolic), the symbolic order itself is not simply absent but maintained in a state of permanent suspension, and the world becomes a world that is not a world.

What is striking about this passage, however, is that it posits having a world as a value in itself. Badiou cannot establish the fact that the historical times when the world still existed were in fact 'better' times for humanity. When the world still existed, it was certainly not a perfect world. On this level, the only thing Badiou can say in defense of the world is that 'the symbolic positions existed and that world was a world'. The tautological nature of this justification ('that world was a world') brings to light Badiou's investment in the category of the world itself. Some of Badiou's readers have already noted the inherent contradictions of this position. One of the first ones to comment on Badiou's political critique of worldlessness was Alberto Toscano, who saw in this move an internal contradiction within Badiou's system: 'In a peculiar inversion of some of the key traits of his doctrine, it seems that Badiou is here advocating, to some extent, an "ordering" task, one that will inevitably, if perhaps mistakenly, resonate for some with the new ubiquitous slogan "Another World is Possible"' (Toscano 2004: 219). When the world was still a fully structured symbolic totality with clearly designated subject positions, emancipatory politics consisted in interrupting and undoing the structures of an unjust world. But when the world no longer exists and the worldlessness of capitalism is the violently enforced norm of our lives, emancipatory politics must embark upon a seemingly paradoxical task: in order to free us, it must construct a new world with clearly designated symbolic positions.

Based on Toscano's insights, Slavoj Žižek takes this analysis a step further and suggests that 'even Nazi anti-Semitism opened up a world: [. . .] Nazism disclosed reality in a way which allowed its subjects to acquire a global "cognitive mapping", inclusive of the space for their meaningful engagement' (Žižek 2006: 318). As far as the fate of the world is concerned, capitalism and Nazism represent here two extreme strategies. If capitalism undermined the very possibility of the world, Nazism represented an attempt to install a unified, stable world against the historical background of worldlessness. The conclusion to be drawn from this opposition, however, is not that both having a world and not having a world are catastrophic prospects for humanity. Just because 'even' Nazism offered a world for its subjects, we should not conclude that every world is the totalitarian approximation of absolute evil on earth. Rather, the fact that Nazism constituted a world should suggest that the world in itself does not carry an inherent value or a guarantee of positive outcomes. In this light, then, what appears to be wrong with Nazism is that it was invested in producing a single unified world at whatever cost, regardless of the human suffering such an enterprise might entail. This fact alone should be enough to caution us against a politics whose ultimate horizon is to create a world *for the sake of having a world*, whatever that world might be. If the only justification of a political project is that it 'at least' offers us a world in face of generalised worldlessness, we are also justified in treating it with a serious amount of scepticism, since the world does not represent an inherent value. Such a world-for-a-world's-sake politics should be treated as the last horrifying cry of world-politics.

Needless to say, this is not Badiou's position, who clearly distinguishes between various actual and possible worlds even as he decries what he considers to be the universal worldlessness of capitalism. But it is now also clear that his argument is organised around an arbitrary investment in the category of the world that does not directly follow from his philosophy. Even if we accept his analysis of the absolute reduction of the symbolic to its perpetual self-cancellation under capitalism, we might ask why this situation is best described by reference to the absence of a world. A flipside of Badiou's argument would be that under such a suspension of the symbolic order the problem is not the *de facto* absence of the world but its infinite multiplication. There is still a symbolic order, but it is now predicated upon the law that it can be replaced anytime by a new order. When capitalism undermines the frameworks of stable representation, it also opens up the possibility of the constitution of an infinite number of possible worlds. In other words, capitalism is worldless in the sense that it produces too many worlds. Under capitalism, there is an excess of worldliness, rather than a simple lack, that tends towards infinity. The extreme fantasy that this infinity sustains is, of course, that every individual will become the sovereign creator of their own private world.

★ ★ ★

What, then, is the relationship between ontology, phenomenology and politics in Badiou's arguments? The project of *Logics of Worlds* is predicated upon the opposition and complementarity of ontology and logic. The point is that mathematics as ontology cannot grasp being in its localisation. It can describe only being as pure multiplicity (mathematics as ontology cannot give us a world). In order to account for appearing, we need to have recourse to another method of formalisation to establish a system of differential networks within being. The point of course is that ontology and logic are addressing the same object: being. But they grant us access to different aspects of being. So, the question concerns the location of Badiou's speculative decision that establishes the relation of ontology to logic. Where is this decision made? We know that the location of this decision cannot be either mathematics or logic. Badiou's clear articulation of the necessity of this speculative decision also demonstrates the necessity for a third system of formalisation in addition to ontology and logic. Using a more traditional language, we could say that we need a third perspective in addition to ontology and phenomenology, a theoretical point of view or a vantage point from which the very relation between logic and mathematics can be articulated.

Even if only indirectly, Badiou does name this third position when he argues that philosophy does not produce its own truths. The fact that he speaks about a 'speculative' decision implies that this act is philosophical in nature. But the content of the decision tells us something else as well: appearing must be anchored in being so that the argument will be able to uphold its 'materialist postulate'. No doubt, this materialism is a purely formal one, but it is clear that the third position from which the relation of being and appearing can be defined in these terms must be one that is consistent with materialism. The essence of this 'formal materialism' is that the infinity of worlds is a necessary outcome of Badiou's ontology, but the infinite multiplication of worlds must still be anchored in something real.

Badiou's political writings on the worldlessness of capitalism have shown that it is his politics that provides the foundation of this speculative decision.[9] Why is it necessary to ground the necessity of appearing in being? Because the worldlessness of capitalism can be rejected in a principled manner only if we can oppose it to a necessity that remains external to the logic capital itself. The infinite multiplication of worlds offered by capitalism cannot be understood as the direct installation of its modes of production in the pure presentation of being if being necessarily produces worlds. The impossibility of atonic worlds implies that there will always be at least one point of resistance that can become the foundation of a new world. The ultimate stake of this argument is to pit against each other two forms of worldlessness: the worldlessness of being and the worldlessness of capital. For Badiou, the frontline of this battle is the necessity of appearing. If politics consists of the forcing of the worldless-ness of being in the domain of appearing in order to oppose the worldlessness of capitalism, we are no longer in the domain of the logics of worlds anymore. This politics should be understood as the logistics of worldlessness.[10]

Notes

1 For an overview of the development of the theory of the event in Heidegger, Blanchot, Derrida and Deleuze, see Rowner (2015: 57–160).

2 For discussions of Badiou's relation to Heidegger, see Bosteels (2011: 174–96), Johnston (2013: 81–2), and Ruda (2015: 32–47).

3 This quotation is taken from a discussion of Deleuze by Badiou. The same passage is examined in Hallward (2003: 115) and Johnston (2013: 98–9). For two different interpretations of Badiou's relation to Deleuze, see Gillespie (2008: 1–23) and Crockett (2013).

4 In a related context, Adrian Johnston speaks about Badiou's 'transcen-dentalism without a subject' that nevertheless refuses to give up on the category of the subject (Johnston 2013: 109). According to Johnston, Badiou attempts to 'elaborate both a nonsubejctive transcendental as well as a nontranscendental subject' (Johnston 2013: 110). See also Toscano (2004: 215) and Hallward (2003: 296–7).

5 For discussions of Badiou's understanding of appearing, see Hallward (2003: 293–315).

6 For relevant discussions of Badiou's conception of life, see Ruda (2009) and Johnston (2013: 83–5).

7 In *Second Manifesto for Philosophy*, Badiou defines the transworldly nature of truth in the following terms: 'In short, this kind of "thing" functions in a transworldly fashion, with "world" here being understood as a materialist totality made up of bodies and languages. Created in one world, it is valid *actually* for other worlds and *virtually* for all' (Badiou 2011: 20–1).

8 In an interview with Oliver Feltham, Badiou summarised this point with the following words: 'What I mean is that the "contemporary world" as a world formatted by the totality of capitalism does not form a world for the women and men from which it is composed. In other words, there is the abstract world of capital, but there is no world which is constituted such that all those who live within it, as fraternal inhabitants, can recognize

each other. Under these conditions philosophy must say "there is one sole world", not as a descriptive statement, but as a prescriptive statement, as what should guide the politics of emancipation today' (Feltham 2008: 136). For similar formulations of the same ideas, see also Badiou (2008: 53–70). Frank Ruda articulated this Badiousian point by reference to Marx's 11th thesis on Feuerbach: '*The philosophers have only interpreted the world, in various ways; the point is to affirm its existence*' (Ruda 2015: 31; emphasis in original).

9 For a systematic examination of the position of politics in Badiou's thought, see Bosteels (2011).

10 I use the term 'logistics' here to refer to the fact that for Badiou politics is simultaneously a form of thought and a praxis of organisation. As Bruno Bosteels put it, for Badiou, 'any politics worthy of its name involves ideas, guidelines, watchwords, and so on that always give much food for thought, but it also inevitably involves an active and material form of organization' (Bosteels 2011: 18).

Contra mundum (A Conclusion)

The critical encounters with the post-Heideggerian tradition presented in the preceding chapters were necessary in order to clear the ground for a new theoretical understanding of world-lessness. In light of these engagements, the following speculative propositions will pave the way towards an affirmative notion of worldlessness:

1. *Worldlessness is not one*: If we accept the thesis that being is worldless because it is not one, it follows that worldlessness itself must be submitted to the same ontological fate: multiplicity. The most important first step for us is to realise that under the category of worldlessness a wide range of often disparate possibilities of being have been and can be subsumed. There are different ways of being worldless. Some of them are more appropriate for a historical moment than others. We need to shift our focus from the plurality and even infinity of worlds to the plurality of forms of worldlessness.

2. *Worldlessness is not the loss of the world*: In spite of what the word itself suggests, we have to understand that worldlessness cannot be defined as the loss of a world. If being is not

one, then the world never existed, and it was not there for us to lose in the first place. Of course, it is possible to lose things, and many things have been lost by humanity in its arduous history. But the positive account of worldlessness depends on trying to understand it on its own terms and not in relation to external categories (like the 'world').

3. *Worldlessness is not necessarily a privative state*: It follows from the previous point that it is possible for us to code certain losses as the disappearance of a world. But when we say that we have lost a world or the world, what we really say is that we have lost a specific set of historical relations or objects that (in spite of our own best intentions) do not actually need to cohere into a world. Most often today, such a claim refers to the loss of a sense of community. In this weak sense of the term, we lose the world on a daily basis. So it is possible to say that, in the midst of the inherent multiplicity of worldlessness, there are states of worldlessness that are in fact produced by the loss of previously highly valued things. But strictly speaking, in its singular being even such a seemingly deficient state is simply what it is in its ontological fullness.

4. *Worldlessness is not the logical negation of the world*: If worldlessness is not the opposite of the world, there is no need for us to look for dialectical mediations between the two opposite poles. The relation of worldlessness and the world is internal to worldlessness itself. When we try to account for the emergence of the idea of the world (why was it possible and maybe even necessary for humanity to produce this idea?), we must start with a description of the worldlessness of being itself. The idea of the world was simply the product of a set of contingent relations inherent in worldlessness itself. The

world itself is merely one object or one being (in the form of an idea) that occurs in the general worldlessness of being.

5. *Worldlessness is not moral negativity*: We cannot assume that the world in itself, by virtue of its mere existence, represents an inherent value. If we accept the proposition that the category of the 'world' cannot be the anchoring point for any morality in an ontology, it follows that our actions need not be guided by what appears to be the self-evident necessity of the existence of the world. While there is an ethics of worldlessness, it cannot consist of assigning inherent values either to the world or its absence.

6. *Worldlessness is not eschatological*: Worldlessness is not the end of the world. Worldlessness is a fundamental determination of being that is coeval with it. Being has always been worldless. A common theological capture of this state of affairs, in fact, consisted of the projection of the end of the world into an imminent future. But the reality is that this catastrophe has always already taken place. Waiting for the advent of worldlessness is simply a waste of time.

7. *Worldlessness is not messianic*: Worldlessness is not the easy answer to Heidegger's desperate conclusion that 'only a god can save us'. Worldlessness is not going to save us if we do not save ourselves. In this sense, worldlessness might be what bears testimony in being to the fact that the world does not need to be saved because being as such is unsaveable.

8. *Worldlessness is not chaos*: The traditional opposition of worldlessness to the world might suggest that we are talking about the presence and absence of order. But worldlessness should not be conceived as the negation of ordering as such. Rather, worldlessness is the result and the location of specific types of operations that we can describe with more

or less accuracy. This is what we could call the logics of worldlessness.

9. *Worldlessness is not the absence of relation*: A common way of justifying our fear of worldlessness is to reduce it to a metaphysical or historical state of autism that systematically eliminates the possibility of meaningful relations with others. But this is simply an unfounded hypothesis. What we have seen is that worldlessness is not the absence of relation but a specific kind of relation that is devoid of any reference to totality. Even in its worldlessness, being produces the conditions of its own organisation.

10. *Worldlessness is not the absence of freedom*: If worldlessness is what there is, we can rightly say that worldlessness is what is given rather than the world. Even if the given enters processes of mediation, it is never simply dissimulated or covered over. It is always readily accessible as it is what constitutes human experience. Yet the givenness of worldlessness does not mean that worldlessness designates an immutable state of things. If being is in fact dynamic, human praxis consists of constructing relations to and in the midst of worldlessness. In this sense, we produce states of worldlessness as much as we find them. There is such a thing as a poetics of worldlessness.

★ ★ ★

Regardless of whether they are critical of worldlessness or more positively inclined towards it, contemporary accounts of its rise and fall seem to share a common theoretical assumption: the emphasis almost always falls on the movement or act of 'withdrawal' that supposedly constitutes the essence of this category.

What follows from the points listed above, however, is that the exclusive focus on withdrawal might in fact be misleading. As a first (but still unsatisfactory) step, we could point out that 'withdrawal' is not always a passive enclosure into a completely isolated self. Withdrawal from the world can be a positive action, a result of a decision that what constitutes a specific world must be rejected. It can be a strategic retreat into another location. In this sense, it is neither passive nor simply negative. At the same time, once the act of withdrawal from a situation is accomplished, it becomes possible to constitute relations with others that are not worldly in nature. To put it differently, it is not necessarily true that the withdrawal from a situation can produce only isolated individuals (manic depressive monads or impoverished Daseins). Withdrawal can establish the conditions of a form of being-together that is not simply the negation of this world that so tortured us but also an emphatic rejection (not even negation but a simple forgetting) of worldliness as such. This latter point is the crucial one. The goal is not to withdraw from the world to move into a new one, but to withdraw from the world in order to inhabit a community that does not know anything of worldliness.

Ultimately, however, the reference to the act of withdrawal remains insufficient even if we redefine it in positive and active terms. The point is rather to imagine worldlessness independently of any act of withdrawal. The problem is that the idea of withdrawal maintains a reference to the world: if withdrawal is by definition an exit from a world, the concept will always lead us back to privative definitions of worldlessness. In essence, it leaves the world intact and simply asks us to step outside the confines of an otherwise stable world. But if our theoretical starting point is the assumption that the world never existed as a genuine ontological determination of existence, we have to also accept the fact that human praxis has always been worldless. The possibilities of human action are actually much wider in worldlessness than what is implied by acts of withdrawal. If the world exists only in the form of an idea, we can also argue that what we used to call a world was (and still is) merely a conceptual limit to human praxis. The world assumes existence for us in those moments when we try to delimit the possibilities of worldlessness. But apart from this manifestation, it has no other existence. The world is an imaginary limit on what is considered to be possible.

The next logical step in the speculative argument, therefore, appears to be the strategic abandonment of any reference to the all-pervasive philosophical motif of the loss of the world in order to categorically assert the thesis that the world never existed in the first place. But if the world never existed, what was the meaning of our long and tumultuous affair with the idea of the world? Was it just a colossal metaphysical mistake? Was it truly nothing more than a form of dogmatic slumber that we must awaken from now? In order to address these questions in a meaningful way, we will have to start with a direct reversal of our perspective in order to assert and reassert the primacy of worldlessness over the world. Even if it does not appear to be obvious, it is nevertheless possible to argue against the idea of the world and still hold that it was something other than one of most cherished yet most embarrassing delusions of humanity. If we accept that worldlessness is what is given and that the world designates something that takes place on the field of this primary worldlessness, we might be able to argue that the world itself was only an episode, a moment, an internal possibility of the history of worldlessness. In this sense, the 'world' is a name that designates specific forms of worldlessness that we find (for whatever reason) desirable. Historically speaking, then, the world named a praxis (a set of mobile strategies loosely gathered together under a vague yet convincing name) that manifested itself as so many strategic interventions in the field of worldlessness. The world divided being into what shows itself to the human being in the form of projected possibilities and that which supposedly falls outside this blessed domain. But this metaphysical struggle remained internal to worldlessness itself as it simply allowed us to strike a path in the midst of beings that was oriented by the conviction that there are more or less authentic ways of charting our possibilities on this earth. To put it simply, the world named the ways of being that we happened to consider to be authentic forms of being together in worldlessness. Everything else was dismissed as inauthentic or simply undesirable. Yet, the fact that the idea of the world remained inseparable from our awareness of the fundamentally precarious nature of any world was a sure sign of this struggle. It showed us that we never truly believed in the world and always suspected that in the end worldlessness will have the last world. There was only one thing more certain than the existence of the world: the fact that the world will end one day.

This reversal can also explain the power that the idea of the plurality of worlds still holds over us.[1] Once we assert that there are several if not an infinite number of possible worlds, we truly only claim that we know for certain that the world does not exist even if we try to mask this admission by the blinding thought of infinity. If our world is not *the* world since it is only one possible world, its very status as a world begins to crumble under the weight of all the other worlds whose (more or less hypothetical) existence it is supposed to support. Since the evidence of my world is the only proof I have of the existence of anything like a world, it is this experience itself that has to remain an anchoring point for my conception of all other possible worlds. But if the experience of my world is never completely free from the possibility of the end of my world, it is precisely the idea of the finitude of my world that justifies the infinite multiplication of other worlds. The idea of the plurality of worlds, therefore, functions as a displacement of worldlessness onto the infinite repetition of the finitude of worlds. Its logic is clear: because not one world is ever a full totality (in other words, because the world is never one), there are an infinite number of incomplete worlds. This argument amounts to a simultaneous acknowledgement of worldlessness (my world is not really the world) and a concomitant covering up of this fact (there are infinite number of worlds). It provides us with some consolation for the fact that we are no longer masters of our world: it suggests that we did not merely lose the world, we gained an infinity of possibilities. The idea of the plurality of worlds, therefore, becomes a seductive thought that, in the end, amounts to a slightly more sophisticated form of apocalypticism. The end of the world is now the guarantee of our endless exposure to different worlds.

But what are we left with if we abandon both of these ideas? What can we say about worldlessness if we reject both positions – both the idea that the world did exist once as a unified totality that we have lost, and the idea that there is an infinite plurality of worlds? Our starting point would have to be the assertion of the multiplicity of worldlessness (and the worldlessness of multiplicity as such). This, however, is not the external plurality of worlds that remain forever alien to each other (even if in felicitous or catastrophic moments they briefly touch) but a multiplicity that is internal to worldlessness itself. The potential internal infinity of worldlessness, however, is conceivable only if worldlessness itself is something other than a complete retreat into the self. This is the point where the inadequacy of common understandings of 'withdrawal' comes into view. The movement of withdrawal does not allow us to pass onto worldlessness if it names the absolute retreat into the self. If the world never existed and the plurality of worlds is merely an inverted image of the immanent plurality of worldlessness, withdrawal cannot be conceived of as a withdrawal from a world into a self (from the pluralised unicity of the world to the singularity of the self). What we find is that withdrawal does not reveal the transcendental ego or a windowless monad, but a constitutive relation to alterity. Withdrawal is not a withdrawal into the self but the withdrawal from the self to the exposure to the other.

★ ★ ★

Since the propositions listed at the opening of this conclusion all assumed a negative form without being negative theses, it might be necessary to conclude here by offering a formally positive rendering of the thesis of worldlessness. In order to accomplish this final task, we need to invert the terms of Deleuze's famous definition of perversion in the appendix to *The Logic of Sense*: 'The world of the pervert is a world without Others, and thus a world without the possible. The Other is that which renders possible. The perverse world is a world in which the category of the necessary has completely replaced that of the possible' (Deleuze 1990: 320). Our definition of worldlessness, therefore, must be the following: it is that in being which opens up our existence to 'Others without a world'. As characteristically subtle as Deleuze's argument is here, it is still limited by an attachment to a specific idea of the world. When Deleuze defines the Other, this concept is immediately inscribed in the construct of a 'possible world'. In a sense, Deleuze collapses the distance between the two categories: if it is possible, it is a world. The possible exists only within a world; and a true world exists only if the possible is allowed to flourish in it. There is no such thing here as the possible without a world.[2]

This identification of the possible with the world can have two different consequences for thinking the world. One possible conclusion that we can draw from it is that it undermines the very concept of the world. If possibility remains an inalienable component of being, the validity of the pervert's world is always undermined by the eventual advent of what it excludes from its composition. In this sense, the category of the possible designates here a form of worldlessness: it names the impossibility of reducing a world to pure necessity. If no world is absolutely necessary, there are only possible worlds. According to this definition, the modality of the world is the possible itself. At the same time, however, the identification of the world with the possible might also reintroduce a perverse limit to the openness of what is. If possibility is possible only as a world, we could argue that there is an inherent limit to the possible. Even if this world is always only a possible world, the necessity of presenting the possible in relation to the world remains an internal determination of the possible itself. The moment we assert the necessity of this possibility, we reach a perverse limit of any possible world. The world is, then, the perverse limit of being itself.

But if we abandon our obsession with 'possible worlds', we might be able to liberate the possible from the constraints of a world. We might see that the Other *is* the possible because the possible, in order to live up to its concept, must always include the possibility of the undoing of the world. There is the possible, because there is no world. The relation to the Other defines a singular relation that simply opens up possibilities without a horizon. The idea of the possible simply refers us to the fact that there are others for the other as well. To use Deleuze's example: when I see a frightened face, I infer from this encounter with the Other the existence of a frightening world for this Other (Deleuze 1990: 307). I do not see this possible world, I merely deduce it from the fact that the Other sees other things that I myself do not see. The encounter with the Other shows that human experience is structured by an inherent opening to alterity. The programme therefore is not to eliminate the Other from our world and, thereby, produce a pure world in itself, but to eliminate the reference to the world in our relations with others. If perversion consists of the disavowal of the structural openness to alterity in the constitution of the world, the goal outlined here might be understood as an inversion of perversion itself since it aims to define the possible in terms of a 'necessary worldlessness'.

★ ★ ★

The expression 'Others without a world', therefore, has an essentially tautological structure: it suggests that the exposure to alterity already implies that the world does not exist. If some Other really exists, the world does not. If the world exists, alterity itself disappears. Hence the common argument that by now has received a number of different philosophical formulations: the originary mark of alterity is not the simple exteriority

303

of the world, but the fact that the self itself fails to cohere into a fully constituted entity ('I is an other', as Rimbaud famously put it). Yet it remains an equally common assumption today that the existence of the Other must be attested to in some kind of a medium. This requirement is, then, often taken to be an unmistakable proof for the necessity of the world. Even if the experience of alterity is essentially shattering, where else would this experience emerge for us if not in the exteriority of a world? According to this logic, worldlessness needs a background against which its vague contours can appear as the shadows of a dark and elusive agency. This is why today the diagnosis of the worldlessness of being is still often considered to be fully compatible with the unequivocal assertion of the necessity of the world.

But the arc of our argument suggests a different direction for thought. In our introduction, we started with the hypothesis that the world is not enough. The question facing us now, however, is how to move on from this initial assumption to a principled and strategic argument against the world that would, by definition, reject any reference to the necessity of the world. In other words, we should question not only the (Deleuzian) total possibilisation of the world but also the common re-assertion of the absolute necessity of the world. One prominent example of the latter position could be found in the works of Emmanuel Lévinas. No doubt, among Heidegger's early critics, Lévinas stands out as a special case since his systematic rejection of Heidegger's philosophy is centred around the insight that Being is worldless.[3] In this sense, Lévinas's starting point is the disavowed conclusion of Heidegger's theses on worldlessness. As might be expected, we can very clearly identify the onto-logical, phenomenological as well as historical dimensions of this argument. For example, *Existence and Existents* opens with the following diagnosis:

> Expressions such as 'a world in pieces' or 'a world turned upside down', trite as they have become, nonetheless express a feeling that is authentic. The rift between the rational order and events, the mutual impenetrability of minds opaque as matter, the multiplication of logical systems each of which is absurd for the others, the impossibility of the I rejoining the you, and consequently the unfitness of understanding for what should be its essential function – these are things we run up against in the twilight of a world, things which reawaken the ancient obsession with an end of the world. (Lévinas 2017: 7)

As a first step, then, Lévinas diagnoses a state of worldlessness in the form of an 'authentic' feeling that is produced by the ominous constellation of historical catastrophes and metaphysical realities. But this argument clearly also bears on the question of phenomenological worldlessness. In the same book, Lévinas suggests that the conditions of intentional consciousness (the transcendental ego) themselves cannot be fully reduced to the world they disclose (the world of light and the world of darkness). Hence the necessary ontological argument which holds that Being in general, as anonymous 'there is', is worldless in a positive sense of the word. In this regard, Lévinas's conclusions are quite clear: 'To take up existence is not to enter into the world. [. . .] Inscription in being is not an inscription in the world' (Lévinas 2017: 105).

Thus, a number of the classic Lévinasian themes allow us to begin to map the domain of worldlessness in positive rather than negative or privative terms.[4] And yet, even though Lévinas discovers the priority of worldlessness of Being and in spite of the fact that he promotes a non-ontological approach to alterity (under the heading 'otherwise than Being'), the onto-logical pathos of his arguments about an existence without a world remain quite obvious. Worldlessness is a non-privative point of origin for Lévinas, but as such it is always reduced to a phenomenologically secondary status – the only way it becomes accessible to us is by the suspension of a world. In the end, worldlessness is still confined here to the thematics of 'withdrawal' ('In our relationship with the world we are able to withdraw from the world' [Lévinas 2017: 45]).

Of course, what is striking in this context is that Lévinas's argument is structured by the thought of necessity rather than that of possibility. In fact, we could speak here of the double necessity: the metaphysical necessity of appearance and the ethical necessity of the reduction of all appearances. As far as the first one is concerned, we should note that for Lévinas the ethical duty of the interruption of ontology is grounded in the necessity of appearing. That which exists in the mode of the 'otherwise than being' remains irreducible to being, but the necessity of its appearance is declared quite bluntly: 'It is necessary' (Lévinas 1998: 43). The duty of philosophy is to ensure that this entry into appearance is never fully ontologised: the appearance of that which is otherwise than being must carry the traces of its constitutive worldlessness. So, the domain of this 'otherwise than being' becomes accessible to us through a reduction. But this reduction does not simply guide us from 'some apparent world to a more real world' as it also does not grant us access to something that is more 'authentic' than the being of entities (Lévinas 1998: 45). It simply exposes us to infinity in the form of a responsibly that can never be absolved.

So, the question is: why does Lévinas need the world? If Lévinas's entire thought is an ethical challenge to ontology, it is clear that the phenomenological argument carries the burden of being a mediating agency between ontology and ethics. There is an unquestionable ethical duty (a categorical imperative) because the appearance of the other of ontology (that leads to the ruin of ontology) is simply necessary. The world becomes here a necessary detour in the ethical adventure of worldlessness. Yet, this way, the question of worldlessness is mostly reduced to the domains of the nocturnal horror of indeterminacy and the ineffable. Its traces survive in language, but it is never accessible as such. It is a pre-originary past, an immemorial memory that haunts our everyday experiences. It is said only by way of the unsaid (which points in the direction of a negative theology of worldlessness). It is a similar set of convictions that leaves many of us today with the melancholy conclusion that the tragic fate of humanity consists of being caught in this contradiction – even if the world is nothing but a thorough disappointment, it is nevertheless the only means for us to access the truth of worldlessness.

But if the world is neither all that is possible nor an absolute necessity, in the end humanity might have always been free from the burden of having to save that which does not need to be and cannot be saved. An 'existence without the world' (to use Lévinas's term) might very well be the opposite of any utopia (in the sense that it is the very *topos* of human history) but it is certainly not by definition a dystopia (as its being exceeds the moral judgement implied by the negative prefix). Reflection on the potentialities that worldlessness harbours could provide us with a chance to reconceive human praxis as well as non-human agency in terms that are simply indifferent to the kind of moral pathos that would forever bind us to the imaginary limits that we impose on existence in the name of world-creation. For, in the end, the world might not have been anything other than what had always hailed us as the *mysterium disiunctionis* (Agamben 2004: 13), the praxis of division rooted in the human being's singular lack of essence, a praxis that consists of separating and sorting out forms of worldlessness in the midst of the inexorable absence of worlds by declaring some of these worldless constellations to be the authentic dwelling places of the human spirit and discarding others in the name of a historical destiny that we could simply not accept as our own.

Notes

1   For useful discussions of the history of this idea, see Dick (1982), Lewis (1986) and Rubenstein (2014).

2   We could argue here that the essence of Badiou's critique of Deleuze is precisely that the latter tries to combine a fundamentally worldly ontology (what Badiou calls Deleuze's 'metaphysics of the One') with a worldless (or, in Badiou's language, 'stoic') ethics of thought driven by a desire for worldless abstraction. To put it differently, in a metaphysical sense, Badiou charges that Deleuze's thought remains too worldly in spite of its worldless orientation (Badiou 2000: 17). Furthermore, for a critique of Deleuze for being too extra-worldly (that is partially inspired by Badiou), see Hallward (2006). For a more positive reading of the possibilities of worldlessness in Deleuze and Guattari's works, see Nealon (2016: 83–108). In its final chapter, 'From the World to the Territory', Nealon's book stages a confrontation between the Derridean definition of the world as a 'necessary fiction' of projected possibilities and the Deleuzogattarian definition of the world as a territory that co-emerges with individualized entities. While this shift from the world to the territory signals a move in the direction of a direct engagement of worldlessness, Nealon nevertheless still formulates his conclusions in terms of world-formation: 'A life is an art of effects, which is not an escape from politics (with Deleuze leading us "out of this world") but an intense, consistently experimental engagement with constructing the world as an emergent territory for living' (Nealon 2015: 106).

3   For example, in his introduction to *Otherwise than Being*, Alphonso Lingis
    contrasted Heidegger and Lévinas precisely in terms of a conflict between
    the world and worldlessness. He claims that, for Lévinas, 'the other is not
    experienced as an empty pure place and means for the world to exhibit
    another perspective, but a contestation of my appropriation of the world,
    as a disturbance in the play of the world, a break in its cohesion' (Lévinas
    1998: xxix).

4   As the most obvious examples, we could list here the early Lévinas's re-
    flections on the necessity of the 'escape from being' (Lévinas 2003), his
    later musings on an 'existence without a world' (Lévinas 2017: 45–60),
    his understanding of 'infinity' (Lévinas 1969) as well as the very idea of
    'otherwise than being' (Lévinas 1998).

References

Abbott, Mathew (2010), 'The Poetic Experience of the World', *International Journal of Philosophical Studies* 18(4), pp. 493–516.

Agamben, Giorgio (2004), *The Open: Man and Animal*, trans. Kevin Attell (Stanford: Stanford University Press).

Agamben, Giorgio (2013), *The Highest Poverty: Monastic Rules and Form-of-Life*, trans. Adam Kotsko (Stanford: Stanford University Press).

Arendt, Hannah (1978), *The Life of the Mind* (New York: Harvest).

Arendt, Hannah (1998), *The Human Condition* (Chicago: University of Chicago Press).

Arendt, Hannah (2004), *The Origins of Totalitarianism* (New York: Schocken).

Badiou, Alain (1994), 'Gilles Deleuze, *The Fold: Leibniz and the Baroque*', in Constantin Boundas and Dorothea Olkowski (eds), *Gilles Deleuze and the Theater of Philosophy: Critical Essays* (London: Routledge), pp. 51–69.

Badiou, Alain (2000), *Deleuze: The Clamor of Being*, trans. Louise Burchill (Minneapolis: University of Minnesota Press).

Badiou, Alain (2005), *Being and Event*, trans. Oliver Feltham (London: Continuum).

Badiou, Alain (2006a), *Polemics*, trans. Steve Corcoran (New York: Verso).

Badiou, Alain (2006b), 'Lacan and the Pre-Socratics', in Slavoj Žižek (ed.), *Lacan: The Silent Partners* (New York: Verso), pp. 7–16.

Badiou, Alain (2008), *The Meaning of Sarkozy*, trans. David Fernbach (London: Verso).

Badiou, Alain (2009a), *Logics of Worlds: Being and Event, 2*, trans. Alberto Toscano (London: Continuum).

Badiou, Alain (2009b), *Theory of the Subject*, trans. Bruno Bosteels (London: Continuum).

310

Badiou, Alain (2011), *Second Manifesto for Philosophy*, trans. Louise Burchill (Cambridge: Polity).

Bajohr, Hannes (2015), 'The Unity of the World: Arendt and Blumenberg on the Anthropology Of Metaphor', *Germanic Review* 90(1), pp. 42–59.

Balmès, Francois (1999), *Ce que Lacan dit de l'être* (Paris: Presses Universitaires de France).

Bataille, Georges (1998), *Inner Experience*, trans. Leslie A. Boldt (Albany: State University of New York Press).

Benhabib, Seyla (1996), *The Reluctant Modernism of Hannah Arendt* (Thousand Oaks, CA: Sage Publications).

Benjamin, Walter (1999), 'Franz Kafka', trans. Harry Zohn, in Michael W. Jennings (ed.), *Selected Writings, Volume 2: 1927–1934* (Cambridge, MA: Harvard University Press), pp. 714–18.

Benjamin, Walter (2003a), 'The Work of Art in the Age of its Technological Reproducibility (Third Version)', trans. Harry Zohn and Edmund Jephcott, in Howard Eiland and Michael W. Jennings (eds), *Selected Writings, Volume 4: 1938–1940* (Cambridge, MA: Harvard University Press), pp. 251–83.

Benjamin, Walter (2003b), 'On the Concept of History', trans. Harry Zohn, in Howard Eiland and Michael W. Jennings (eds), *Selected Writings, Volume 4: 1938–1940* (Cambridge, MA: Harvard University Press), pp. 389–400.

Bernauer, James William, ed. (1987), *Amor Mundi: Explorations in the Faith and Thought of Hannah Arendt* (Dordrecht: Martinus Nijhoff).

Birmingham, Peg (2006), *Hannah Arendt and Human Rights: The Predicament of Common Responsibility* (Bloomington: Indiana University Press).

Blanchot, Maurice (1988), *The Unavowable Community*, trans. Pierre Joris (New York: Station Hill).

Blumenberg, Hans (1983), *The Legitimacy of the Modern Age*, trans. Robert M. Wallace (Cambridge, MA: MIT Press).

Bosteels, Bruno (2011), *Badiou and Politics* (Durham, NC: Duke University Press).

Boym, Svetlana (2009), 'From Love to Worldliness: Hannah Arendt and Martin Heidegger', *The Yearbook of Comparative Literature* 55, pp. 106–28.

Brassier, Ray (2007), *Nihil Unbound: Enlightenment and Extinction* (New York: Palgrave Macmillan).

Brient, Elizabeth (2000), 'Hans Blumenberg and Hannah Arendt on the "Unworldly Worldliness" of the Modern Age', *Journal of the History of Ideas* 61(3), pp. 513–30.

Bryant, Levi (2011), *The Democracy of Objects* (Ann Arbor: Open Humanities Press).

Butler, Judith (2015), *Notes Toward a Performative Theory of Assembly* (Cambridge, MA: Harvard University Press).

Butler, Judith, and Stephanie Berbec (2017), 'We Are Worldless without One Another: An Interview with Judith Butler', *The Other Journal*, 26 June 2017, <https://theotherjournal.com/2017/06/26/worldless-without-one-another-interview-judith-butler/> (last accessed 9 August 2019).

Calarco, Matthew (2008), *Zoographies: The Question of the Animal from Heidegger to Derrida* (New York: Columbia University Press).

Cerbone, David R. (1994), 'World, World-Entry, and Realism in Early Heidegger', *Inquiry* 38(4), pp. 401–21.

Clark, Timothy (2013), 'What on World is Earth?: The Antropocene and Fictions of the World', *Oxford Literary Review* 35(1), pp. 5–24.

Copjec, Joan (2004), *Imagine There is No Woman: Ethics and Sublimation* (Cambridge, MA: MIT Press).

Crary, Jonathan (2014), *24/7: Late Capitalism and the Ends of Sleep* (New York: Verso).

Crockett, Clayton (2013), *Deleuze beyond Badiou: Ontology, Multiplicity, and Event* (New York: Columbia University Press).

Crockett, Clayton (2017), *Derrida after the End of Writing: Political Theology and New Materialism* (New York: Fordham University Press).

Cutrofello, Andrew (2002), 'The Ontological Status of Lacan's Mathematical Paradigms', in Suzanne Barnard and Bruce Fink (eds), *Reading Seminar XX: Lacan's Major Work on Love, Knowledge, and Feminine Sexuality* (Albany: State University of New York Press).

Deleuze, Gilles (1990), *The Logic of Sense*, trans. Mark Lester and Charles Stivale (London: Athlone Press).

Deleuze, Gilles, and Félix Guattari (2009), *Anti-Oedipus: Capitalism and Schizophrenia*, trans. Robert Hurley (New York: Penguin).

Derrida, Jacques (1978), 'Freud and the Scene of Writing,' trans. Alan Bass, in *Writing and Difference* (Chicago: University of Chicago Press), pp. 196–231.

Derrida, Jacques (1982), 'Différance', trans. Alan Bass, in *Margins of Philosophy* (Chicago: University of Chicago Press), pp. 1–27.

Derrida, Jacques (1989), *Of Spirit: Heidegger and the Question*, trans. Geoffrey Bennington and Rachel Bowlby (Chicago: University of Chicago Press).

Derrida, Jacques (1994), *The Specters of Marx: The State of Debt, the Work of Mourning, and the New International*, trans. Peggy Kamuf (New York: Routledge).

Derrida, Jacques (2002), 'Force of Law: The "Mystical Foundation of Authority"', trans. Mary Quaintance, in Gil Anidjar (ed.), *Acts of Religion* (New York: Routledge), pp. 230–98.

Derrida, Jacques (2008a), *The Animal That Therefore I Am*, ed. Marie-Louise Mallet, trans. David Wills (New York: Fordham University Press).

Derrida, Jacques (2008b), '*Geschlecht I:* Sexual Difference, Ontological Difference', trans. Ruben Bevezdivin and Elizabeth Rottenberg, in Peggy Kamuf and Elizabeth Rottenberg (eds), *Psyche: Inventions of the Other, Volume II* (Stanford: Stanford University Press), pp. 7–26.

Derrida, Jacques (2011a), *The Beast and the Sovereign, Volume II*, trans. Geoffrey Bennington (Chicago: University of Chicago Press).

Derrida, Jacques (2011b), *Voice and Phenomenon: Introduction to the Problem of Sign in Husserl's Phenomenology*, trans. Leonard Lawlor (Evanston: North-western University Press).

Dick, Steven J. (1982), *Plurality of Worlds: The Origins of the Extraterrestrial Life Debate from Democritus to Kant* (New York: Cambridge University Press).

Dickinson, Colby (2011), 'The Logic of the "As If" and the (Non)Existence of God: An Inquiry Into the Nature of Belief in the Work of Jacques Derrida', *Derrida Today* 4(1), pp. 86–106.

Diprose, Rosalyn, and Ewa Plonowska Ziarek (2018), *Arendt, Natality and Biopolitics: Toward Democratic Plurality and Reproductive Justice* (Edinburgh: Edinburgh University Press).

Dreyfus, Hubert L. (1990), *Being-in-the-World: A Commentary on Heidegger's Being and Time, Division I* (Cambridge, MA: MIT Press).

Eyers, Tom (2012), *Lacan and the Concept of the 'Real'* (New York: Palgrave Macmillan).

Feltham, Oliver (2008), *Alain Badiou: Live Theory* (London: Continuum).

Fink, Bruce (1995), *The Lacanian Subject: Between Language and Jouissance* (Princeton: Princeton University Press).

Foucault, Michel (2012), *The Courage of Truth: The Government of Self and Others II; Lectures at the Collège de France, 1983–1984*, trans. Graham Burchell (New York: Palgrave Macmillan).

Freud, Sigmund (1957a), 'On Narcissism: An Introduction', in *The Standard Edition of the Complete Psychological Works of Sigmund Freud, Volume 14*, trans. James Strachey et al. (London: Hogarth Press), pp. 67–102.

Freud, Sigmund (1957b), 'The Unconscious', in *The Standard Edition of the Complete Psychological Works of Sigmund Freud, Volume 14*, trans. James Strachey et al. (London: Hogarth Press), pp. 159–215.

Freud, Sigmund (1989a), *Beyond the Pleasure Principle*, trans. James Strachey et al. (New York: Norton).

Freud, Sigmund (1989b), *An Outline of Psycho-Analysis*, trans. James Strachey et al. (New York: Norton).

Freud, Sigmund (1989c), 'The Question of a *Weltanschauung*', in *New Introductory Lectures on Psycho-Analysis*, trans. James Strachey (New York: Norton), pp. 195–225.

Freud, Sigmund (2010), *The Interpretation of Dreams*, trans. James Strachey et al. (New York: Basic Books).

Gabriel, Markus (2015), *Why the World Does Not Exist*, trans. Gregory Moss (Cambridge: Polity).

Gadamer, Hans-Georg (1994), *Heidegger's Ways*, trans. John W. Stanley (Albany: State University of New York Press).

Gaston, Sean (2013), *The Concept of World from Kant to Derrida* (New York: Rowman and Littlefield.

Gillespie, Sam (2008), *The Mathematics of Novelty: Badiou's Minimalist Metaphysics* (Melbourne: re.press).

Glynos, Jason, and Yanis Stavrakakis, eds (2003), *Lacan and Science* (New York: Routledge).

Gordon, Peter Eli (2009), 'Realism, Science, and the Deworlding of the World', in Hubert L. Dreyfus and Mark A. Wrathall (eds), *A Companion to Phenomenology and Existentialism* (Oxford: Blackwell Publishers), pp. 425–44.

Hägglund, Martin (2008), *Radical Atheism: Derrida and the Time of Life* (Stanford: Stanford University Press).

Hallward, Peter (2003), *Badiou: A Subject to Truth* (Minneapolis: University of Minnesota Press).

Hallward, Peter (2006), *Out of this World: Deleuze and the Philosophy of Creation* (New York: Verso).

Hamacher, Werner (2017), 'The One Right No One Ever Has', trans. Julia Ng, *Philosophy Today* 61(4), pp. 947–62.

Hardt, Michael, and Antonio Negri (2011), *Commonwealth* (Cambridge, MA: Harvard University Press).

Harman, Graham (2011), *The Quadruple Object* (New York: Zero Books).

Heidegger, Martin (1977), *The Question Concerning Technology and Other Essays*, trans. William Lovitt (New York: Harper and Row).

Heidegger, Martin (1995), *The Fundamental Concepts of Metaphysics: World, Finitude, Solitude*, trans. William McNeill and Nicholas Walker (Bloomington: Indiana University Press).

Heidegger, Martin (1998a), 'What is Metaphysics?', in *Pathmarks*, trans. William McNeil (Cambridge: Cambridge University Press), pp. 82–96.

Heidegger, Martin (1998b), 'Postscript to "What is Metaphysics?"', in *Pathmarks*, trans. William McNeil (Cambridge: Cambridge University Press), pp. 231–8.

Heidegger, Martin (1999), *Contributions to Philosophy (Of the Event)*, trans. Parvis Emad and Kenneth Maly (Bloomington: Indiana University Press).

Heidegger, Martin (2000), *Introduction to Metaphysics*, trans. Gregory Fried and Richard Polt (New Haven: Yale University Press).

Heidegger, Martin (2001), 'The Thing', in *Poetry, Language, Thought*, trans. Albert Hofstadter (New York: Harper Collins), pp. 161–84.

Heidegger, Martin (2002), 'The Origin of the Work of Art', in *Off the Beaten Track*, trans. Julien Young and Kenneth Haynes (Cambridge: Cambridge University Press), pp. 1–56.

Heidegger, Martin (2010), *Being and Time*, trans. Joan Stambaugh and Dennis J. Schmidt (Albany: State University of New York Press).

Heidegger, Martin (2014), *Gesamtausgabe, Überlegungen VII–XI (Schwarze Hefte 1938/39)*, Vol. 95 (Frankfurt am Main: Klostermann).

Irigaray, Luce (2008), *Sharing the World* (New York: Continuum).

Johnston, Adrian (2009), *Badiou, Žižek, and Political Transformations: The Cadence of Change* (Evanston: Northwestern University Press).

Johnston, Adrian (2013), *Prolegomena to Any Future Materialism: The Outcome of Contemporary French Philosophy* (Evanston: Northwestern University Press).

Kateb, Georg (1984), *Hannah Arendt: Politics, Conscience, Evil* (Totowa, NJ: Rowman and Allanheld).

Kristeva, Julia (2001), *Hannah Arendt: Life is a Narrative*, trans. Frank Collins (Toronto: University of Toronto Press).

Krell, David Farrell (2013), *Derrida and Our Animal Others: Derrida's Final Seminar*, The Beast and the Sovereign (Bloomington: Indiana University Press).

Krell, David Farrell (2016), *Ecstasy, Catastrophe: Heidegger from Being and Time to the Black Notebooks* (Albany: State University of New York Press).

Lacan, Jacques (1992), *The Seminar of Jacques Lacan, Book VII, The Ethics of Psychoanalysis, 1959–1960*, trans. Dennis Porter (New York: Norton).

Lacan, Jacques (1993), *The Seminar of Jacques Lacan, Book III, The Psychoses, 1955–1956*, trans. Russell Grigg (New York: Norton).

Lacan, Jacques (2006a), 'The Function and Field of Speech and Language in Psychoanalysis', in *Écrits*, trans. Bruce Fink (New York: Norton), pp. 197–268.

Lacan, Jacques (2006b), 'The Instance of the Letter in the Unconscious, or Reason Since Freud', in *Écrits*, trans. Bruce Fink (New York: Norton), pp. 412–41.

Lacan, Jacques (2006c), 'On a Question Prior to Any Possible Treatment of Psychosis', in *Écrits*, trans. Bruce Fink (New York: Norton), pp. 445–88.

Lacan, Jacques (2006d), 'Response to Jean Hyppolite's Commentary on Freud's "Verneinung"', in *Écrits*, trans. Bruce Fink (New York: Norton), pp. 318–33.

Lacan, Jacques (2014), *The Seminar of Jacques Lacan, Book X, Anxiety*, trans. A. R. Price (Cambridge: Polity).

Lafont, Cristina (2000), *Heidegger, Language and World Disclosure*, trans. Graham Harman (Cambridge: Cambridge University Press).

Lawlor, Leonard (2002), *Derrida and Husserl: The Basic Problem of Phenomenology* (Bloomington: Indiana University Press).

Lawlor, Leonard (2007), *This Is Not Sufficient: An Essay on Animality and Human Nature in Derrida* (New York: Columbia University Press).

Lévinas, Emmanuel (1969), *Totality and Infinity: An Essay on Exteriority*, trans. Alphonso Lingis (Pittsburgh: Duquesne University Press).

Lévinas, Emmanuel (1990), 'Heidegger, Gagarin, and Us', in *Difficult Freedom: Essays on Judaism*, trans. Seán Hand (Baltimore: Johns Hopkins University Press), pp. 231–4.

Lévinas, Emmanuel (1998), *Otherwise than Being or Beyond Essence*, trans. Alphonso Lingis (Pittsburgh: Duquesne University Press).

Lévinas, Emmanuel (2003), *On Escape: De l'évasion*, trans. Bettina Bergo (Stanford: Stanford University Press).

Lévinas, Emmanuel (2017), *Existence and Existents*, trans. Alphonso Lingis (The Hague and Boston: Martinus Nijhoff).

Lewis, David K. (1986), *On the Plurality of Worlds* (New York: Blackwell).

Malabou, Catherine (2008), *What Should We Do with Our Brain?*, trans. Sebastian Rand (New York: Fordham University Press).

Malpas, Jeff (2006), *Heidegger's Topology: Being, Place, World* (Cambridge, MA: MIT Press).

Marder, Michael (2009), *The Event of the Thing: Derrida's Post-Deconstructive Realism* (Toronto: University of Toronto Press).

Marrati, Paola (2005), *Genesis and Trace: Derrida Reading Husserl and Heidegger* (Stanford: Stanford University Press).

Meillassoux, Quentin (2010), *After Finitude: An Essay on the Necessity of Contingency*, trans. Ray Brassier (London: Continuum).

Mendieta, Eduardo (2017), 'Metaphysical Anti-Semitism and Worldlessness: On World Poorness, World Forming, and World Destroying', in Andrew J. Mitchell and Peter Trawny (eds), *Heidegger's Black Notebooks: Responses to Anti-Semitism* (New York: Columbia University Press), pp. 36–51.

Milner, Jean-Claude (1991), 'Lacan and the Ideal of Science', in Alexandre Leupin (ed.), *Lacan and the Human Sciences* (Lincoln: University of Nebraska Press), pp. 27–42.

Milner, Jean-Claude (2000), 'The Doctrine of Science', trans. Oliver Feltham, *Umbr(a): Science and Truth* 1, pp. 33–63.

Mitchell, Andrew (2015), *The Fourfold: Reading the Late Heidegger* (Evanston: Northwestern University Press).

Morel, Geneviève (2000), 'Science and Psychoanalysis', trans. Karen M. Fisher, *Umbr(a): Science and Truth* 1, pp. 65–79.

Morriston, Wesley (1972), 'Heidegger on the World', *Man and World* 5(4), pp. 452–67.

Morton, Timothy (2013), *Hyperobjects: Philosophy and Ecology after the End of the World* (Minneapolis: University of Minnesota Press).

Naas, Michael (2015), *The End of the World and Other Teachable Moments: Jacques Derrida's Final Seminar* (New York: Fordham University Press).

Nancy, Jean-Luc (2000), *Being Singular Plural*, trans. Robert Richardson and Anne O'Byrne (Stanford: Stanford University Press).

Nancy, Jean-Luc (2007), *The Creation of the World or Globalization*, trans. Francois Raffoul and David Pettigrew (Albany: State University of New York Press).

Nealon, Jeffrey (2016), *Plant Theory: Biopower and Vegetable Life* (Stanford: Stanford University Press).

O'Byrne, Anne (2010), *Natality and Finitude* (Bloomington: Indiana University Press).

O'Connor, Patrick (2010), *Derrida: Profanations* (London: Continuum).

Oliver, Kelly (2015), *Earth and World: Philosophy after the Apollo Mission* (New York: Columbia University Press).

Rubenstein, Mary-Jane (2014), *Worlds Without End: The Many Lives of the Multiverse* (New York: Columbia University Press).

Ruda, Frank (2009), 'Humanism Reconsidered, or Life Living Life', *Filosofski Vestnik* 30(2), pp. 175–93.

Ruda, Frank (2015), *For Badiou: Idealism without Idealism* (Evanston: Northwestern University Press).

Scarry, Elaine (1987), *The Making and Unmaking of the World* (Oxford: Oxford University Press).

Schreber, Daniel Paul (2000), *Memoirs of My Nervous Illness*, trans. Ida Macalpine and Richard A. Hunter (New York: New York Review Books).

Sloterdijk, Peter (2013), *In the World Interior of Capital: Towards a Philosophical Theory of Globalization*, trans. Wieland Hoban (Cambridge: Polity).

Stengers, Isabelle (2010), *Cosmopolitics*, trans. Robert Bononno (Minneapolis: University of Minnesota Press).

Stiegler, Bernard (2008), *Technics and Time, 2: Disorientation*, trans. Stephen Barker (Stanford: Stanford University Press).

Stiegler, Bernard (2009), *Acting Out*, trans. David Barison, Daniel Ross and Patrick Crogan (Stanford: Stanford University Press).

Tauber, Alfred (2010), *Freud, the Reluctant Philosopher* (Princeton: Princeton University Press).

Toscano, Alberto (2004), 'From the State to the World? Badiou and Anti-Capitalism', *Communication & Cognition* 37(3–4), pp. 199–224.

Trawny, Peter (2015), *Heidegger and the Myth of a Jewish World Conspiracy*, trans. Andrew J. Mitchell (Chicago: University of Chicago Press).

Végső, Roland (2012), *The Naked Communist: Cold War Modernism and the Politics of Popular Culture* (New York: Fordham University Press).

Végső, Roland (2018a), 'Towards an Aesthetics of Worldlessness: Béla Tarr and the Berlin School', in Marco Abel and Jaimey Fischer (eds), *The Berlin School and Its Global Contexts* (Detroit: Wayne State University Press), pp. 317–34.

Végső, Roland (2018b), 'A World Without the Novel', *Continental Thought and Theory* 2.3, pp. 70–90.

Villa, Dana R. (1996), *Arendt and Heidegger: The Fate of the Political* (Princeton: Princeton University Press).

Villa, Dana R. (2001), *Politics, Philosophy, Terror: Essays on the Thought of Hannah Arendt* (Princeton: Princeton University Press).

Young, Julian (2001), *Heidegger's Later Philosophy* (Cambridge: Cambridge University Press).

Young-Bruehl, Elisabeth (2006), *Why Arendt Matters* (New Haven: Yale University Press).

Žižek, Slavoj (2006), *The Parallax View* (Cambridge, MA: MIT Press).

Žižek, Slavoj (2008), *The Ticklish Subject: The Absent Centre of Political Ontology*, 2nd edn (New York: Verso).

Žižek, Slavoj (2015), *Absolute Recoil: Towards a New Foundation of Dialectical Materialism* (New York: Verso).

Index

319